Network Intrusion Alert:

An Ethical Hacking Guide to Intrusion Detection

Ankit Fadia

Manu Zacharia

THOMSON

COURSE TECHNOLOGY

Professional ■ Technical ■ Reference

ISBN-10: 1-59863-414-3

ISBN-13: 978-1-59863-414-3

Library of Congress Catalog Card Number: 2007927291

Printed in the United States of America

08 09 10 11 12 TW 10 9 8 7 6 5 4 3 2 1

Publisher and General Manager, Thomson Course Technology PTR:
Stacy L. Hiquet

Associate Director of Marketing:
Sarah O'Donnell

Manager of Editorial Services:
Heather Talbot

Marketing Manager:
Mark Hughes

Acquisitions Editor:
Mitzi Koontz

Marketing Assistant:
Adena Flitt

Project Editor:
Kezia Endsley

Technical Reviewer:
Arlie Hartman

PTR Editorial Services Coordinator:
Erin Johnson

Copy Editor:
Kezia Endsley

Interior Layout Tech:
Danielle Foster

Cover Designer:
Mike Tanamachi

Indexer:
Katherine Stimson

Proofreader:
Kim Benbow

THOMSON

™

COURSE TECHNOLOGY

Professional ■ Technical ■ Reference

Thomson Course Technology PTR,
a division of Thomson Learning Inc.
25 Thomson Place
Boston, MA 02210
http://www.courseptr.com

To my mum and dad.

About Ankit Fadia

Ankit Fadia, 22 years old, is an independent computer security and digital intelligence consultant with definitive experience in the field of Internet security based out of Silicon Valley in California, USA. He has authored 11 internationally best-selling books on numerous topics related to computer security that have been widely appreciated by both professionals and industry leaders the world over. His books have sold a record 2 million copies across the globe; have been translated into Japanese, Korean, Portuguese, and Polish; and are also being used as reference textbooks in some of the most prestigious academic institutions in Asia and North America. Fadia is also a widely recognized computer security guru and cyber terrorism expert.

Fadia is, however, better known for his significant work in the field of digital intelligence, security consultancy, and training. Fadia has been involved in numerous classified projects pertaining to international security and computer networks. He handles the Asia operations of the classified intelligence agency.

Widely traveled, Fadia provides customized cyber security training and consulting solutions to clients all across Asia, Australia, North America, and the Middle East, including Google, Citibank, Shell, Volvo, Thai Airways, UOB Bank, PT Cisco Systems, and many other organizations in the government, police, and corporate sectors. He has also conducted more than 1,000 different training sessions across 25 countries on various topics related to cyber security to an audience comprised of CEOs, CIOs, top-level management, entrepreneurs, technical specialists, defense personnel, and students.

With a strong belief in the integration of security and education, Fadia closely works with the School of Information Systems at Singapore Management University and San Jose State University and advises them on the design and structure of the course material of their computer security courses. He also offers a widely respected certification course on computer security entitled *Ankit Fadia Certified Ethical Hacker*.

Fadia is a senior at Stanford University.

About Manu Zacharia

Manu Zacharia has excelled in the field of security for more than 12 years, working with both the private sector and the armed forces. He has practical experience in network security, intrusion detection, forensics, and corporate investigations. His passion for computer security has also inspired him to set up two Web portals—The Admins (http://www.theadmins.info) and Port8080 (http://www.port8080.info). One of the exceptional performers in the Ankit Fadia Certified Ethical Hacking Course (AFCEH) certification program, he has played an instrumental role in conceptualizing the Information Security Day —http://www.informationsecurityday.com. Manu has also been involved with the state police for various cyber forensic investigations, some of which attained nationwide attention. Manu has written many security-related articles for industry publications/Web portals. He is currently working as a network administrator for a U.S.-based information technology firm.

Contents at a Glance

Contents

The Beginnings

This book is a product of *Project Hacking Kitaab* started by Ankit Fadia in late 2006. The vision and motivating force behind this project is to research, develop, and publish insightful cutting edge material on important issues related to computer security. *Project Hacking Kitaab* aspires to make the Internet a safer placer to be in by bringing useful computer security knowledge into everybody's hands. Not only has the Internet deeply impacted our lives, but it has also completely revolutionized the way we lead our personal and professional lives. Unfortunately, as more and more individuals become dependent on the Internet, the grave threat of cyber attack comes to the foreground. Within a few minutes, a single computer intrusion is capable of causing losses amounting to millions of dollars. Most users continue to remain clueless about the threat posed by computer criminals, espionage, identity theft, privacy invasion, and cyber terrorism. Globally, with a tremendous rise in cyber crime, there is a rapidly growing demand for highly skilled *ethical hackers* who can safeguard the Internet. This is where the books in the *Project Hacking Kitaab* series come into the picture. All books in this project contain tips, tricks, and secrets that help readers to make their life a lot safer. *Project Hacking Kitaab* would not have been possible without the hard work, dedication, and intellect of the highly talented stars who have been selected through the competitive Ankit Fadia Certified Ethical Hacker certification course (http://www.ankitfadiacertified.com). The stars that should be given credit for championing the books in this project at all stages from concept to release are Diwakar Goel, Manu Zacharia, and Jaya Bhattacharjee. The talented star behind this book in particular is Manu Zacharia. Kudos to each one of them!

Introduction

The access to the Internet has increased in the past few years and organizations have increasingly put critical information resources online. This has given rise to the activities of cyber criminals, and virtually all organizations face increasing threats to their network resources and services they provide.

This book was written to give its readers an introductory picture of the intrusion detection capabilities that are currently available. The goal is to go beyond learning how a product works, while focusing on how to use the information it gives you. Three of the most popular intrusion detection systems are covered. The reader learns to implement the product, understand essential administration and maintenance tasks, fine-tune, and use the data appropriately.

This book is organized into two sections—the first section deals with the various security concepts, the basics of security attacks and related issues, an introduction to IDS and its working concepts, the principles of IDS and the IDS architecture. The second section of the book deals with the installation and configuration of various IDS tools, including TCPdump, ISA Server 2004, and Snort.

When you are learning a new security topic or technology, it is always important to have all of the basics at your disposal. *Network Intrusion Alert: An Ethical Hacking Guide to Intrusion Detection* provides the building blocks of IDS technologies that will help you establish yourself in the security environment. The book offers an introduction and detailed overview of Intrusion Detection Systems (IDS) technology. Using real-world examples and step-by-step instructions, this book walks you through the lifecycle of an IDS project.

Whether you are evaluating IDS technologies or want to learn how to deploy and manage IDS in your network, this book is an invaluable resource for anyone who needs to know how IDS technology works, what kind of attacks it can or cannot detect, how it is deployed, and where it fits in the large security scenario.

This book is designed to teach the fundamentals of Intrusion Detection Systems and related network security topics to people who are fairly new to the topic:

- People interested in learning more about IDS and network security.
- Decision-makers who need to know the fundamentals in order to make valid and effective security choices.
- Administrators who feel they are missing some of the foundational information about information security.
- Those interested in learning more about why computer security is a problem and what IDS can do to mitigate the issue.
- Instructors teaching a network security fundamentals course.
- Students enrolled in a network security fundamentals course.

Happy Ethical Hacking!
—Ankit Fadia
fadia.ankit@gmail.com

CHAPTER 1

Computer Security and Intrusion Detection

There is no security on this earth, there is only opportunity.
—General Douglas MacArthur

Introduction

It is 3 AM in the morning when the SMS beep wakes up the System Admin from his sound sleep. He is startled to see the customized alert message that was originated from his network. The message is an alert indicating a Secure Shell overflow attempt, outbound from one of the machines in his network.

Welcome to the world of computer security and intrusion detection. This book covers the various aspects of the emerging discipline of computer security—intrusion detection, with an introduction to intrusion prevention.

Over time, attackers have become more sophisticated in the methodologies they use to intrude into corporate networks. These intruders spend a large part of their time and effort seeking ways to exploit weaknesses in the communication methods and systems used by common services, such as Web sites and email. Attackers routinely send abnormal commands or data to these services in an attempt to exploit both known and unknown weaknesses. Traditional firewalls cannot assess the validity of such communications because they do not understand them.

Computer Security and Intrusion Detection

This chapter attempts to give you a more systematic view of system security requirements and the potential means to satisfy them. I will be defining the properties of a secure computer system and will provide a classification of potential threats to them.

Security Policy

A *security policy* can be defined as the framework within which an organization establishes needed levels of information security to achieve the desired confidentiality goals. A *policy* is a statement of information values, protection responsibilities, and organization commitment for a system. Before you can evaluate attacks against a system and decide on appropriate mechanisms to repulse these threats, it is necessary to specify your security policy. A security policy that is sufficient for the data of one organization might not be sufficient for another organization. The biggest challenge for the system administrator is striking a balance between convenience and security. Many times system administrators have to take the hard decision of blocking certain services (that make life easy for employees) because they must keep the overall security concerns in mind. Security policies are also usually a tussle between the top-level management and the IT department. Being able to convince the top-level management to spend more on security is a constant battle for all system administrators. Unfortunately, budget issues often get in the way of having the correct security policies and mechanisms in place.

Security Attacks and Security Properties

The graphical representation of the communication process and some of the attacks are shown in the following figure.

Figure 1.1 Information Flow

Interruption

Interruption can be defined as a state where the asset of a system is destroyed or becomes unavailable. This kind of attack targets the source or the communication channel and prevents the information from reaching its intended target. For example, the attacker could cut the physical wire, thus preventing the information from reaching its destination. Another commonly used technique by the attacker is to overload the carrying media so that pertinent information is dropped due to the congestion. Attacks in this category attempt to perform a kind of *denial of service* (DOS).

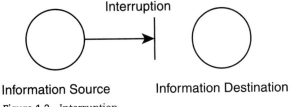

Figure 1.2   Interruption

Interception

Interception happens when an unauthorized party gets access to the information by eavesdropping into the communication channel. Wiretapping is a good example of an interception.

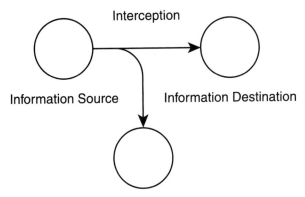

Figure 1.3   Interception

Modification

With *modification*, the information is not only intercepted, but modified by an unauthorized party while in transit from the source to the destination. (The unauthorized party modifies the message content and sends the modified content to the destination.)

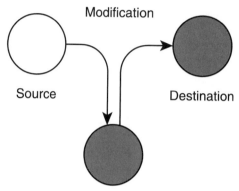

Figure 1.4   Modification

Fabrication

Fabrication occurs when an attacker inserts forged objects into the system without the senders' knowledge or involvement. Fabrication can be categorized as:

- **Replaying**—When a previously intercepted entity is inserted, this process is called replaying. For example, replaying an authentication message.

- **Masquerading**—When the attacker pretends to be the legitimate source and inserts his/her desired information, the attack is called masquerading. For example, adding new records to a file or database.

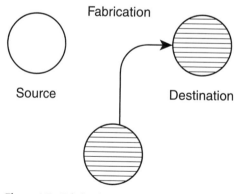

Figure 1.5   Fabrication

Security Property

A security property describes a desired feature of a system with regard to certain types of attacks. The four classes of attacks—Interruption, Interception, Modification, and Fabrication—violate the various security properties of a computer system. Some of the security properties and their descriptions are defined in the following sections.

Confidentiality

Confidentiality is defined by the International Organization for Standardization (ISO) as "ensuring that information is accessible only to those authorized to have access" and is one of the cornerstones of information security. Confidentiality covers the protection of transmitted data against its release to unauthorized parties. It is one of the design goals for many cryptosystems, made possible in practice by the techniques of modern cryptography.

In addition to the protection of the content itself, the information flow should also be resistant against traffic analysis. *Traffic analysis* is the process of intercepting and examining messages in order to deduce information from patterns in communication. Traffic analysis is used to gather other information than the transmitted values themselves from the data flow. For example, the following information can be collected using a simple traffic analysis:

- The source of the communication
- The destination of the communication
- The timing of the data
- The frequency of particular messages
- The type of data/communication

Integrity

When data has *integrity,* it means that the data has not been altered or destroyed in an unauthorized manner or by unauthorized users; it is a security principle that protects information from being modified or otherwise corrupted, either maliciously or accidentally. This property ensures that a single message reaches the receiver just as it left the sender. Integrity means that no messages are lost, duplicated, or re-ordered, and it makes sure that messages cannot be replayed. Because this property also contains information about whether or not data has been destroyed en route to the destination system, it plays a very important role in verifying that all data is received successfully.

Availability

High availability refers to a system or component that is continuously operational for a desirably long time. Availability can be measured relative to "100% operational" or "never failing." A widely held but difficult-to-achieve standard of availability for a system or product is known as "five 9s" (99.999 percent) availability. Availability characterizes a system whose resources are always available for use. This property makes sure that attacks cannot prevent resources from being used for their intended purpose.

Authentication

Authentication is defined as a security measure designed to establish the validity of a transmission, message, or originator, or a means of verifying an individual's authorization to receive specific categories of information. Authentication is mainly concerned with making sure that the information is authentic. A system implementing the authentication property ensures the recipient that the data is from the source that it claims to be. The authentication system must make sure that no third party can masquerade successfully as another source.

Nonrepudiation

Nonrepudiation is the concept of ensuring that a contract, especially one agreed to via the Internet, cannot later be denied by one of the parties involved. This property describes the mechanism that prevents either sender or receiver from denying a transmitted message. Nonrepudiation means that it can be verified that the sender and the recipient were, in fact, the parties who claimed to send or receive the message, respectively. In other words, nonrepudiation of origin proves that data was sent, and nonrepudiation of delivery proves it was received.

Security Mechanisms

The security properties discussed previously are the core qualities of any information system. Various security mechanisms can be used to enforce the security properties. A smart security professional has to anticipate the various attacks and apply various countermeasures to safeguard the security properties of the information system. The various measures that can be initiated to counter the attacks on the security properties are as follows:

- Attack prevention
- Attack avoidance
- Attack detection

Attack Prevention

Hackers and individuals with malicious intent commonly target corporate networks and services that constitute the corporate information system. By overwhelming these critical applications and networks with bogus service requests, denial-of-service attacks (DoS), and distributed denial of service (DDoS) attacks can severely disrupt the business, resulting in lost communications, failed business transactions, reduced business productivity, and lower profitability.

Attack prevention is defined as a series of security mechanisms implemented to prevent or defend against various kinds of attacks before they can actually reach and affect the target system. An important mechanism in this category is access control. *Access control* is the process of limiting access to the resources of an IS to authorized users, programs, processes, or other systems. Access control can be applied at different levels such as the operating system, the network layer, or the application layer.

> ## Access Control
>
> Access control is the ability to permit or deny the use of an object (a passive entity, such as a system or file) by a subject (an active entity, such as an individual or process).
>
> Access control includes authentication, authorization, and audit. It also includes additional measures such as physical devices, including but not limited to biometric scans and metal locks, hidden paths, digital signatures, encryption, social barriers, and monitoring by humans and automated systems (for all newbies reading this book, just do a simple Google or Wikipedia search for detailed information on these access control mechanisms). Authorization can also be implemented using role-based access control, access control lists, or a policy language such as XACML.
>
> Access control systems provide the essential services of identification and authentication (I&A), authorization, and accountability, where identification and authentication determine who can log on to a system, authorization determines what an authenticated user can do, and accountability identifies what a user did.

A *firewall* is also an important access control system that is implemented at the network layer. The concept behind a firewall is to separate the trusted network (internal network) from the untrusted network (an external network or Internet). The firewall prevents the attack from the outside world from reaching the machines in the inside network by preventing connection attempts from unauthorized entities located outside. Firewalls also perform the additional role of preventing the internal users from using certain services. All these are based on certain rules and criteria.

Attack Avoidance

The expansion of the connectivity of computers makes ways of protecting data and messages from tampering or reading important. *Attack avoidance* is the technique in which the information is modified in a way that makes it unusable for the attacker. This is performed under the assumption that the attacker can access the subject information. The sender pre-processes the information before it is sent through the unsecure communication channel and the same is post-processed at the receiver end. During this communication process, if an intruder manages to capture or access the data, it will be of no use to him, as it is modified in a specified manner at the source level. However, the attacker is still able to perform the attacks on the availability of the data. In case of any manipulation en route, the same can be detected while post-processing the data at the receiver end. The errors that may occur en route can also be detected in the same manner. If the data is not modified during the transfer, the data received is identical to the data transferred from the source.

Cryptography is one of the technologies used in the parlance of attack avoidance.

Cryptography

Cryptography (or *Cryptology*) is the study of message secrecy. The noted cryptographer Ron Rivest has observed that "cryptography is about communication in the presence of adversaries."

Cryptography is the discipline that embodies principles, means, and methods for the transformation of data in order to hide its information content, prevent its undetected modification, or prevent its unauthorized use. Cryptanalysis is the art of breaking these methods. Cryptology is the study of cryptography and cryptanalysis.

The cryptographic algorithms can be categorized into three areas based on the number of keys that are employed for the encryption and decryption. They are:

- **Secret key cryptography (SKC)**—Uses a single key for both encryption and decryption. Most modern day encryption technologies do not solely use secret key cryptography due to its susceptibility to attack. It is typically used in conjunction with public key cryptography.

- **Public key cryptography (PKC)**—Uses one key for encryption and another for decryption. For example, Secure Sockets Layer (SSL) is a system commonly used by e-commerce Web sites.

- **Hash functions**—Use a mathematical transformation to irreversibly "encrypt" information. For example, Message Digest Algorithm 5 (MD5).

Secret key (symmetric) cryptography uses a single key for both encryption and decryption

Public key (asymmetric) cryptography uses two keys, one for encryption and the other for decryption

Figure 1.6   Types of Cryptography

Cipher text is another name for encrypted text.

Notes

Attack Detection

The methods of *attack detection* assume that the attacker has bypassed the installed security measures and can access the desired target/information. When such incidents occur, attack detection reports that something went wrong and, in some cases, identifies the type of attack that occurred. However, on the other hand, attack detection is not effective in providing confidentiality of information. When the security system specifies that interception of information has a serious impact on the information system, attack detection is not an applicable mechanism. In the next level of attack detection, counter measures are initiated to recover from the impact of the attack. The most important member of the attack detection class is the intrusion detection system (IDS).

Intrusion Detection

Intrusion detection encompasses a range of security techniques designed to detect (and report on) malicious system and network activity or to record evidence of intrusion. Because this book is focused on intrusion detection, the remaining sections of this book are dedicated to a more detailed view into the inner workings of IDS.

Summary

This chapter covered the basics of computer security and the various types of security attacks and prevention mechanisms. Connecting to a network/Internet exposes your valuable assets to the insecure world. A better understanding of computer security concepts will help you arm yourself against these risks.

## CHAPTER 2

Attack Framework

If you know the enemy and know yourself, you need not fear the result of a hundred battles. If you know yourself but not the enemy, for every victory gained you will also suffer a defeat. If you know neither the enemy nor yourself, you will succumb in every battle.
—Sun Tzu

Introduction

The current trend in information security shows that new types of attacks are evolving at a faster rate. As the level of automation in attack tools continues to increase, the complexity also increases proportionally, making the life of a security professional very challenging. However, before proceeding toward an effective intrusion detection system, it is mandatory that you understand the various factors of an attack:

- What is an attack?
- What are the various types of attacks?
- How are they classified?
- How are these attacks carried out?

Without a sound knowledge of these factors, it would be nearly impossible for a security professional to detect the attacks and then prevent the negative impact of these attacks on the information system.

Security Events

During the normal operation of a system, various activities occur in the background without the user even knowing about them. However, from a security point of view, these activities are categorized as *actions* and *targets*. Actions are defined as the steps initiated by a specific *subject* (a service, thread, a user, and so on) in order to achieve a specific result. The following are examples of an action: reading a file, copying a file, modifying a file, accessing a folder, and so on. On the other hand, a target is defined as a logical (user account, group account, process, data on the system, and so on) or physical (client, network components, and so on) system object.

A user accessing a file can be an example of an *event*. When the subject event occurs within the security boundary of the established rules, it is considered a normal event. When a specific event violates the boundaries of the established security policy, it is considered (part of) an attack.

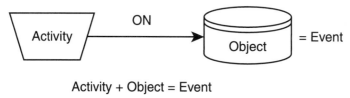

Activity + Object = Event

Figure 2.1   Security Event

An *auditable security event* is defined as any event that can be logged using the audit subsystem such as a logger, sniffer, or other mechanism. Examples of security-relevant events include the creation of a file, the building of a network connection, or a user logging in. Auditable events are either *attributable*, meaning that they can be traced to an authenticated user, or *nonattributable* if they cannot be. Examples of nonattributable events are any events that occur before authentication in the login process, such as bad password attempts.

Vulnerabilities

Vulnerability is defined as the existence of a weakness, design, or implementation error that can lead to an unexpected, undesirable event compromising the security of the system, network, application, or protocol involved. From a penetration tester's point of view, vulnerability is defined as a security weakness in a *target of evaluation*. It is the existence of a characteristic in an information system that might result in the realization of a threat if exploited by an intruder. On the other hand, a threat (to the information system) is defined as any possible event, action, process, or phenomenon that can potentially inflict damage on system resources. The following figure shows the relationship of these terms.

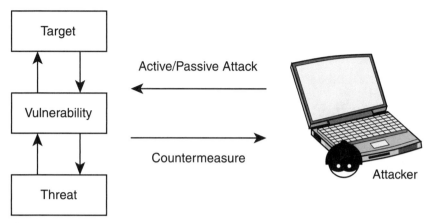

Figure 2.2   Target, Vulnerability, and Threat Relationship

Real-Life Case Study—
An Expensive Bug and a Crash

Sometimes a bug is more than an error message. It took almost 10 years and $7 billion for the European Space Agency (http://www.esa.int/) to build the Ariane 5, a giant rocket capable of placing a pair of three-ton satellites into orbit with each launch with the aim of Europe achieving overwhelming supremacy in the commercial space market. The unmanned Ariane 5 was launched on June 4, 1996.

Immediately after its launch (in less than a minute), the giant Ariane 5 exploded into flames, scattering fiery rubble across the mangrove swamps of French Guiana. The cause of the explosion—in simple terms—was a very small computer program trying to stuff a 64-bit number into a 16-bit space. Technically explaining the crash—the cause of the explosion was a software error in the inertial reference system, specifically, a 64-bit floating point number relating to the horizontal velocity of the rocket with respect to the platform was converted to a 16-bit signed integer. The number was larger than 32,767, the largest integer storable in a 16-bit signed integer, causing the conversion to fail.

Vulnerabilities can be classified as follows:

- Design vulnerabilities
- Implementation vulnerabilities
- Configuration or operational vulnerabilities

Design Vulnerabilities

A vulnerability is classified under the design category when it's said to be inherent to the project or design. Because the vulnerability is inherent to the project/product, it is very difficult to detect and eliminate. A proper implementation of the product will not get rid of such a flaw.

A very simple example is the TCP/IP protocol stack vulnerabilities, which refer to the various vulnerabilities that exist in the TCP/IP protocol suite. When someone unscrupulous exploits these vulnerabilities, this leads to various security attacks. The security requirements/scenarios were not taken into consideration while developing the TCP/IP protocol stack, which resulted in the detection of new vulnerabilities every time. The most serious fact about a design vulnerability is that it cannot be eliminated or rectified once and for all with a patch or service pack. The only possible solution to this problem is to take temporary preventive measures. Because the flaw lies in the design of a system, there exists many potential ways to bypass the default security mechanism to compromise the system. IDS plays a vital role in detecting design vulnerabilities by reporting the intrusion attempts to compromise the integrity of the system.

Implementation Vulnerabilities

When an error is introduced into the components of a system during the implementation stage of a project or algorithm, whether it is hardware-based or software-based, this error is called an implementation vulnerability. Buffer overflows that are introduced into a system during the realization phase are examples of implementation vulnerabilities.

Wikipedia defines buffer overflow as follows:

- In computer security and programming, a *buffer overflow,* or *buffer overrun,* is a programming error that can result in a memory access exception and program termination, or in the event of the user being malicious, a breach of system security.

- A buffer overflow is an anomalous condition where a process attempts to store data beyond the boundaries of a fixed-length buffer. The result is that the extra data overwrites adjacent memory locations. The overwritten data may include other buffers, variables, and program flow data.

- Buffer overflows can cause a process to crash or produce incorrect results. They can be triggered by inputs specifically designed to execute malicious code or to make the program operate in an unintended way. As such, buffer overflows cause many software vulnerabilities and form the basis of many exploits. Sufficient bounds-checking by the programmer or the compiler can prevent buffer overflows. *Bounds checking* involves simple checks that can be introduced into an application that check whether the input data can be accepted, stored, and processed securely without any major security infiltration or application crash. For example, if a user tries to access the eleventh variable in an array of length 10, the application being used might behave unpredictably.

Real-Life Example of Buffer Overflow— eBay Picture Manager Vulnerability

In July 2006, a major bug was detected in the *EPUImageControl* object of the eBay's Picture Manager. The hole lies within the way in which ActiveX controls are integrated in the Web page. The exploitation of such a vulnerability causes a buffer overflow on the Picture Manager, eventually permitting the execution of remote arbitrary code.

The vulnerability in eBay Picture Manager ActiveX control could allow an attacker to use specially crafted HTML to trigger to buffer overflow in the *EPUImageControl* COM object in EUPWALcontrol.dll. Such an attempt makes the target machine vulnerable to the execution of arbitrary code with the same privileges as the target user.

Configuration/Operational Vulnerabilities

The last category of vulnerability is *configuration vulnerability,* also known as *operational vulnerability*. These types of vulnerabilities are introduced into the system when the administrator responsible does not perform the proper configuration or sometimes uses the default configuration settings. Because the default passwords to most systems are well known, attackers can easily enter such a system. Not disabling unwanted services, allowing weak passwords, and not checking for invalid password attempts are all examples of configuration/operational vulnerabilities.

Oracle 9iAS SOAP Default Configuration Vulnerability

In the default installation of Oracle 9iAS v.1.0.2.2, it is possible to deploy or un-deploy SOAP services without the need of any kind of credentials. This is due to SOAP being enabled by default after installation in order to provide a convenient way to use SOAP samples. However, this feature poses a threat to HTTP servers with public access because remote attackers can create SOAP services and then invoke them remotely. Because SOAP services can contain arbitrary Java code in Oracle 9iAS, an attacker can therefore execute arbitrary code in the remote server.

Attacks

An *attack* is defined as an assault on a system's security that derives from an intelligent threat, that is, an intelligent act that is a deliberate attempt to evade security services and violate the security policy of a system. Examples of attacks include denial-of-service attacks, penetration, and sabotage. The difference between a security event and an attack boils down to user access or privileges. For example, an example of a security event is a user directing a document to a print server to which he is authorized. However, if the user accesses a CD writer or a USB drive that he or she is normally not authorized to access, thereby bypassing the permissions, this event is categorized as an attack.

An attack consists of the following components:

- **Attack realization tool**—An attacker will be using some kind of security tool to perform/prepare the attack. For example, to perform a port scan, an attacker might be using nMap.

- **Vulnerability**—The attacker might exploit one of the types of vulnerabilities discussed in the previous section to carry out an attack.

- **Security event**—When an attacker performs some action on the target system, an event occurs. For example, when the attacker bypasses the security infrastructure and accesses the protected resources, a security event is said to have occurred. To implement an attack, the intruder models a specific security event.

- **Result of the attack**—When an attacker exploits a vulnerability and generates a security event, the outcome is known as the result of an attack. The results of an attack might vary depending upon the security event and vulnerability chosen.

Attack Models

To effectively implement an Intrusion Detection System, it is always ideal to understand the nature of an attack and the various attack models. An attack generally consists of the elements illustrated in Figure 2.3.

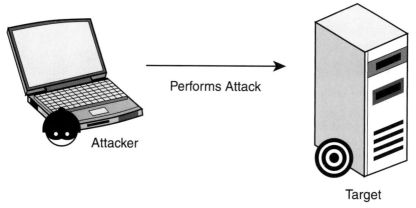

Figure 2.3   Attack Model

In some cases, the attacker and the target represent the same entity. That means the attacker has gained accessed to the host or group of hosts that represent the target entity. Both the attacker and the target entity can represent a single host or a group of hosts (for example, a network segment).

Figure 2.4   Attacker and Target Are on the Same Entity

In such a scenario, the ideal solution to prevent such an attack is either to eliminate the attacker or the target host or groups of hosts. It is not practical to eliminate the target, as without a target there is no scope for an attack. The only available option is then to concentrate on the attacker.

The attack model is classified into two categories, which are categorized as shown here:

- Traditional attack model

  One-to-one attack model

  One-to-many attack model

- Distributed attack model

  Many-to-one attack model

  Many-to-many attack model

Traditional Attack Models

The traditional attack model is based on the one-to-one and one-to-many concept. This kind of attack always originates from a single point. The traditional attack model implements a single-tier architecture, which means that there is only a single layer between the attacker and the target.

- **One-to-one (traditional attack model)**—In the one-to-one attack model, the attacker, and the target are having a one-to-one relationship. The attack originates from a single machine, as shown in Figure 2.5.

Figure 2.5   One-to-One Attack (Traditional Attack Model)

- **One-to-many (traditional attack model)**—In a one-to-many attack model, the attacker and the target are having a one-to-many relationship. The attack originates from a single machine; however, there is more than one target, as shown in Figure 2.6.

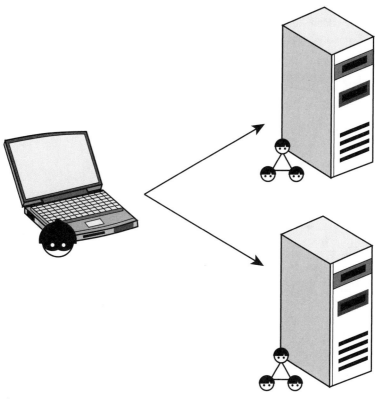

Figure 2.6   One-to-Many Attack (Traditional Attack Model)

Distributed Attack Models

The distributed attack model is based on the many-to-one and many-to-many relationships, in which the source of the attack is always more than one entity. The most important feature of this attack model is that the data packets originate from intermediate systems that are compromised by the attacker rather than from the attacker's own system.

- **Many-to-one (distributed attack model)**—In this attack, the attacker and target are having a many-to-one relationship. The source of the attack is in a distributed mode and is attacking a single target, as shown in Figure 2.7.

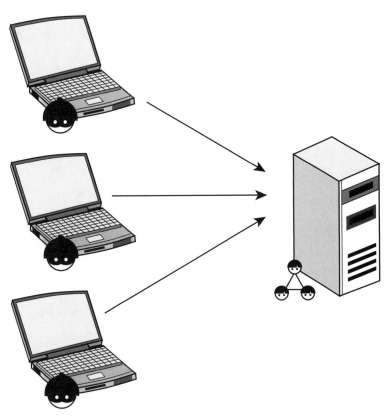

Figure 2.7   Many-to-One Attack (Distributed Attack Model)

- **Many-to-many (distributed attack model)**—In this attack, the attacker and the target are having a many-to-many relationship. There is more than one source and more than one target, as displayed in Figure 2.8.

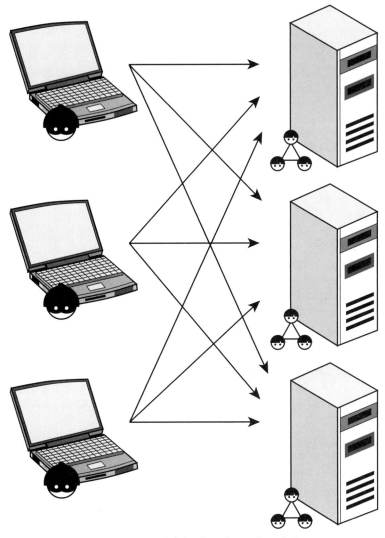

Figure 2.8   Many-to-Many Attack (Distributed Attack Model)

A distributed attack is implemented in three stages:

- Reconnaissance
- Compromise the system
- Attack initiation

Reconnaissance

During this stage, the attacker performs a reconnaissance (inspection) on the Internet, searching for suitable hosts that could be used for initiating the distributed attacks. The efficiency of the attack is directly proportional to the number of compromised systems at the attacker's disposal. Hence, the attacker always tries to find the maximum number of hosts for this purpose.

Compromise the System

During this phase, the attacker compromises the system by getting into the host system and installing back doors and tools for initiating the distributed attacks. These compromised systems that the attacker uses to perform distributed attacks are generally known as *zombies*.

Attack Initiation

Once the attacker has acquired a sufficient number of hosts at his or her disposal, the attacker is ready to start the attack using the compromised system. Because the attack originates from more than one source, it is very difficult to identify and block the attack from its source.

It is important to note that all compromised systems that an attacker gains control over are called zombies. Distributed attacks are performed using special types of agents (installed on these zombies) that fall into two categories:

- *Masters* are examples of compromised systems or zombies that are used typically to control the daemons. In other words, a single attacker controls multiple masters, and each master controls multiple daemons.
- *Daemons* are examples of zombies that usually are controlled by the masters, which are actually controlled by the attacker. All attacks seem to originate from the daemons.

To recapitulate, each attacker controls multiple masters, each of which control multiple daemons. These daemons actually are the points from which the attack packets are originated. The distributed attack model implements a three-tier architecture, which means that there are three layers between the attacker and the target. These layers make tracing the origin of the attack very difficult.

Distributed DoS with Reflectors (DRDoS)

The latest and the most dangerous transformation of the DoS/DDoS attack model is the Distributed DoS with Reflectors (DRDoS) model. As is evident from its name, reflectors are the new elements included in the model. Instead of providing more computational power for the attacker, reflectors help the attackers to execute a more effective and secure attack, resulting in a more harmful and harder-to-trace attack.

The reflector's goal is to deflect any response to the attack onto itself, which is accomplished by having the zombies list a reflector as the originator of the traffic instead of the actual origin. This DoS model allows the zombies to be free to attack at all times, and also decreases the possibility of trace-back, because the target server assumes the reflectors are the originator of traffic, and thus forwards all responses to them. Reflectors can be introduced into an attack if the zombies use spoofed addresses as the source address for all data packets sent to the victim system. There are many packet-generation tools available that can be used by the attacker to carry out a DRDoS attack.

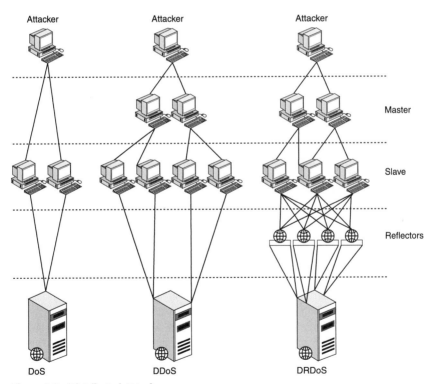

Figure 2.9   Distributed Attacks

Noted Advantages of the Distributed Attack Model

The distributed attack model provides the attacker with the following advantages:

- **Attack effect**—A well-coordinated attack that originates from multiple locations can have a devastating effect on the target. Because the attack effect is directly proportional to the number of attacking systems, the distributed attack model typically delivers the desired results from an attacker's point of view.

- **Anonymity**—Because the actual attack originates from multiple locations, the distributed attack model provides the attacker a high ground for covering his tracks.

- **Hard-to-stop attacks**—The distributed attacks are sometimes referred to as hard-to-stop attacks. The level of anonymity involved and the dimensions at which the attack is carried out makes the distributed attack very difficult to stop without bringing down or disconnecting the target system from the network.

Intruders

The *intruder* (also known as the attacker) is the first element in the attack model. An intruder is a person who attempts to gain unauthorized access to a system, to damage that system, or to disturb data on that system. Basically, this person attempts to violate the security code by interfering with system availability, data integrity, or data confidentiality.

Intruders and their activities can be categorized as follows:

- **Black hat hackers**—A black hat (also called a cracker or dark side hacker) is a person who uses their skills with computers and other technological knowledge in a malicious or criminal manner.

- **Hacker spies supported by governments**—These are hackers supported by governmental organizations attempting to get into enemy systems for information gathering.

- **Cyber terrorists**—Cyber terrorists attack the computers and information systems of their enemies to cause physical, real-world harm or to sever disruption with the aim of advancing the attacker's own political or religious goals.

- **Corporate spies**—These kinds of intruders are funded by corporate agencies to get into the systems of rivals for the purposes of gathering information about upcoming projects, accessing research and development work, defacing Web sites, bringing down critical services, and so on.

- **Professional criminals**—These intruders target financial (including e-commerce) organizations. Their activities include transferring funds illegally from banks and other financial organizations, getting hold of customer information such as credit card details and social security numbers, and more.

- **Vandals**—Vandals are intruders without any specific goals, motives, or targets. Their only aim is to produce as much damage as possible to absolutely any system that they can get their hands on. Unlike black hat hackers, vandals don't have any particular targets in mind.

Incidents

An incident is defined as a violation or imminent threat of violation that could or does result in a loss of data confidentiality, disruption of data or system integrity, or disruption or denial of availability. Every abnormal event and malfunction is not an incident. An incident must clearly be a breach of network security.

Examples of incidents include but are not limited to:

- **Denial of service**—An attacker sends specially crafted packets to a Web server, causing it to crash. An attacker directs hundreds of external compromised workstations to send as many Internet Control Message Protocol (ICMP) requests as possible to the organization's network.

- **Malicious code**—A worm uses open file shares to quickly infect several hundred workstations within an organization.

- **Unauthorized access**—An attacker runs an exploit tool to gain access to a server's password file or a perpetrator obtains unauthorized administrator-level access to a system and then threatens the victim that the details of the break-in will be released to the press if the organization does not pay a designated sum of money.

- **Inappropriate usage**—A user provides illegal copies of software to others through peer-to-peer file sharing services or a person threatens another person through email.

Summary

This chapter covered the attack framework and the various attack models. A better understanding of the attack framework discussed in this chapter will enable a security administrator to effectively equip his or her arsenal with proper tools for fighting against the evil forces of the underground network community.

## CHAPTER 3

Introduction to IDS and IPS

When meditating over a disease, I never think of finding a remedy for it, but, instead, a means of preventing it.
—Louis Pasteur (1822–1895)

Introduction

Intrusion detection encompasses a range of security techniques designed to detect (and report on) malicious system and network activity or to record evidence of intrusion. To understand intrusion detection, one must first understand what intrusion is. Webster's dictionary defines an intrusion as "the act of thrusting in, or of entering into a place or state without invitation, right, or welcome." For the purposes of this book, I define *intrusion* as any unauthorized system or network activity on one (or more) computer(s) or network(s). This can be an instance of a legitimate system user trying to escalate his privileges so that he can gain greater access to the system that he is currently assigned, a legitimate user trying to connect to a remote port of a server to which he is not authorized to, a remote or an unauthenticated user trying to compromise a running service in order to create an account on a system, a virus running uncontrolled through the email and instant messenger system, or many other similar scenarios. These intrusions can originate from the outside world, from a disgruntled ex-employee who was fired last week, or from your own trusted staff.

What Is an IDS?

Intrusion detection systems (IDSs) are software- or/and hardware-based systems that detect intrusions to your network/host based on a number of telltale signs. Active IDSs attempt to block attacks and respond with countermeasures that are already pre-programmed into the IDS system, or at least alert administrators while the attack progresses in a pre-defined way. Passive IDSs merely log the intrusion or create audit trails that are apparent after the attack has succeeded.

The term *intrusion detection* covers a wide range of technologies that are involved in the detection, reporting, and correlation of system and network security events. Intrusion detection technologies are detective rather than preventive, but they can help mitigate the following types of risks by providing a security administrator with information on attempted or actual security events:

- Data destruction
- Denial-of-service attacks
- Hostile code, for example, buffer overflow attempt
- Network or system eavesdropping
- System or network mapping
- System or network intrusion
- Unauthorized access

Intrusion detection systems are weapons in the arsenal of system administrators, network administrators, and security professionals, allowing real-time reporting of suspicious and malicious system and network activity. Although they are not perfect and will not show you every possible attack, IDSs can provide much-needed intelligence about what's really going on in your hosts and your network. IDS is not a standalone protection system, but part of an overall protection system that is installed around a system or device.

Types of IDS Systems

The intrusion detection systems are categorized into three types:

- Host-based intrusion detection system (HIDS)
- Network-based intrusion detection system (NIDS)
- Hybrid intrusion detection systems

Host-Based Intrusion Detection Systems (HIDS)

An HIDS is an IDS that resides on the host. The HIDS scans the host systems for activities. Typically, the HIDS scan the operating system log files, application log files, or DBMS log files for activity traces. This makes them completely dependent on the contents of the log files. As a result, if the log file data is corrupt or, in the worst case, if the attacker is able to manipulate the log file information, these systems will not be able to detect the occurrence of an attack. The results of the scan performed by the host-based intrusion detection system are logged into a secure database and compared with the knowledge base to detect any malicious activity.

There are various types of host-based intrusion detection systems that work at the various levels. They are:

- Operating system level HIDS
- Application level HIDS
- Network level HIDS

Operating System Level

These types of host-based intrusion detection systems function by working on the operating system's log files These HIDS determine unauthorized activities based on the following criteria:

- Applications initiated on a system
- Logon and logoff credentials like date and time, login location, and so on
- Addition/deletion/modification of system entities
- Access to system resources such as files/folders/memory locations/the Registry

The information collected from the log files are compiled and compared to the signatures available in the database using special algorithms.

Application Level

These types of HIDS are very similar to the OS level HIDS. The main difference is that HIDS concentrate more on the application level log files rather than on the system level log files. These types of HIDS are good for detecting intrusion attempts on a database application residing on a host machine.

Network Level

Even though the name of these HIDS looks very similar to NIDS (discussed in the next section), they are different. A network level HIDS works on the network packets that are addressed to or sent from the particular host. If a packet is not addressed to the host, the network level HIDS will not collect and work on the network packet.

Advantages of HIDS

The advantages of using HIDS are several:

- **HIDS are cost effective**—HIDS are more cost effective when compared to NIDS for a small to medium sized network.
- **HIDS provide an additional layer of protection**—In a multi-tiered security architecture, HIDS can provide an additional level of security by detecting attacks missed by other security tools in the architecture.
- **HIDS provide direct control over system entities**—Because HIDS work at the host level, you have more control and command over the system entities like the memory, the Registry, system files, and the like.

Network-Based Intrusion Detection Systems

Network-based intrusion detection systems are IDSs responsible for detecting inappropriate, anomalous, or any other kind of data that's considered unauthorized or inappropriate for a subject network. The NIDS is designed to receive all packets on a particular network segment. In the case of a switched network, various methods like taps and port mirroring are used to receive all the packets in the network.

Most NIDS are pattern based, which means that they require signatures to alert any intrusion attempt, or a set pattern in the payload. The accuracy of these approaches depends on the level to which the NIDS is fine-tuned.

Hybrid Intrusion Detection Systems

Hybrid intrusion detection systems are IDSs that combine the features of host-based IDS and network-based IDS. The host-based IDS monitors events occurring at the host level, and the network-based IDS is configured to monitor the network activities.

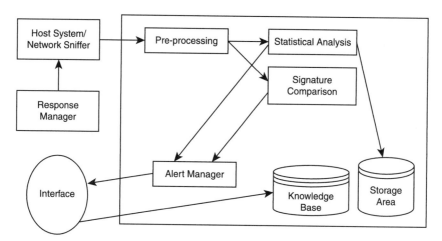

Figure 3.1   Intrusion Detection Process

What Is an IPS?

Almost all of the corporate networks (and in fact personal systems) are protected by firewalls. However, these firewalls are not always effective against the emerging intrusion attempts. The average firewall is designed to deny clearly defined or suspicious traffic—such as an attempt to telnet to a device when corporate security policy forbids telnet access completely. The same firewall is also designed to allow some traffic through, for example, Web traffic to an internal Web server.

The problem with conventional firewalls is that many new generation exploits attempt to take advantage of the existing weaknesses in the very protocol that is allowed through the perimeter firewall. Assuming that one of the internal Web servers has been compromised, the Web server can now be used as a launch pad to initiate additional attacks on other internal servers or external networks.

At this time, the hacker installs the *root kit* or *back door*. The best way to understand how a root kit works is by using an analogy from a real-life robbery. Imagine that you break into a bank and leave the bathroom window slightly open. That open window becomes a *root kit* that allows you to keep entering the bank again in the future until it is discovered and fixed by the security authorities. These root kits allow hackers to have unfettered access to the compromised system at any point of time.

Another important factor to remember is that the firewalls are typically positioned only at the network perimeter. But many attacks, intentional or unintentional, are launched from within an organization/network. Hotspots, wireless access points, virtual private networks, laptops—they all provide access to the internal network that often bypasses the firewall protection. Intrusion detection systems may be effective at detecting suspicious activity, but they do not provide *protection* against such attacks. The propagation speeds of recent computer worms such as *Slammer* and *Blaster* (if you do a simple Google or Wikipedia search you will realize how much damage these worms inflicted on millions of systems worldwide) are so fast that by the time an alert is generated, the damage is already done, and it is moving toward its next target.

The innate shortcomings in the current security systems have driven the development of a new breed of security solutions known as *intrusion prevention systems*. These systems are proactive defense mechanisms designed to detect malicious packets within normal network traffic (something that the current breed of firewalls do not actually do, for example) and stop network intrusion/penetration by blocking the unauthorized traffic automatically before it does any damage rather than by simply raising an alert and sending messages all over.

Intrusion prevention systems are sophisticated classes of network security implementations that not only have the ability to detect the presence of intruders and their actions, but also can prevent them from successfully launching any attack. Intrusion prevention systems incorporate the security features of firewall technology and those of intrusion detection systems. They can be viewed as a successful integration of both security technologies for higher and broader security measures. One of the negative points associated with intrusion prevention systems is that they may not be as fast and robust as some of the conventional firewalls and intrusion detection systems. For this reason, they might not be appropriate solutions when speed is of high importance. Intrusion prevention systems are a constant area of research and could be a sought-after technology in the future.

Categories of IPS

Intrusion prevention systems are categorized as follows:

- Host IPS (HIPS)
- Network IPS (NIPS)

Host Intrusion Prevention Systems (HIPS)

Host intrusion prevention systems (HIPS) involve security software that is loaded on each PC and server you want to protect. This security software monitors and tracks how processes running on each system interact with each other and with the operating system itself. This software control mechanism has policy-based rules configured by the security staff that controls how applications are allowed to run. These rules vary in their functions but can control how processes access the Registry, COM components, network, disk drives, memory, and various programming APIs, among other items. This allows you to have extremely granular control over how systems and their software function and interact with each other. By implementing a host IPS, you can not only protect your systems from unauthorized access and Trojan horse–like behavior (including day-zero attacks, which are examples of security vulnerabilities that are misused by attackers before knowledge of the vulnerability becomes public information), but also implement a software package capable of enforcing your corporate security policy and acceptable usage documents.

The benefits of using HIPS are as follows:

- **Attack prevention**—The most important benefit of using HIPS is that it can stop both well-known and new attacks. This drastically reduces the inoculation and remedial costs.

- **Patch relief**—Applying patches to the systems is a costly affair. Also, the time between the discovery of a vulnerability and the creation of an exploit that takes advantage of it is shrinking. A HIPS can stop new and unknown attacks so that patching does not have to be as high a priority.

- **Internal attack propagation prevention**—The Internet is always a source of attack for any network, and many network administrators focus their attention on the attacks that originate from the Internet. However, when an internal host is compromised, it takes the role of an attacker. The propagation vector now changes from Internet to host and becomes internal host to internal host. The only feasible way to address the issue of internal attack propagation is to use software that resides on the host itself instead of on the network. HIPS can prevent a protected host from attacking others, and it can prevent the host from being a victim of an attack.

- **Policy enforcement**—HIPS also helps ensure that the corporate security policy is enforced in the right spirit. For example, the corporate security policy might state that removable storage devices should not be used to store data. To enforce this policy, you could remove all the removable storage device drives. But this is not practical. Using HIPS, this can be achieved by controlling the flow of data from the hard drive or the network to removable storage devices. You can prevent anything from being written to removable storage, but at the same time, anything can be read. This allows the devices to be used for legitimate purposes, but the user cannot violate the policy. The following figure shows the message displayed when the user tries to violate the policy.

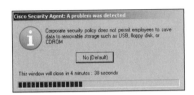

Figure 3.2   Cisco Security Agent

- **Regulatory requirements**—Most of the HIPS can be configured to fulfill the various government regulatory requirements. For example, the Administrative Simplification provisions of the United States Health Insurance Portability and Accountability Act of 1996 (also popularly known as HIPAA) defines standards for the security and privacy of health data, most of which can be met by the proper configuration of HIPS.

Hack Notes: How to Bypass/Disable HIPS

The Windows operating system includes a troubleshooting tool called *Safe mode.* When the system is running in Safe mode, most of the applications are disabled for troubleshooting purposes. In most cases, Safe mode also disables HIPS. Once it is disabled, the user can remove it entirely or disable HIPS.

Network Intrusion Prevention System (NIPS)

Network intrusion prevention systems (NIPS) can be defined as proactive components that effectively integrate into your overall network security framework. A robust, defense-in-depth network security solution (explained later in this chapter) can be built by combining a network intrusion prevention system with other security components such as a host intrusion prevention system (HIPS), an intrusion detection system (IDS), and perimeter firewalls.

An NIPS allows you to stop the intruders and unauthorized traffic from entering your network by placing the sensors as Layer 2 (Ethernet layer) forwarding devices in the network. (A *switch*, for example, is a common forwarding device on a network. It receives traffic on one of its ports and then passes that traffic to another one of its ports. Unlike routing at Layer 3, which rewrites the Ethernet header at each hop, Layer 2 forwarding simply passes the frame to the destination system without modification.) A typical IPS Sensor implementation is shown in Figure 3.3. Typically, an IPS sensor has two interfaces.

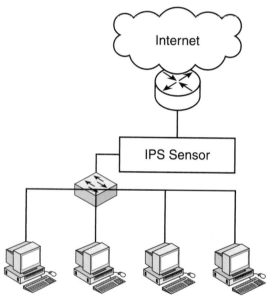

Figure 3.3   Basic NIPS

The IPS sensor has the capability to examine any packet that passes through it. The capability of an IPS to drop (modify) traffic that is received on one of its interface differentiates an IPS from an IDS. This capability prevents the original traffic (if it is malicious/unauthorized) from reaching its destination. The dropping of packets can be categorized as follows:

- **Dropping a single packet**—This is the simplest form of intrusion prevention in which each packet is scanned and, if identified as unauthorized or suspicious, is dropped before it reaches the target system/network. However, the attacker might be sending bad packets repeatedly. Here is the catch. The IPS will be analyzing each packet originated by the attacker to determine whether the same needs to be passed or dropped, which will consume the resources on the IPS device.

- **Dropping all packets from a connection**—The second category is that the IPS can be configured to drop all packets for a specific connection for a configured period of time rather than dropping each single packet. In this scenario, when a suspicious packet is detected, it is dropped along with all subsequent packets that belong to the same connection. The parameters used in this scenario are as follows:

  - Source IP address

  - Destination IP address

  - Destination port

  - Source port (optional)

  - The advantage of using the connection drop option is that the subsequent packets that match the connection can be dropped automatically without performing the packet analysis. This saves IPS resources, which in turn increases the performance of the IPS device.

  - The disadvantage is that the attacker can still manipulate his or her connection parameters and attack by sending packets that do not match the connection being dropped for example, by attacking another port or service or system on the same network. If any of the parameters are changed, the attacker can easily send packets to the network.

- **Dropping all traffic from a source IP**—In this case, all the traffic originating from a specific source IP address is dropped. In this scenario, if a suspicious packet is detected, it is dropped. Also, all the packets originating from the same IP address are also dropped for a configured period of time.

  - *Advantages*—Because all the packets originating from a particular source IP can be dropped with a minimum examination, the IPS device uses very few resources.

  - *Disadvantages*—If the attacker is able to spoof the source address, he or she can immediately change the parameters and bypass the dropping feature of the IPS. Also, if the attacker is able to spoof the source address and pretend to be an important system, such as a business partner or a machine where trust relationships are established, he or she can perform a DoS attack by denying the legitimate traffic.

The History of Intrusion Detection and Prevention

Any book written on intrusion detection and prevention is not complete without talking about its origin and history. Intrusion prevention systems are a fairly new and evolving branch of network security, whereas intrusion detection has a bit more history associated with it. The basic concept of both IDS and IPS originated from auditing. The first reference to this is the technical report called *Computer Security Threat Monitoring and Surveillance* submitted by James Anderson in 1980 for the U.S. Air Force. The report suggested that audit records could be used to help identify the misuse of computers and identify threat calculation. The report also offered suggestions to improve auditing of systems to identify the misuse. With the release of this paper, the concept of "detecting" misuse and specific user events emerged. This insight into audit data and its importance led to tremendous improvements in the auditing subsystems of virtually every operating system. (A copy of this report—*Computer Security Threat Monitoring and Surveillance*—can be found at http://seclab.cs.ucdavis.edu/projects/history/papers/ande80.pdf, if you are interested.)

In 1983, a team from SRI International (http://www.sri.com/) lead by Dr. Dorothy Denning, began working on a government project that launched a new effort into intrusion detection development. The project was funded by the U.S. Navy. Their main goal was to analyze audit trails from government mainframe computers and create profiles of users based upon their system activities. One year later, the first model for intrusion detection, the Intrusion Detection Expert System (IDES), was developed. This provided the foundation for the IDS technology development that was soon to follow.

In 1984, SRI also developed a means of tracking and analyzing audit data containing authentication information of users on ARPANET, the original Internet. Soon after, SRI completed the Navy SPAWAR contract and this in turn realized the first functional intrusion detection system, IDES. In 1987, Dr. Denning published a paper called *An Intrusion Detection Model* for the 1986 IEEE Symposium on security and privacy that helped describe the basic workings of behavioral analysis. Behavioral analysis looks for deviations from the type of behavior that has been statistically baseline, such as relationships in packets and in what is being sent over a network. Her paper is the basis for most of the work in IDS that followed. (A copy of this paper—*An Intrusion Detection Model*—can be found at http://www.cs.georgetown.edu/~denning/infosec/ids-model.rtf, if you are interested.)

While SRI was working on IDES for the Navy in 1987, Los Alamos National Laboratory was working on the Haystack Project. The project produced an IDS system with the capability to analyze audit data against pre-defined patterns. Several team members from the Haystack Project worked with designers and developers from the University of California, Davis and Lawrence Livermore National Laboratory (http://www.llnl.gov/) (and later Trident Data Systems) to develop an IDS called the Distributed Intrusion Detection System (DIDS) for the U.S. Air Force. DIDS became the basis for a commercial IDS (Net Stalker), with similar functionality by Haystack Labs.

In 1989, Todd Heberlein, a student at the University of California, Davis, built an IDS system called Network Security Monitor (NSM). NSM was different from IDES and DIDS in that it would analyze network traffic rather than system logs.

A great deal of developments happened in the 1990s. The U.S. Air Force Commissioned Science Applications International Corporation (SAIC) to develop the Computer Misuse Detection System (CMDS). Some of the other products that were developed during this period include the commercial IDS called Network Flight Recorder (NFR) and Automated Security Incident Measurement (ASIM) by the U.S. Air Force Cryptologic Support Center. ASIM is the first IDS to incorporate both software and hardware based solutions.

Some of the developers of ASIM formed the Wheel Group, acquired by Cisco in 1998, which ultimately led to Cisco Systems developing IDS to be included in their router's functionality. At this time, the Centrax Corporation released the host-based intrusion detection for Windows NT called eNTrax.

The intrusion detection system markets started getting popular and generating revenues by 1997. The security market leader, ISS, developed a network intrusion detection system called RealSecure. In 1998, Cisco recognized the importance of network intrusion detection and purchased the Wheel Group. Likewise, the first visible host-based intrusion detection system company, Centrax Corporation, emerged as a result of a merger of the development staff from Haystack Labs and the departure of the CMDS team from SAIC.

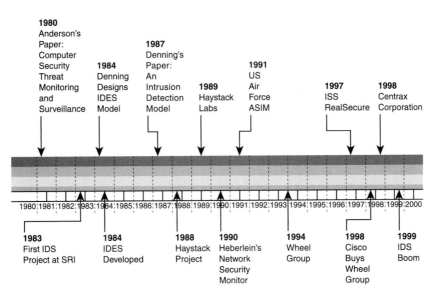

Figure 3.4 IDS Timeline

Why Choose an IDS or IPS?

> *But a lot of businesses out there don't see the return on investment, they look at it as a liability, and until they can understand that proactive security actually returns, gives them a return on investment, it's still a hard sell for people.*
> —Kevin Mitnick, *Controversial Computer Hacker*

The initial design and function of the intrusion detection system was aimed at protecting the network and its vital information from the outside network/Internet. However, this is slowly changing as more and more organizations want to monitor their internal networks—studies show the majority of losses in the commercial sector involve insiders. The information industry now wants to use the IDS in any of the following combinations: to track down insiders, catch them in the act, get the evidence needed for prosecution, fire them, or take them to court for indictment.

Another reason why you should consider not deploying an IDS is that the technology is still in its infancy and intrusions get missed due to its immaturity. New attack techniques are coming out each month, and the IDS technology must adapt to these rapid changes. IDS and IPS offer many benefits, including:

- Provide worthwhile information about malicious traffic.
- Greater proficiency in detecting intrusions than by doing it manually.
- Help identify the source of the incoming probes or attacks.
- Ability to deal with large volumes of data.
- Real-time detection and alerting capabilities that help reduce potential damages.
- Automated responses, for example, logging off a user, disabling a user account, or launching automated scripts.
- Forensic evidences can be collected, which could be used to identify intruders.
- Built-in reporting capabilities.
- Help in meeting the requirements for various legal and regulatory issues.
- Help in quantifying the attacks against the network.
- Help in establishing an overall defense-in-depth security strategy.

The IDS is an important tool of a good security architecture and multi-layered defense strategy. The quantity of information that passes through a typical corporate network and the level of activity on most corporate servers make it practically impossible for a single person to continually monitor it by hand. Traditional network management and system monitoring tools do not address the issues of helping to ensure that systems are not misused and abused. Nor can they help detect theft of a company's critical data from important servers. The potential impact of computer-based crime is significant to most corporations; their entire intellectual property often resides on servers. A properly configured IDS, one that can detect security-related threats and attacks as they occur, can significantly ease the burden that most network administrators face.

Understanding IDS/ IPS and the Analysis Schemes

IDSs and IPSs are just two of many methods that should be configured and positioned in a strong security program. These systems are indispensable components of a network that is based on the layered security approach, also known as *defense-in-depth.*

IDSs work at the network layer of the OSI model (see Chapter 6 for more information on the OSI layer). Passive network sensors are placed at the various applicable network points where they analyze data packets to find specific patterns in network traffic. If the network sensors find any suspicious packets that match the criteria or patterns, an alert is initiated and logged and a response can be initiated based on the data recorded.

For any IDS or IPS system, a baseline is first set. In simple English, a *baseline* is defined as a known value or quantity with which an unknown is compared when measured or assessed. Taking this definition into the IDS scenario, a group of network activities/characteristics are categorized as baseline for an IDS system. Any activity that falls outside the boundaries of the defined baseline is scrutinized for malicious activity.

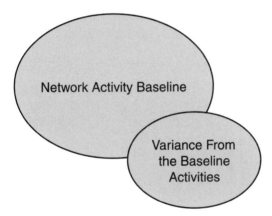

Figure 3.5 Network Baseline Activity

As part of detecting the intrusions, the IDSs perform various types of analysis. In intrusion detection systems, analysis is the process of organizing the various elements of data related to IDS and their inter-relationships to identify any irregular activity of interest. The intrusion analysis process is divided into four phases as follows:

- Pre-processing
- Analysis
- Response
- Refinement

Defense-In-Depth

Defense-in-depth (also known as *elastic defense*) is a military strategy that seeks to delay rather than prevent the advance of an attacker, buying time by yielding space. In information security, defense-in-depth represents the use of multiple computer security techniques to help mitigate the risk of one component of the defense being compromised or circumvented. An example is an HIPS installed on individual workstations when there is already NIPS and firewall protection on the network and perimeter within the same environment.

If a layered security approach is followed, an intruder who is able to penetrate the first line of defense (a firewall) does not gain complete access to the assets (systems). Intruders must successfully penetrate a series of layered defenses, each of which is equipped with the suitable defense/preventive mechanisms to detect that an attack is underway. The time and effort the attackers must expend provides the security staff the opportunity to respond to the attack, possibly eliminating it or at least taking actions to contain it.

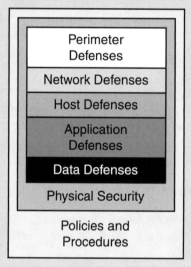

Figure 3.6   Defense-in-Depth

Pre-Processing

Pre-processing is the organization of data in a particular pattern for the purpose of classification. This function is performed on the data that is collected from the IDS or IPS Sensors. The data is put into some canonical format or a structured database format based on the pre-processing. Once the data is formatted as mentioned above, they are further broken down into classifications which depend upon the analysis scheme used. (Analysis scheme is covered later in this chapter.)

Once the data is classified, the data is concatenated and used along with a predefined detection template in which the variables are replaced by the real-time data. These templates define the framework for the baseline. Some examples are:

- Detection of unexpected privilege escalation
- Detection of the modification of system log files
- ACKDOOR Matrix 2.0 client connect
- DDoS stream handler to client

Analysis

Once the pre-processing is completed, the analysis stage begins where the data record is compared to the knowledge base. After the comparison, the record data is logged as an intrusion or is discarded and the next data record is taken for analysis.

Response

Once the information is categorized as an intrusion, a response will be generated. In the case of an IDS, it will be in the form of an alert.

The response phase is the differentiating factor between an IDS and an IPS. In the case of an IDS, in this phase, a response is generated in the form of an alert. However, in IPS a response is specific to the type of intrusion detected or it is based on the different analysis schemes used. It could be one of the various intrusion prevention techniques that are pre-configured and are based on the analysis and outcome results. The response can be configured either to be initiated automatically, or it can be performed manually after someone has analyzed the situation.

Refinement

This is an important phase as far as the fine-tuning of an installed IDS or IPS is concerned. In this stage, the fine-tuning of the IDS/IPS is performed based on previous usage and intrusion detection history. This helps in reducing the false-positive levels and to have a more accurate and refined intrusion detection/prevention system. An example of a tool used at this phase is the Cisco Threat Response (CTR).

Rule-Based Detection (Misuse Detection)

Misuse detection (also known as *rule-based detection*) is the first scheme that was used in early intrusion detection systems. They are also referred to as *signature detection* and *pattern matching*.

Misuse detection is the process of attempting to identify instances of network attacks by comparing current activity against the expected actions of an intruder. Most current approaches to misuse detection involve the use of rule-based expert systems to identify indications of known attacks. However, these techniques are less successful in identifying attacks that vary from expected patterns.

Anomaly Detection

By definition, an *anomaly* is a deviation or variation from the normal or common order, form, or rule. Detecting an anomaly depends on what you are specifically trying to detect. A baseline or a profile is a fundamental requirement for conducting any anomaly detection.

As mentioned, in anomaly detection, a *profile* is created for each user group on the system. These profiles can be created automatically or manually depending upon the requirement. How a profile is created is not important as long as the profiles accurately define the characteristics for each user group or user on your network. The profiles created are then used as baselines to define the user activity. If any network activity deviates from these baselines, the activity generates an alarm. Anomaly detection is also known as *profile-based detection* as the same principles apply to user profiles. Some of the common anomaly detection techniques are as follows:

- Behavior anomaly detection
- Network behavior anomaly detection
- Protocol anomaly systems

Behavior Anomaly Detection

Behavior anomaly detection basically looks for anomalies in user behavior. These systems are characteristic dependent rather than statistical. For example, these systems monitor the type of application used, protocols used, and database queries performed during a particular period of time. Based on the results of the monitoring, behavioral baselines are created.

Network Behavior Anomaly Detection (NMAD)

Network behavior anomaly detection (also known as *traffic anomaly systems*) is the process of continuously monitoring a proprietary network for unusual events or trends. An NBAD program tracks critical network characteristics in real time and generates an alarm if a strange event or trend is detected that could indicate the presence of a threat. Examples include traffic volume, bandwidth usage, and protocol usage. These systems are primarily statistical rather than characteristic.

Protocol Anomaly Systems

Protocol anomaly systems look for deviations from the set protocol standards. These systems are primarily characteristic. Unfortunately, this system is not very reliable as many vendors do not comply with protocol standards, which can lead to false positives.

One of the main differences between the anomaly detection and other analysis schemes is that anomaly-based schemes not only define activities that are not allowed, but also define activities that are allowed. Additionally, anomaly detection is used to collect statistical behavior and characteristics behavior.

Target Monitoring Systems

With target monitoring, the systems do not actively monitor for anomalies or misuse, but instead look for the modification of specified files or objects. This is more of a corrective control that is designed to reveal an unauthorized action after it occurs in order to revert it. This is usually done through a cryptographic algorithm that computes a checksum value for each target file. This checksum is compared at regular intervals to detect any changes. This is the easiest system to implement because it does not require constant monitoring by the administrator.

Stealth Probes

Stealth probes are also referred to as "low and slow" attacks. In this technique, the system attempts to detect any attacks that span over a prolonged period of time. Stealth probes collect a wide variety of data throughout the system, checking for any methodical attacks over a long period of time. They take a wide-area sampling and attempt to discover any correlating attacks. In effect, this method combines anomaly detection and misuse detection in an attempt to uncover suspicious activity.

Heuristics

In IDS terminology, heuristics refers to the use of Artificial Intelligence (AI) in detecting intrusions. In theory, an IDS will identify anomalies to detect an intrusion based on the traffic pattern and analysis carried out over a period of time. To use heuristics, an AI scripting language can apply the analysis to the incoming data. Heuristics is still in its initial stages and is developing. The concentration is now on a pattern-matching language that can use programming constructs to learn and identify malicious activity more accurately.

Hybrid Approach

Any system that uses a combination of the previously mentioned analysis is called a *hybrid approach*. There are various opinions as to which IDS methods are best. However, as you now know, all these approaches have their own advantages and disadvantages. Depending upon the situation and the requirement, when they are used in a mixed approach, they provide a more robust and secure security system.

Some Myths

Keep these myths in mind as you consider and prepare your own IDS approach:

- **Intrusion detection and intrusion prevention are two separate solutions.** The misconception that prevails in the industry is that the IDS and the IPS are two separate solutions. However, the reality is that both are part of a secure security infrastructure. Due to the inherent performance limitations, many IPS products have been designed with a very restrictive signature set on board with very little scope to expand them without seriously affecting the performance. Because the detection capabilities of an IPS are limited, compared to IDS, it is always a good practice to use an IDS and an IPS together.

- **IDSs and IPSs will catch or stop all network intrusions.** No network security device can ensure 100 percent security. There is a misconception that after the installation of a firewall, IDS, and IPS, a network is 100 percent secure.

- **Intrusion detection systems give too many false positives.** It is true that the intrusion detection systems give too many false alarms if it is not properly configured. The success of any security device lies in the proper configuration of its security settings. This is applicable to IDS also. If it is not properly configured, there is a likely chance that the intrusion detection systems may give too many false positives.

- **Intrusion detection will eventually replace firewalls.** Some people mistakenly think intrusion detection is the next generation of firewalls and assume that the firewalls will be replaced by IDS. However, as discussed in the defense-in-depth section, each network device is unique and has distinct functions to perform.

- **When an organization implements IDS or IPS, it should need fewer security professionals.** It is true that the IDS or IPS performs an excellent job in detecting and preventing intrusions. However, there is a need for trained professionals who can interpret and react to the information provided by the IDS or IPS systems.

Summary

Intrusion detection systems are like burglar alarms for your computer network. They detect unauthorized access attempts and other related security events. They are the first line of defense for your computer systems and networks. This chapter introduced the IDS and IPS and the IDS/IPS analysis process.

CHAPTER **4**

Principles of IDS

All warfare is based on deception. Hence, when able to attack, we must seem unable; when using our forces, we must seem inactive; when we are near, we must make the enemy believe we are far away; when far away, we must make him believe we are near.
—Sun Tzu, Author of *The Art of War*

Introduction

Intrusion detection is based on the following concepts:

- How to detect an intrusion
- What to detect
- Where to detect it

The three detects are also known as the *detect triangle*.

Detect Triangle—Principles of IDS

Figure 4.1   Detect Triangle

Concepts of Intrusion Prevention System

Intrusion prevention is based on four concepts. The first three concepts are the same as intrusion detection. The fourth one asks "when to detect?" The main aim of an intrusion prevention system is to prevent an intrusion before the actual infringement occurs. Any delayed information is of no use as far as an IPS is concerned.

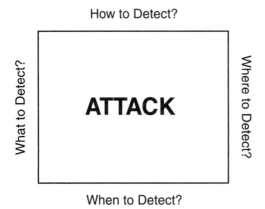

Figure 4.2   The IPS System

Symptoms of an Attack

Before you can prevent your system from an intrusion, you must know how to determine the symptoms of an attack. Generally the symptoms are very clear—users can no longer log into the database server or the Web site. Sometimes, however, the symptoms are not so obvious.

To effectively implement an intrusion detection system, it is mandatory that the intrusions be identified and differentiated from normal security events. The following sections discuss different symptoms of an attack.

Unexpected Changes in Network Performance and Irregular Network Traffic

Unexpected changes in network performance—such as variations in traffic load at specified times—can be a positive indication that the network is under some kind of scanning or attack. If you experience a sudden increase in the network traffic, you should monitor for malicious activities.

Be sure to take any of the following possible symptoms seriously: any major changes in the network load, typical packet size, average number of fragmented packets, and so on. These deviations could indicate an attack or could indicate a network problem caused by the network device(s). Irregular network traffic is categorized in two ways:

- **Traffic originating from/to a particular host**—In this case, the traffic originating from a particular host or traffic destined for a particular host is irregular. A simple example is an infected/compromised host that continuously transfers data to its master server.

- **Traffic independent of any host**—A simple example of traffic that is independent of any host is the one that contains unexpected protocols. Another example is traffic with addresses that do not belong to the internal network.

Any unusual problem or incident that happens in an internal network should also be taken seriously. The root cause of such problems will have a positive influence on reliability of the security systems. For example, problems with hardware and software components should be taken seriously. Router failure, server reboots, or the inability to start one of the system services might be an indication of an attempt to implement a denial-of-service attack (DoS attack).

Poor System Performance

Poor system performance is a possible symptom that your system is under attack or is compromised and utilized for an attack. An example of an attack that causes poor system performance is a denial-of-service attack.

Repeated or Multiple Occurrences of a Specific Event(s)

One of the best ways to detect an intrusion is to differentiate the normal security events from security events that occur repeatedly within a stipulated time frame. This method is based on the assumption that if the first attack originated by an attacker fails, the attacker will repeat the same process with or without the same parameters to gain illegal access to the subject resource. An example that falls under this activity is a port scan that covers multiple ports of a system. During a port scan, the intruder scans the target system for open ports and details of services running on the target system. The port-scanning event can be easily detected, because it's basically the same event repeated, with different parameters.

Threshold Values Controls

This method is very similar to the repeated or multiple occurrence of a specific event in that it monitors the threshold value for a repeated event to distinguish between authorized repeated events and the unauthorized ones. Whatever the case may be, the system tracks and detects when the threshold value has been exceeded. A simple example is the Account Lockout Threshold feature in Windows XP/2003. The Account Lockout Threshold sets the number of invalid logon attempts that are allowed before an account is locked out.

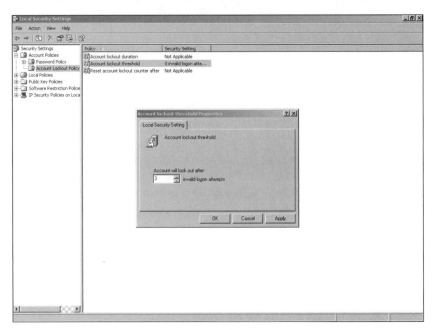

Figure 4.3   Security Policy for Threshold Value Controls

Time Intervals Between the Events

Monitoring the number of security events occurring within a stipulated period of time can be a useful methodology for detecting an intrusion. A simple example is monitoring the number of attempts to access a particular port or a range port within a specified period of time. For example, simple port scanners scan port numbers in ascending order, incrementing the port number by one. These kinds of events can be easily detected, because the source and destination are the same and the port number is sequentially accessed.

Hacking the Time Interval Factor

Generally, the IDS is configured to detect continuous port scans that are incremented by one. However, the new generation port scanners are intelligent enough to overcome this security feature. In some cases, the number of the scanned port is not incremented by 0 but is randomly generated. To complicate this process more, the port number is both increased and decreased at random intervals. In some cases, port numbers are scanned repeatedly with the aim of deceiving intrusion detections systems.

Another method to evade IDS detection is to use sophisticated port scanning methods, also known as *stealth scanning*. Stealth scanning exploits the various design-inherent vulnerabilities in the TCP/IP stack.

The next method used to avoid IDS detection involves increasing the time interval between two scans. Scanning is generally performed at 5 to 10 ports per second. However, if you change the default value to some custom value, the chances of the IDS detecting the scan becomes unlikely.

(*nMap* is one of the most popular network reconnaissance tools commonly used by computer hackers. It is available for download at www.insecure.org/nmap. The latest version of this tool has more than 10 scanning algorithms that are capable of bypassing simple IDS rules like the one discussed here.)

Invalid Commands or Request for Nonexisting Web Components

Scrutiny of log files for invalid commands or user parameters is the next best option for identifying or detecting attacks. A good example is the request for nonexisting files to a Web browser.

Unauthorized Scans and Probes

Any attempt to perform a security scan from an unauthorized source can be considered an attempt to intrude into the system. This also could be an indication of a system-wide vulnerability that any attacker could exploit.

Digital Fingerprints

Digital fingerprints are similar to the signatures used in anti-virus detection. The security analyzer compares the digital fingerprints of installed software with the default fingerprint in its database. If the parameter value does not match the standard one, this is an indication that the object has changed, which could be the result of an attack.

Passing of Network Packets with Invalid Parameters

Attackers sometimes try to exploit the design vulnerability that exists in the TCP/IP stack to generate network packets with invalid parameters. Some of the examples of such activities are:

- Traffic coming from and going to unexpected locations
- Network connections made at unusual times
- Repeated, failed connection attempts
- Nonstandard or malformed packets (protocol violations)

Let's discuss the malformed packets in more detail with some simple examples.

Source Address Spoofing (Inbound Traffic)

In this scenario, the incoming network packets arriving at the protected local area network from an outside network appear to have a source address that corresponds to the address range of the internal trusted network. These kinds of packets are easily detected by security systems.

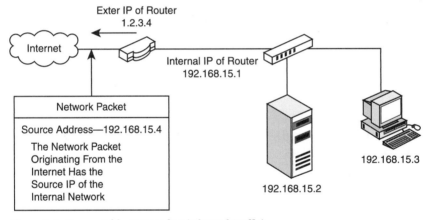

Figure 4.4   Source Address Spoofing (Inbound Traffic)

Source Address Spoofing (Outbound Traffic)

In this scenario, a packet originating from the internal LAN has a source address of an external network. The aim of this is generally to conceal an attacker's who originates from an internal network.

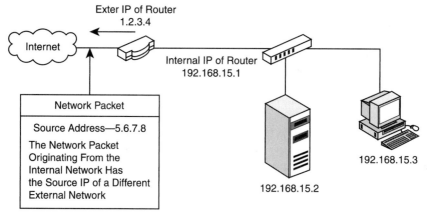

Figure 4.5   Source Address Spoofing (Outbound Traffic)

Unexpected Internet Protocol (IP) Addresses

Some IP addresses are not routed or used in the Internet. For example, the Internet Assigned Numbers Authority (IANA) has reserved the following three blocks of the IP address space for private Internets (also known as local networks):

> 10.0.0.0 –10.255.255.255
>
> 172.16.0.0–172.31.255.255
>
> 192.168.0.0–192.168.255.255

These IP address ranges are described in RFC 1918, which deals with the address allocation for private internets.

Also, IP addresses in the range of 169.254.0.0 to 169.254.255.255 are reserved for Automatic Private IP Addressing (also known as APIPA).

What Is Automatic Private IP Addressing (APIPA)?

Automatic Private IP Addressing (APIPA) is the Microsoft Windows term for fallback to the "link local" addresses, as prescribed in RFC 3330.

In simple terms, APIPA is a feature of later Windows operating systems, with which DHCP clients can automatically self-configure an IP address and subnet mask when a DHCP server is not available. Upon boot-up, a client machine that is configured to obtain its IP address from a DHCP server first looks for a DHCP server in order to obtain an IP address and subnet mask. If the client machine can't find the information, it uses APIPA to automatically configure itself with an IP address from a range that has been reserved especially for Microsoft. The IP address range is 169.254.0.1–169.254.255.254. The client also configures itself with a default class B subnet mask of 255.255.0.0. The client uses the self-configured IP address until it can contact a DHCP server.

There are other sets of IP address ranges that are reserved by the Internet Assigned Numbers Authority, or the IANA, including:

0.0.0.0/8	#IANA; reserved for hosts on "this" network. See RFC3300 and RFC1700
1.0.0.0/8	#IANA; reserved
2.0.0.0/8	#IANA; reserved
5.0.0.0/8	#IANA; reserved
7.0.0.0/8	#IANA; reserved
10.0.0.0/8	#IANA; reserved for private use. See RFC1918
23.0.0.0/8	#IANA; reserved
27.0.0.0/8	#IANA; reserved
31.0.0.0/8	#IANA; reserved
36.0.0.0/8	#IANA; reserved
37.0.0.0/8	#IANA; reserved
39.0.0.0/8	#IANA; reserved originally for "Class A Subnet Experiment." Available for allocation to Registries. See RFC1797
41.0.0.0/8	#IANA; reserved
42.0.0.0/8	#IANA; reserved
49.0.0.0/8	#IANA; reserved

```
50.0.0.0/8      #IANA; reserved
73.0.0.0/8      #IANA; reserved
74.0.0.0/8      #IANA; reserved
75.0.0.0/8      #IANA; reserved
76.0.0.0/8      #IANA; reserved
77.0.0.0/8      #IANA; reserved
78.0.0.0/8      #IANA; reserved
79.0.0.0/8      #IANA; reserved
89.0.0.0/8      #IANA; reserved
90.0.0.0/8      #IANA; reserved
91.0.0.0/8      #IANA; reserved
92.0.0.0/8      #IANA; reserved
93.0.0.0/8      #IANA; reserved
94.0.0.0/8      #IANA; reserved
95.0.0.0/8      #IANA; reserved
96.0.0.0/8      #IANA; reserved
97.0.0.0/8      #IANA; reserved
98.0.0.0/8      #IANA; reserved
99.0.0.0/8      #IANA; reserved
100.0.0.0/8     #IANA; reserved
101.0.0.0/8     #IANA; reserved
102.0.0.0/8     #IANA; reserved
103.0.0.0/8     #IANA; reserved
104.0.0.0/8     #IANA; reserved
105.0.0.0/8     #IANA; reserved
106.0.0.0/8     #IANA; reserved
107.0.0.0/8     #IANA; reserved
108.0.0.0/8     #IANA; reserved
109.0.0.0/8     #IANA; reserved
110.0.0.0/8     #IANA; reserved
111.0.0.0/8     #IANA; reserved
112.0.0.0/8     #IANA; reserved
```

113.0.0.0/8	#IANA; reserved
114.0.0.0/8	#IANA; reserved
115.0.0.0/8	#IANA; reserved
116.0.0.0/8	#IANA; reserved
117.0.0.0/8	#IANA; reserved
118.0.0.0/8	#IANA; reserved
119.0.0.0/8	#IANA; reserved
120.0.0.0/8	#IANA; reserved
121.0.0.0/8	#IANA; reserved
122.0.0.0/8	#IANA; reserved
123.0.0.0/8	#IANA; reserved
124.0.0.0/8	#IANA; reserved
125.0.0.0/8	#IANA; reserved
126.0.0.0/8	#IANA; reserved
127.0.0.0/8	#IANA; reserved for host loopback address. See RFC3300 and RFC1700
128.0.0.0/16	#IANA; reserved originally for classful network purposes. Available for allocation to registries. See RFC3300
169.254.0.0/16	#IANA; reserved for the "link local" block. For DHCP and IPv4 auto configuration. See RFC3300 and the IETF
172.16.0.0/12	#IANA; reserved for private use. See RFC1918
173.0.0.0/8	#IANA; reserved
174.0.0.0/8	#IANA; reserved
175.0.0.0/8	#IANA; reserved
176.0.0.0/8	#IANA; reserved
177.0.0.0/8	#IANA; reserved
178.0.0.0/8	#IANA; reserved
179.0.0.0/8	#IANA; reserved
180.0.0.0/8	#IANA; reserved
181.0.0.0/8	#IANA; reserved
182.0.0.0/8	#IANA; reserved
183.0.0.0/8	#IANA; reserved
184.0.0.0/8	#IANA; reserved

185.0.0.0/8	#IANA; reserved
186.0.0.0/8	#IANA; reserved
187.0.0.0/8	#IANA; reserved
189.0.0.0/8	#IANA; reserved
190.0.0.0/8	#IANA; reserved
191.255.0.0/16	#IANA; reserved originally for classful network purposes. Available for allocation to Registries. See RFC3300
192.0.0.0/24	#IANA; reserved originally for classful network purposes. Available for allocation to Registries. See RFC3300
192.0.2.0/24	#IANA; reserved for "test net." Designed to be used in documentation and sample code. See RFC3300
192.88.99.0/24	#IANA; reserved for 6 to 4 relay anycast addresses. See RFC3068
192.168.0.0/16	#IANA; reserved for private use. See RFC1918
197.0.0.0/8	#IANA; reserved
198.18.0.0/16	#IANA; reserved for network device benchmark testing. See RFC2544
223.0.0.0/8	#IANA; reserved
224.0.0.0/4	#IANA; reserved for IPv4 multicast. Formerly known as "Class D" addresses. See RFC3171
240.0.0.0/4	#IANA; reserved. Formerly known as "Class D" addresses. See RFC3300

Information source for this table is http://www.liquifried.com/docs/security/ reservednets.html.

If a packet has a source IP address belonging to any of the IP address ranges mentioned here, it could indicate an attack.

Default Values and Information

Another indication that a machine has been attacked is the existence of certain values or attributes associated with common viruses. These attributes can be names of files at particular locations, process names, used ports, custom messages or dialog boxes, and so on. Most Trojans and viruses have default names and processes associated with them. If your system contains these files or process, it could very well be an indication that your machines have been attacked and infected. Another tell-tale sign is the list of open ports. Many Trojans/worms have ports associated with their activities. If your system shows that these ports are or have been opened, your machine might be compromised. Please refer to Appendix E for a list of known Trojans and their respective port numbers.

Date and Time Factor

The date and time factor can also be used to identify an attack or violation. For example, when a user logs in to a system, a log entry is made. Log entries, then, can be searched for questionable time entries, such as log entries made when the system was down or closed. These entries should be investigated as to whether the user was authorized to work during that time or whether was it an attempt from an attacker. Here, the key entity that holds the clue is the date and time factor.

Location Factor

The location of a security entity plays a critical role in identifying an attack. Let's look at a real-life example. In an Active Directory setup, users can be configured to log in to the network only from certain machines. This means that if users try to log in to the network from any other system, they will get a message box saying that they are not authorized to log in from the particular system. If auditing is enabled, these messages can be used to detect unsuccessful login attempts.

Another example is the dial-up server setup. Users generally connect to their corporate networks from their homes using a single telephone number through dial up. These numbers are categorized under the authorized dial-in numbers. The appearance of unauthorized telephone numbers on the log file can therefore be an indication of a dial-in attack attempt originating from that unauthorized telephone number.

Another example is the use of FTP and FTP logs. In a typical corporate network setup, the clients and the branch office are allowed to log in to the FTP server for various business purposes. The IP addresses of the clients and the branch offices are categorized under the green list. Any attempt to connect to the FTP from any other IP address indicates that some kind of log in attempt took place.

User and System Parameters

The user and system have certain system parameters associated with their daily activities. For example, normal logon and logoff timings, session duration, maximum, average, minimum workloads, and so on. Any major deviations from these parameters can be grounds to suspect an attack. Also, if a user is all of a sudden trying to access a resource that the user has never accessed before, this might well mean that the attacker now has some kind of access to the legitimate user's login credentials and is attempting to access important data disguised as that user.

The best way to determine which activity should be considered malicious is by actively monitoring user and file activity on your network. Every network has different user and file activity (which could differ from time to time), hence it is important to understand your network activity really well.

Information Sources about Attacks

To reach the conclusion that an attack has occurred, you need some kind of information related to the system's security events. Information about attacks can be collected from the following sources.

Log Files

Log files are the first place to look for any information related to security events. The log file is one of the most important and often-neglected sources of information. Without a detailed and careful analysis of the log files, the security administrator will be more or less blind and oblivious to the activities and threats that are happening in the network. The log file is your primary source of information, even if you do not have an intrusion detection system installed. The need for registering the system and security events in a log file is now a regulatory requirement.

Each system uses its own log formats. It is the duty of the Security Administrator to become accustomed with the log format of the system in place. Consider the following sample log file formats.

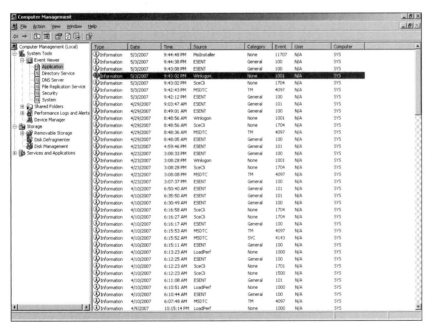

Figure 4.6   Windows Server 2003 Log Files

The following Cisco log file illustrates several packets that matched the DENY ICMP access list rule, which is commonly used to block out data packets from a particular IP address range. In the following example, you can clearly see that the DENY ICMP access list rule has managed to block out a number of data packets from different IP addresses:

```
%SEC-6-IPACCESSLOGDP: list 169 denied icmp 192.168.45.142
   (Serial0 *HDLC*) -> 10.2.3.7 (0/0), 1 packet

%SEC-6-IPACCESSLOGDP: list 169 denied icmp 192.168.45.113
   (Serial0 *HDLC*) -> 10.2.3.7 (0/0), 1 packet

%SEC-6-IPACCESSLOGDP: list 169 denied icmp 192.168.212.72
   (Serial0 *HDLC*) -> 10.2.3.7 (0/0), 1 packet

%SEC-6-IPACCESSLOGDP: list 169 denied icmp 172.16.132.154
   (Serial0 *HDLC*) -> 10.2.3.7 (0/0), 1 packet

%SEC-6-IPACCESSLOGDP: list 169 denied icmp 192.168.45.15
   (Serial0 *HDLC*) -> 10.2.3.7 (0/0), 1 packet

%SEC-6-IPACCESSLOGDP: list 169 denied icmp 192.168.45.142
   (Serial0 *HDLC*) -> 10.2.3.7 (0/0), 1 packet

%SEC-6-IPACCESSLOGDP: list 169 denied icmp 172.16.132.47
   (Serial0 *HDLC*) -> 10.2.3.7 (0/0), 1 packet

%SEC-6-IPACCESSLOGDP: list 169 denied icmp 192.168.212.35
   (Serial0 *HDLC*) -> 10.2.3.7 (0/0), 1 packet

%SEC-6-IPACCESSLOGDP: list 169 denied icmp 192.168.45.113
   (Serial0 *HDLC*) -> 10.2.3.7 (0/0), 1 packet

%SEC-6-IPACCESSLOGDP: list 169 denied icmp 172.16.132.59
   (Serial0 *HDLC*) -> 10.2.3.7 (0/0), 1 packet

%SEC-6-IPACCESSLOGDP: list 169 denied icmp 192.168.45.82
   (Serial0 *HDLC*) -> 10.2.3.7 (0/0), 1 packet

%SEC-6-IPACCESSLOGDP: list 169 denied icmp 192.168.212.56
   (Serial0 *HDLC*) -> 10.2.3.7 (0/0), 1 packet

%SEC-6-IPACCESSLOGDP: list 169 denied icmp 172.16.132.84
   (Serial0 *HDLC*) -> 10.2.3.7 (0/0), 1 packet

%SEC-6-IPACCESSLOGDP: list 169 denied icmp 192.168.212.47
   (Serial0 *HDLC*) -> 10.2.3.7 (0/0), 1 packet

%SEC-6-IPACCESSLOGDP: list 169 denied icmp 192.168.45.35
   (Serial0 *HDLC*) -> 10.2.3.7 (0/0), 1 packet

%SEC-6-IPACCESSLOGDP: list 169 denied icmp 192.168.212.15
   (Serial0 *HDLC*) -> 10.2.3.7 (0/0), 1 packet

%SEC-6-IPACCESSLOGDP: list 169 denied icmp 172.16.132.33
   (Serial0 *HDLC*) -> 10.2.3.7 (0/0), 1 packet
```

Network Traffic

Network traffic is the next source of information related to security events. Network traffic consists of packets that are transferred across the network. The packet consists of the following three parts:

- Packet header (service information, source address, destination address, and so on)
- Data field of the packet
- Packet trailer (check sum, delimiter, and so on)

An analysis of these specified characteristics can help the IDS detect an intrusion.

What Is a Frame?

The term *frame* is most frequently used to describe a chunk of data created by network communication hardware such as a network interface card (NIC cards) and router interfaces. Switch ports primarily forward existing frames and do not usually create frames of their own (unless they are participating in spanning tree or dynamic VLANs).

There are different types of frames, including Ethernet frames, token ring frames, FDDI frames, and so on. A frame is simply a chunk of data, frequently with some sort of pattern of bit at the start (called a *header*) and bits at the end (called a *trailer*). Frames are created by hardware protocols that do not have separate control circuits in the physical media to which they are attached.

The frame generally contains the hardware addresses, such as a MAC address, frame delimiters, and data.

What Is a Packet?

Request For Comments (RFC) documents frequently use the term *packet* to describe a stream of binary octets of data of some arbitrary length. Packet is typically used to describe chunks of data created by the software, not by the hardware. An example is the Internet Protocol (IP), which creates packets.

Packets contain logical addressing information such as an IP address and its data.

Information from the Attacker

In some cases, the attacker leaves some clues or information regarding the attack carried out. This can include the details of the existing vulnerabilities, the details of the exploited vulnerability, and the like.

Information from End Users

In certain cases, the information is provided by the end user. These information bits can help reveal problems that cannot be detected using other methods.

External Information Sources

Information about attacks can be collected from many outside sources as well, including the following:

- IRC channels
- Mailing lists
- Hacking resources on the Internet (AntiOnline, NewOrder, BugTraq, BSRF, and others)
- Hacker magazines (like *Phrack*, *2600*, and others)
- Books (*Hacking Exposed, The Unofficial Guide to Ethical Hacking,* and others)
- Internet conferences and seminars (like DEFCON, HACKED, and others)

Summary

The future of information safety rests with people and products. This chapter covered the IDS principles, the symptoms of an attack, and how to find information about various attacks.

## CHAPTER 5

IDS Architecture

According as circumstances are favorable, one should modify one's plans.
—Sun Tzu, Author of *The Art of War*

Introduction

In the recent years, intrusion detection systems have become an integral part of an organization's information system infrastructure. Business giants and government organizations are in the process of designing and deploying enterprise-wide IDS solutions. As they move toward the practical side of IDS implementation, organizations are experiencing numerous obstacles related to deployment, management, data collection, and data correlation.

For an effective intrusion detection/prevention system, organizations typically use multiple systems and components that perform a variety of sophisticated intrusion-detection and intrusion-prevention functions. The roles performed by each component, and the relationship among machines, devices, applications, and processes, including the conventions used for communication between them, define the security architecture for that system.

The IDS architecture is the most important component in an intrusion detection implementation. An effective architecture is one in which each machine, device, component, and process performs its role in an effective and coordinated manner, resulting in the following:

- Efficient information processing and output
- Appropriate responses that meet the business and operational needs of an organization

On the other hand, a poorly designed and implemented architecture can create network havoc, such as lack of appropriate and timely responses, data not being available or not being available when needed, network slowdowns, and more.

The following sections cover the intrusion-detection architectures, the associated tiered models, how servers are deployed, the functioning of sensors and agents, the functions of management consoles in intrusion-detection architecture, and the various constraints associated with their implementation.

Tiered Architectures

The IDS architecture can be categorized as three types:

- Single-tiered architecture
- Multi-tiered architecture
- Peer-to-peer architecture

Single-Tiered Architecture

The single-tiered architecture is the simplest form of architecture used for IDS implementation. This architecture is ideal for small business segments or home-based installations.

In a single-tiered architecture, a single component in an IDS collects and processes data, rather than passing the output it collects to another set of components. An example of a single-tiered architecture is a host-based intrusion-detection tool that takes the output of system logs and compares it to known patterns of attack.

The advantages of using a single-tiered architecture include:

- Simple and easy to install and configure
- Less maintenance, monitoring, and administration required
- Low cost (lots of open source and freeware tools available)
- Independent from other components

However, the single-tiered architecture also has some disadvantages, as follows:

- Not ideal for medium- to large-sized networks.
- The spectrum of attacks the IDS can detect is very limited or low.
- It has components that are not aware of each other, thus reducing the potential for efficiency and sophisticated functionality.
- It is easy to compromise a single-tiered IDS when compared to other architectures.

Multi-Tiered Architecture

As evident from the title, a multi-tiered architecture involves multiple components that pass information to each other. The intrusion-detection systems that fall under this category generally consist of three primary components:

- Sensors
- Analyzers or agents
- Manager

Sensors

The sensors in an intrusion-detection system perform the duty of data collection. Sensors are programs that are responsible for collecting data from network interfaces, system logs, and other information sources, such as personal firewalls and TCP wrappers.

Sensors are the most critical component of any intrusion-detection and intrusion-prevention system. They are the beginning point of intrusion detection and intrusion prevention, because they supply the initial data about the security event in the network. Sensors are usually (but not always) the lowest end components in an intrusion detection system. They do not have sophisticated functionality and are usually designed to collect certain types of data and pass them to the next level/component in an IDS. There are two types of sensors:

- Network-based sensors
- Host-based sensors

Network-Based Sensors

Network-based sensors are programs or hardware network devices that capture data in packets traversing a local network (the network could be Ethernet, token ring, or a network switching point). The greatest advantage of using a network-based sensor is that it can provide data to a large number of hosts. However, if the sensor is overburdened, the chances are likely that the sensor will miss a considerable amount of data that might be critical to an intrusion-detection and intrusion-prevention system.

Advantages of network-based sensors:

- Capable of providing data to large numbers of hosts
- Cost effective

Disadvantages of network-based sensors:

- Additional traffic if not properly configured—If the network-based sensor is not properly configured for the network, it can generate additional network traffic that might slow down the performance of the network.
- If the network-based sensor is overburdened, there are chances that the sensor might miss considerable amounts of possibly critical data.

TCPdump and libpcap are frequently used as sensors in intrusion detection and intrusion prevention. TCPdump (more info at http://www.tcpdump.org) captures data from packets and prints packet headers that match a particular filter (or Boolean) expression. If you are administering an IDS or IPS, it is always better to completely understand the following packet parameters:

- Time
- Source address
- Destination address

- Source port

- Destination port

- TCP flags

- Initial sequence number from the source IP for the initial connection

- Ending sequence number

- Number of bytes

- Window size

TCPdump versus libpcap

TCPdump is an application whereas libpcap is a library called by an application. libpcap (http://sourceforge.net/projects/libpcap/) is designed to gather packet data from the kernel of the operating system and then transfer/distribute that data to one or more applications—in this particular case, to intrusion-detection and intrusion-prevention applications.

libpcap provides intrusion-detection and intrusion-prevention applications with the payload data so that these applications can analyze the content to look for attack signatures, malicious data/code, and so on. Let's see how the libpcap library works:

- An Ethernet card gets the packet data traversing through the network.

- The libpcap library, working along with the underlying operating system, processes each packet received by the network interface card by first determining the type of packet. This is done by removing the Ethernet header and getting to the next layer up the stack.

- Assuming that the next layer is an IP layer, the IP header is removed to determine the protocol at the next layer of the stack.

- Assuming that the packet is a TCP packet, the TCP header is removed and the contents of the packet are then passed on to the next upper layer—the application layer. In the case here, the application running at this layer is the IDS or IPS. The libpcap provides IDS and IPS applications with the extracted data (payload).

The advantage of using libpcap is that it is an open source project and is freely available on the public domain software.

Apart from TCPdump and the libpcap library, many IDS vendors develop and include their own proprietary sensors in the IDS. These proprietary sensors sometimes provide more functionality than TCPdump and libpcap, because they are fine-tuned for a particular application (IDS).

Host-Based Sensors

Host-based sensors are also capable of receiving packet data captured by network interface cards and then sending the data to the concerned application/process. However, the difference lies in the operating mode of the sensor. Host-based sensors work in non-promiscuous mode, which means that the network interface on each host has to be set to capture only data sent to that particular host.

Sensor Deployment

To deploy the sensor, many sensors require that the host be running one or more network interfaces in promiscuous mode. Sensors can be placed in three different patterns:

- **Outside of exterior firewalls**—Sensors that are placed outside the exterior firewall record information about attacks that originate from the Internet.

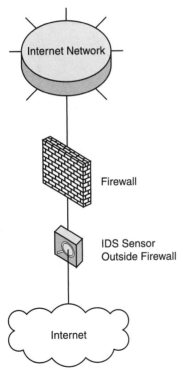

Figure 5.1   IDS Sensor Outside the Firewall

Promiscuous Mode

Promiscuous mode refers to a configuration of a network card wherein a setting is enabled so that the card passes all traffic it receives to the CPU rather than just passing packets addressed to it. Inside each packet is a hardware (MAC) address. When a computer receives a particular packet, it checks the hardware address to determine whether the packet is addressed to it. If not, the network card normally drops the packet. When in promiscuous mode, the network card doesn't drop the packet, thereby enabling it to read all packets.

Promiscuous mode is commonly used to diagnose network connectivity issues. Some applications that use promiscuous mode are:

- **KisMAC**—A wireless network discovery tool for Mac OS X. Product home page is http://kismac.de/.

- **AirSnort**—A Linux utility (using GTK+) for decrypting WEP encryption on an 802.11b network. Product home page is http://airsnort.shmoo.com/.

- **Wireshark**—A free software protocol analyzer (also known as a packet sniffer) used for network troubleshooting, analysis, software, and protocol development, and R&D and educational purposes. It has all of the standard features of a protocol analyzer. Product home page is http://www.wireshark.org/.

- **TCPdump**—Covered in detail throughout this book. Product home page is http://www.tcpdump.org/.

- **PRTG**—Paessler Router Traffic Grapher (PRTG) is a network monitoring and bandwidth use software for Microsoft Windows by Paessler AG. Product home page is http://www.paessler. com/prtg/.

- **Kismet**—A network detector, packet sniffer, and intrusion detection system for 802.11 wireless LANs. Kismet will work with any wireless card that supports raw monitoring mode, and can sniff 802.11b, 802.11a, and 802.11g traffic. The program runs under Linux, FreeBSD, NetBSD, OpenBSD, and Mac OS X. The client can also run on Windows. Product home page is http://www.kismetwireless.net/.

- **Inside the network protected by a firewall**—Sensors that are placed inside the network protected by a firewall mainly record information about attacks that originate from the internal network, as well as any attacks that were able to bypass the security fencing implemented by the external firewall.

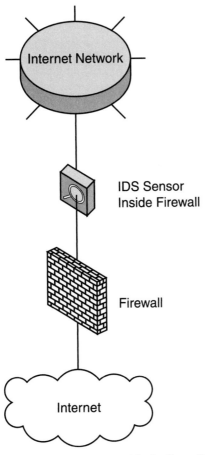

Figure 5.2   IDS Sensor Inside the Firewall

- **Both the locations (outside and inside of firewall protected network)**—These kind of sensors are used for highly secure networks like defense establishments, research organizations, and so on, where a high degree of security and monitoring is required.

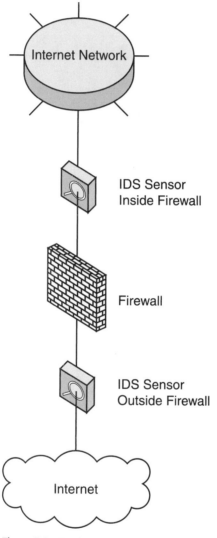

Figure 5.3 IDS Sensor at Both Locations

Issues Related to Sensor Deployment

Some of the issues related to sensor deployment are as follows:

- **Administrative/superuser privileges**—Applications that capture the network data or read these captured data require certain administrative level privileges and access rights. For example, to access the captured data files at /var/log/ messages, root privileges are required. Similarly, running windump, the windows equivalent of TCPdump, requires administrator level privileges.

- **Security factor**—The administrative/superuser requirement can also be a security issue, because, if an attacker is able compromise the application, he can get full control of the system using *privilege escalation*. Another interesting point to note here is that, out of the three major components of a multi-tiered architecture, sensors are the most frequently attacked. The security of the host on which the sensors are configured/installed should be hardened by tightening the file permissions, restricting privileges, restricting access to the system itself, reducing the number of services running to the barest minimum, managing patches, monitoring continuously, and so on. Each sensor should be placed where it is most suited from a security perspective.

 *Privilege escalation* is the act of exploiting a bug in an application to gain access to resources that normally are protected from an application or user. The result is that the application performs actions with a higher security context than intended by the application developer or system administrator.

- **Disk management**—Continuously capturing data that traverses the network could consume a large amount of hard disk/storage space. Having an adequate amount of storage space, regularly checking the storage space occupied by the system, monitoring the performance of the disk system, and archiving and purging the contents of the system are basically the inevitable parts associated with intrusion detection and prevention.

- **Throughput rate**—Sometimes, the rate at which the sensor receives data is too much for it to process. Many types of sensors have difficulty in handling throughput much greater than 350–400 Mbps. This could cause the sensor to drop the excess packets or the sensor to crash, requiring a reboot to return to operation.

- **Switched network**—In a switched network, network-based sensors cannot capture packet data by simply putting an interface in promiscuous mode. The most commonly used work-around for the problem is to deploy a special kind of port known as a *spanning port* between a switch or similar device and a host used to monitor network traffic. A spanning port configures the switch to behave like a hub for a specific port. Using a spanning port is also known as switch port mirroring, port mirroring, monitoring port, SPAN port, and link mode port.

- **Encrypted traffic**—The next common challenge faced by the IDS sensor is the encrypted network traffic. The ideal way to overcome this complication is to place a sensor at an endpoint where the traffic is in its unencrypted form.

- **Secure communication channel**—A secure communication channel between the sensors and the other IDS components is highly recommended. If an intruder intercepts the communication between sensors and other components, it would defeat the whole purpose of an intrusion-detection system. The attackers can utilize the IDS system for their purposes. The easiest way to tackle such a situation is to establish an authenticated and encrypted channel between the sensors and the other IDS components.

- **(Status) monitoring**—In the case of a sensor failure, there should be some mechanism in place to generate the notification to the IDS manager component. An IDS or IPS that attempts to contact all sensors at frequent, scheduled times to discover failed sensors can tackle this issue.

Agents

After the data is collected by the IDS sensors, the data is passed to agents (also known as *analyzers*). In simple terms, the primary function of an agent is to analyze the input provided by the sensors. An *agent* can be defined as a group of processes that run independently of other components and that are programmed to analyze system behaviors or network events or both to detect anomalous events and violations of an organization's security policy.

The agents are responsible for monitoring the intrusive activity on their assigned individual hosts. Typically, an agent is specialized to perform one and only one function. For example, one agent might be examining only TCP traffic whereas, another might watch for HTTP traffic only. Each sensor and agent is configured to run on a particular operating environment in which it is placed. Each agent is independent of the others, which means that if one agent crashes or is taken down in some form, the others will continue to perform their assigned function normally. This also means that the agents can be added to or deleted from an IDS or IPS as needed without affecting the performance of the other agents.

Basic Functions of an IDS Agent

An IDS agent should provide the following three basic functions:

- **Provisioning of a communication interface**—An IDS agent is supposed to provide a communication interface that allows the agent to communicate with other components of IDSs and IPSs.

- **Provisioning of a listener interface**—The IDS agent also functions as a listener interface that waits in the network background for data from IDS sensors and messages from other IDS agents and receives them.

- **Provisioning of a sender interface**—The IDS agent's function as a sender interface mainly deals with transmitting data and messages to other components, such as other agents and the manager component of IDS, using established means of communication.

Some of the advantages of using an IDS agent are:

- **Independence**—As discussed previously, the agents are implemented in an independent pattern, which means that if some of the agents go down due to any reason, the other IDS agents aren't affected.

- **Scalability and adaptability**—Agents are highly adaptable and can be deployed to both large- and small-scale intrusion-detection and intrusion-prevention deployments.

- **Efficient**—Because an IDS agent is simple and deals with independent functions, it is a more efficient implementation.

Some of the disadvantages associated with agents are as follows:

- **False alarms**—Agents are known to generate a large number of false alarms, which causes a variety of problems in the security framework.

- **Dedicated administration**—Maintaining an IDS agent requires continuous administration, because the agents need to be changed according to an organization's requirement. They must be configured to minimize the number of false alarms, and their performance must be continuously monitored for any bottlenecks—all these require a dedicated administration.

- **Resource consumption**—The IDS agents cause system overhead in terms of memory consumption and CPU allocation, which in turn will cause IDS performance bottlenecks. This might affect the performance and reliability of an IDS.

You can also use third-party tools to increase the efficiency of the IDS analysis pattern. Third-party tools include:

- Connection-tracing tools

- Network monitoring tools

- Neural networks

Issues Related to Agent Deployment

Some of the issues related to the deployment of IDS agents are:

- **Agent security**—Security is always the buzzword. The agents are more powerful and dynamic when compared to sensors. If a hacker successfully attacks an IDS agent, he or she can then control the type of analysis the agent performs. The attacker could also access other information through the compromised agent. Always place an IDS agent in secure zones within networks.

- **Dedicated system**—It is advisable to run the IDS agent in a dedicated system. There are two reasons for this. First, it's for better performance, as all the resources will be available for the IDS agent. The second reason is from a security point of view. If another application is running on the same system, attackers might be able to access the system/agent via the other application and then use privilege escalation to gain control over the system/agent.

- **Encrypted traffic**—It is always advisable to encrypt the traffic between an IDS agent and other agents and to encrypt the traffic between IDS agents and other IDS components.

Manager

The basic purpose of this component is to provide the master control capability for an IDS or IPS. When an agent determines that an attack has occurred or is occurring, it transfers the related information to the manager component of the IDS (also known as the *server component*). The manager component of the IDS then performs a variety of functions, including (but not limited to) the following:

- **Providing a management console/user interface to the IDS manager component**—The basic function of an IDS manager component is to provide an interface/management console for the existing system setup. This is the interface through which the user/administrator interacts with the IDS manager component. The IDS management console should display critical information, including the alerts generated, the status of each component, the interface used to access/control each IDS component, data in individual packets, audit log data, network traffic details, and so on.

- **Generating an alert as configured**—The IDS manager is responsible for generating alerts when a threatening event occurs. Even though the IDS agents are capable of providing intrusion-detection alerts, they do not tend to do so. It is always more efficient to generate the alert from a central location such as an IDS manager than to generate multiple events from different locations (sometimes about a single intrusion), making the IDS process more complex. Agents usually send the collected information to a central server, which in turn sends alerts when a predefined criteria is met. This also indirectly implies that there should be an alert mechanism associated with the IDS manager to cater for this need. Also, the IDS manager should have the addresses of the operators who need to be notified when an alert is generated.

This alert could be in the form of a log entry, an application or batch file running, triggering a pager message, an SMS, or calling a cellular phone number.

- **Assembling and displaying alerts on a console/user interface**—Once an attack has been identified or detected, the same has to be conveyed to the concerned administrator/person. The IDS manager component performs this role by collecting and displaying the related information about the alerts on a specified console/user interface.

- **Correlating events**—Correlation of events reported by the other components is an important function of an IDS. The manager component correlates the events reported by the various components to determine whether they have a common source and destination, whether they belong to the same series of attacks/security events, and so on.

- **Adding the information regarding the incident to a database**—After the attack has been conveyed to the concerned by generating the console alerts and other information transfer mechanism, the next step is to store all the available information to a central data repository/database. A relational database, such as Oracle or Sybase, is ideal for this purpose. This is basically performed for various reasons:

  - For future investigations on the attack scenario
  - Regulatory compliance
  - Studying the attack patterns
  - For fine-tuning the IDS analysis pattern using the previous traffic/attack patterns

- **Managing policies**—The IDS manager component is responsible for generating, updating, distributing, and enforcing IDS manager policy. An IDS manager policy refers to the settings that affect how the various components of an intrusion-detection and intrusion-prevention system function. The policy that is generated and distributed is dependent on the data received by the IDS manager component. For example, a manager might create a policy instructing each host not to accept input from a particular source IP address or not to execute a particular system call.

- **Monitoring the components**—As discussed, the IDS needs various components to function, including its agents and sensors. These components need to be monitored on a regular basis. For monitoring distributed entities like the agents and sensors, a centralized component is ideal. In IDS, the manager performs the function of centrally monitoring the various components associated with it.

  One way the IDS manager performs this function is by sending packets to each sensor and agent to determine that each is responsive to input on the network. Additionally, the manager can also initiate individual connections to each IDS sensor and IDS agent to determine whether each of them is up and running. If the IDS manager component determines that an IDS component is not functioning, it notifies its alerting facility to generate an alert log.

- **Retrieving additional information related to the incident**—Once the basic information is collected and stored in the database, some IDS manager components collect additional information related to the attack incident that can be used for future analysis and study purposes.

- **Sending information/control instructions/commands to a system**—Some IDS manager components issue certain kinds of commands or control instructions to the systems under *limelight* based on the intrusion pattern detected. (Limelight is basically a mechanism wherein each time an IDS detects any suspicious activity, it compares it with the existing database of security infiltrations and then takes relevant action against the matches that come out of this comparison.)

- **Sending commands to a firewall or router**—When an attack is detected, some IDS manager components issue commands and control instructions to firewall or routers in the network. The nature of these commands depends upon the pattern of the intrusion attempt. These commands generally result in the modification of the access control list that matches the situational requirements.

The availability of all the log files at a central location makes it easy to perform the log analyzing and parsing functions. Additionally, writing log data to a different system (the system on which the IDS manager component is installed/configured) from the one that generated them is an additional security feature. When attackers compromise the original system, they might also be able to tamper or destroy the log data, thereby helping to masquerade their presence on the system. However, if the data is stored in a central server—the IDS manager component—the log data is still available at the central data depository. Finally, the management console provided by the IDS manager component enables the administrator to remotely change policies and parameters and perform other important functions.

IDS Manager Deployment Considerations

As discussed earlier, out of the three major components of an IDS, the sensors are the most attacked component of any IDS system. However, if an attacker compromises an IDS manager, the whole IDS system will go down, due to the very simple fact that the IDS is centrally managed from the IDS manager component. A successful attack on the IDS manager can also destroy all the logs, analysis patterns, policies, and data collected. Hence, it is very evident that sufficient security controls should be implemented to safeguard the IDS manager component. Some of the security controls recommended for hardening the security of IDS management components include:

- **Physical access**—Unauthorized physical access to the IDS manager component host should be restricted.

- **Protection from DoS**—The server should be protected from malicious network activities like denial-of-service attacks. This can be achieved by using both internal and external firewalls.

- **Dedicated server**—The host on which the IDS manager component is running should not be used for running any services or applications that are not required for IDS functioning.

- **Authentication**—Simple authentication controls can be easily bypassed by a skilled intruder. It is always advisable to go for third-party authentication such as smart cards and tokens.

- **Encryption**—All communication between the IDS manager component and any other component needs to be encrypted using 192- or 256-bit Advanced Encryption Standard (AES).

- **Storage space**—The IDS and IPS gather a huge amount of data as part of their security operations. Managing this data efficiently is always a challenging task for the IDS and IPS administrators. The solution of compressing and archiving is not an ideal solution, as it is always better to have an online access for carrying out the on-the-fly analysis. Having sufficient storage space for management purposes is of utmost importance when it comes to IDS data management. A good solution is to go for RAID (Redundant Array of Inexpensive Disks, now also known as Redundant Array of Independent Disks), which writes data to multiple disks and provides redundancy in case of any disk failing. Optical media, such as a worm drive, is also an option for storage.

- **Alerting**—When an alert is generated, it is either sent via email or it is logged at a central repository like the UNIX syslog facility.

  If the alerts are sent via email, the email content should be encrypted using some form of message encryption like PGP (Pretty Good Privacy). If an attacker gets hold of the alert email containing the information of the detected intrusions or shunned IP addresses, it can alter their operating strategies, which in turn will affect the future detection process.

The syslog has many security loopholes. Due to its flexibility, the syslog can send messages about nearly anything to just about everybody. These messages sent by the syslog are not currently encrypted. However, a project called syslog-ng intends to develop encrypting for TCP connections between the clients and the *loghost* systems, either via *stunnel* or a *virtual private network* (VPN). You can find more information about syslog-ng at http://freshmeat.net/projects/syslog-ng/.

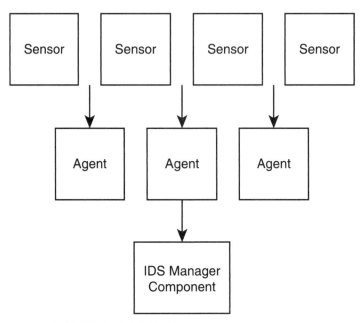

Figure 5.4   Multi-Tiered Architecture

Advantages of Multi-Tiered IDS Architecture

One of the main advantages of using a multi-tiered architecture is greater efficiency and in-depth analysis. Because it has multiple components independent of each other but that work toward a common function, an appropriately designed multi-tiered architecture can provide a degree of efficiency not possible with the simple single-tiered architecture. Because the multi-tiered architecture is deployed at more than one location, it can provide a much more complete picture of an organization's entire network and its hosts.

Disadvantages of Multi-Tiered IDS Architecture

The disadvantages of using a multi-tiered architecture are:

- Increased setup cost
- Complex architecture and requires skilled manpower to maintain
- Requires continuous administration, monitoring, and troubleshooting
- Increased maintenance cost

Peer-to-Peer Architecture

In a peer-to-peer architecture, there exists more than one pair of IDS components in a peer-to-peer structure that exchange intrusion-detection and intrusion-prevention information between the peer components. These peer components perform the same kind of IDS functions.

Peer-to-peer architecture is generally used by cooperating firewalls, whereby one firewall obtains information about events that are occurring and passes the information to the other peer firewalls, which may cause a change in an access control list or addition of restrictions on connections. The second firewall on the peer network can also send information that causes changes to the first firewall. None of the components in the peer-to-peer architecture acts as the central server or master repository of information.

Advantages of a Peer-to-Peer Architecture

Advantages of the peer-to-peer architecture include:

- Simple architecture
- Any peer can participate
- Each participating peer can benefit from the information supplied by the others

Disadvantages of Peer-to-Peer Architecture

Disadvantages of the peer-to-peer architecture include:

- Lack of sophisticated functionality due to the absence of specialized components.
- If a single peer is compromised by attackers, they can bring the whole network under their control by sending false information to the compromised peer's components.

Implementing a Network-Based IDS in a Heavily Switched Environment

Hubs and switches are the basic components that connect the various systems and servers in a network. A hub works at the physical layer of the OSI model and simply echoes every packet it receives to every port on the hub, excluding only the port the packet came in on. A switch, however, is based on connections. When a packet comes in, a temporary connection in the switch is made to the destination port, and the packets are forwarded. So in a hub environment, you can place your sensors almost everywhere, whereas with switches, you must do specific workarounds to ensure that the sensor can see the traffic required.

To overcome this constraint, you must use one or a combination of the following:

- Spanning ports
- Hubs
- TAPs (Test Access Ports)

Spanning Ports

A *spanning port* configures the switch to behave like a hub for a specific port. Let's look at one example. In the following figure, you want to set up the IDS to monitor the connection between the switch and the client machine—Client A. In a normal switched network, the IDS cannot monitor the connection between the switch and the client machine. To resolve this problem, you can configure the switch to span the data from the resource machine port to the IDS port. This can be configured for transmitting the data, receiving the data, or both.

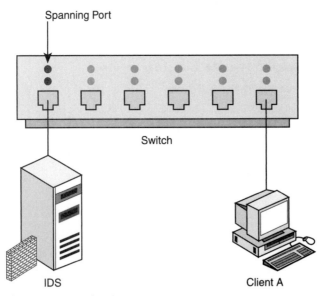

Figure 5.5   Spanning Port

Some of the disadvantages of using a spanning port are as follows:

- Not all switches support spanning ports.

- Spanning ports are not 100% reliable.

- Monitoring multiple machines is not possible, because switches allow only one port to be spanned at a time.

Hubs

The next option for monitoring a connection between two network objects in a switched network is to place a hub between the connections to be monitored, as shown in the following figure.

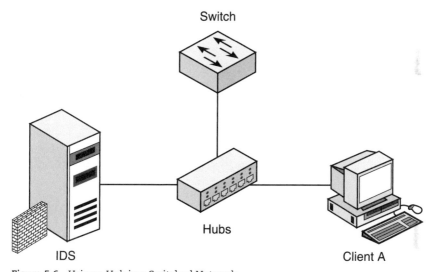

Figure 5.6   Using a Hub in a Switched Network

In this network setup, the traffic flows between the client machine and the switch. The hub placed between the client machine and the switch will enable the IDS to copy the traffic going through the hub.

Some of the disadvantages of using a hub in a switched network for IDS purposes are as follows:

- Like the span port, this solution is suitable only for a single machine.

- Multiple machines on the hub would cause network problems and negate the benefits and features of a switched network.

- Setting up a fault-tolerant hub is a costly affair.

Test Access Ports (or TAPs)

Network TAPs are used to create permanent access ports for passive monitoring. A TAP can be installed for monitoring the traffic between any two network devices, such as between switches, routers, and firewalls. It can function as an access port for any monitoring device used to collect in-line data, including intrusion detection, protocol analysis, denial-of-service, and remote monitoring tools. The TAP can send traffic data to the subject device by splitting or by regenerating the network signal received by the TAP. Splitting or regenerating the traffic will not delay or change the content, structure, or strength of the network packets, because they modify the strength of the transmitted signal.

TAPs fall under the passive network devices category, because they do not act on network traffic directly. If a TAP fails or stops functioning, traffic continues to run, and the network operations are not affected. Refer the next figure for a network setup using TAP for monitoring.

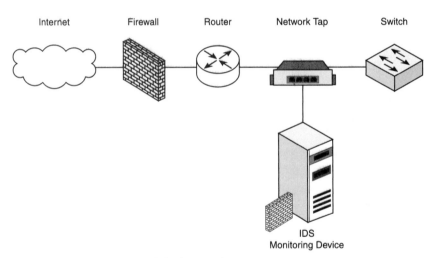

Figure 5.7   Using TAP in a Switched Network

This figure shows a simple installation of TAP. For a detailed installation diagram of network TAPs for monitoring, visit http://www.logixcomms.co.uk/t_net_tap_passive.htm.

Summary

This chapter has attempted to dig into the basics of IDS architecture, discussing various kinds of IDS architecture and its associated advantages and disadvantages. Understanding the IDS architecture and its inner working is critical for effectively administering an IDS. With this knowledge under your belt, you can feel more at ease when troubleshooting IDS issues and be more active in tuning the system for better performance.

Understanding TCP/IP for IDS

In battle, there are not more than two methods of attack—the direct and the indirect—yet these two in combination give rise to an endless series of maneuvers.
—Sun Tzu, Author of *The Art of War*

Introduction

The *Internet Protocol (IP)* family of protocols has been designed to provide a range of services, from low-level networking functions that interact with the system hardware, to routing data through various networks, reliability functions, and scaling capabilities, to application-level transparency in a layered approach.

The current version of Internet Protocol (IP) is Version 4 (IPv4). IPv4 was designed with little attention to security. The IP protocol is designed in such a way that an implicit trust relationship can be established based on the information received from other communication partners, which can lead to subversion by malicious parties. False information can be easily supplied to the trusting hosts that can eventually open the doors to these systems.

Layered Approach

The various functions that the network hardware and software must perform can be categorized as a series of functional layers, with each layer built on and depending on the proper functioning of the layers above and below it. The layered approach gives applications a great deal of independence, as they do not have to be concerned with the implementation complicacies.

Advantages of the Layered Approach

The layered approach to network communications provides the following benefits:

- Reduced complexity
- Improved teaching and learning
- Modular engineering
- Accelerated evolution
- Interoperable technology
- Standard interfaces

The Open Systems Interconnection (OSI) reference model is such a framework that is based on the layered approach concept.

The Open Systems Interconnection Reference Model

To materialize a communication network, hundreds of interrelated issues need to be addressed by a set of protocols. Evaluating and working with these large number of issues would be a Herculean and impractical task. As a result, in 1977, the International Organization for Standardization (ISO) adopted the Open Standards Interconnection (OSI) model. The OSI model breaks down the many issues involved and divides them into seven smaller, more manageable groups of sets. These seven groups are known as the *OSI layers.*

By breaking down the huge task of data communication into seven layers, the task seems more manageable. As the name implies, the OSI reference model is a model for reference and is not a product. It functions as a baseline for comparison to any protocol suite.

The Seven Layers of the OSI Model

The ultimate aim of the OSI reference model is to break down the task of data communication into easily manageable steps. These steps are known as layers and the OSI reference model is divided into seven distinct layers, as follows:

- Application layer
- Presentation layer
- Session layer
- Transport layer
- Network layer
- Data-Link layer
- Physical layer

The purpose of each layer in the OSI reference model is to provide services to the next layer above it while shielding the upper level from the complicacies of the layer below it. The higher layers do not need to know how the data came there or what kinds of technologies were used at the lower layers.

Application Layer

Also known as the *layer 7,* the Application layer is the topmost layer of the OSI model. The purpose of this layer is to manage communication between the applications and end-user processes. In other words, an application that communicates with other computers is implementing OSI Application layer concepts. This is the layer through which applications receive and request data. For example, if a spreadsheet application needs to transfer a file across the network, the spreadsheet application would need to implement the OSI layer 7 features/specifications. Examples include HTTP, Telnet, FTP, WWW browsers, NFS, SMTP gateways, SNMP, X.400 mail, and FTAM.

Presentation Layer

The Presentation layer is the layer below the Application layer and above the Session layer. The primary function of this layer is to define data formats such as EBCDIC text, ASCII text, binary, BCD, and JPEG, to name a few. The Presentation layer adds structure to packets of data being exchanged and ensures that the message gets transmitted in a format or syntax that the receiving system can understand. Data encryption is also defined by the OSI reference model at the presentation level of service.

An example of the Presentation layer is the process of FTP transfer. In a typical FTP file transfer, you are presented with two options for transferring the files—binary transfer and ASCII transfer. If you use binary, the sender and receiver do not modify the contents of the file. On the other hand, if you use ASCII, the sender translates the text from the sender's character set to a standard ASCII format and sends the data. At the receiver end, the receiver translates back from standard ASCII to the character set used on the receiving computer. Examples include MIDI, MPEG, encryption, PICT, ASCII, EBCDIC, TIFF, GIF, and JPEG. The Presentation layer is also known as *layer 6.*

Session Layer

The Session layer, also known as *layer 5*, is below the Presentation layer. This layer is responsible for controlling the "dialogues" during the communication processes. The Session layer defines how to start/establish a connection, how to use and control a connection, and how to break down the connection when a session is completed. The Session layer also checks for transmission errors once a connection is established. It also adds control headers to the data packets during the exchange of data. Some examples that fall under this layer include DECnet SCP, AppleTalk ASP, NetBIOS names, SQL, NFS, and RPC.

Transport Layer

The Transport layer, also known as *layer 4* of OSI reference model is below the Session layer. Layer 4 includes the choice of protocols, only some of which provide error recovery. Multiplexing of incoming data for different types to applications on the same host (TCP sockets) is also performed at this layer. In some cases, data is not received at the destination in the same order it is sent. The Transport layer performs the re-ordering of the incoming data stream when packets arrive out of order. Transmission Control Protocol (TCP), User Datagram Protocol (UDP), and SPX are examples of Transport layer processes.

Network Layer

The Network layer, which is below the Transport layer, is responsible for routing the packet based on its logical address. Also known as *layer 3*, the Network layer defines the end-to-end delivery of packets. To uniquely identify the end points, the Network layer defines logical addressing. It also defines how the routing of packets work and how the routes are learned so that the packets are delivered to the right destination. The Network layer also defines how to fragment a packet into smaller packets so that the packets can be accommodated in the transmission media with smaller MTU (maximum transmission unit) sizes. In simple terms, the fragmenting and re-assembling of packets is performed by the Network layer. Examples include Internet Protocol (IP), IPX, AppleTalk, DDP, and ICMP.

The Data-Link Layer

The Data-Link layer, which is below the Network layer, is responsible for preparing the data for final delivery to the network. The Data-Link layer specifications are concerned with getting data across one particular link or medium. The protocols associated with this layer are concerned with the type of medium. The packets are encapsulated into frames, and the protocols associated with the layer help address and detect data errors when transferred across the medium. The Data-Link layer is also known as *layer 2* of the OSI reference model.

The Data-Link layer is composed of two sub-layers:

- Logical Link Control (LLC) sub-layer
- Media Access Control (MAC) sub-layer

The LLC sub-layer functions as the interface between Network layer protocols and the media access methods such as the Ethernet or token ring. The MAC sub-layer is responsible for handling the connection to the physical medium such as twisted-pair or coaxial cabling. Examples related to the Data-Link layer are IEEE 802.3/802.2, HDLC, Frame Relay, PPP, FDDI, ATM, IEEE, and 802.5/802.2.

The Physical Layer

At the bottom of the OSI reference model is the Physical layer, also referred to as *layer 1* of the OSI reference model. The function of this layer is to determine how the bits of data move along the network's communication medium (or in simple language, the wire).The Physical layer specifications are basically standards from other organizations that are referred to by the OSI reference model. Electrical currents, connectors, pins, encoding, and light modulation are all part of the Physical layer's specifications. Examples that fall under this layer are EIA/TIA-232, V.35, EIA/TIA-449, V.24, RJ45, Ethernet, 802.3, 802.5, FDDI, NRZI, NRZ, and B8ZS.

Control is passed from one layer to the next, starting at the Application layer in one system, and proceeding to the bottom layer, over the stack to the next system and back up the hierarchy. The following figure shows how the data travels through the seven layers of the OSI reference model.

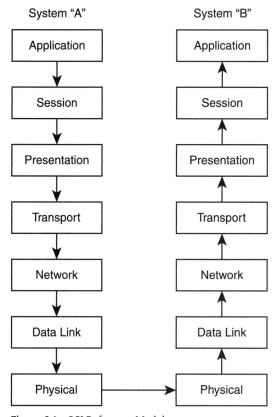

Figure 6.1   OSI Reference Model

The representation or transformation of data at each layer of the OSI reference model is shown in the following figure.

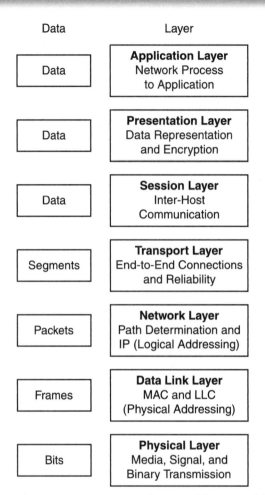

Data	Layer
Data	**Application Layer** Network Process to Application
Data	**Presentation Layer** Data Representation and Encryption
Data	**Session Layer** Inter-Host Communication
Segments	**Transport Layer** End-to-End Connections and Reliability
Packets	**Network Layer** Path Determination and IP (Logical Addressing)
Frames	**Data Link Layer** MAC and LLC (Physical Addressing)
Bits	**Physical Layer** Media, Signal, and Binary Transmission

Figure 6.2   Data Type at Each Layer of the OSI Model

Notes

Use these mnemonics to remember the seven layers of the OSI reference model:

From Top to Bottom: All People Seem To Need Data Processing

From Bottom to Top: Please Do Not Take Sales Persons' Advice

TCP/IP Model and the OSI Reference Model

Even though the OSI reference model is the ideal framework for understanding and describing the various network functions that come into play during a network communication, the IP suite of protocols does not conform to the reference model described by the OSI. The TCP/IP model was developed independently of the OSI reference model.

The TCP/IP protocol suite allows systems of all sizes, from many different system vendors, running totally different operating systems, to communicate and exchange data with each other. It is an open system in the sense that the definition of the protocol suite and many of its implementations are publicly available at little or no cost. As discussed earlier, the networking protocols are normally developed in layers, with each layer responsible for a different facet of the communication phase. The TCP/IP is generally considered as a four-layer system:

- Application layer
- Transport layer
- Network layer
- Link layer

Application Layer

The top layer in the Internet reference model is the Application layer. The Application layer deals with the details of a particular application. This layer is responsible for providing the functions for users or their programs—functions that are highly specific to the application being performed. This layer provides the services that user applications need to communicate over the network. These processes include all of those that users interact with directly, as well as other processes of which the users are not aware. Some of the examples of common TCP/IP implementation include:

- SMTP (Simple Mail Transfer Protocol)
- FTP (File Transfer Protocol)
- Telnet
- TFTP

Transport Layer

The Transmission Control Protocol (TCP) and the User Datagram Protocol (UDP) operate at the Transport layer. TCP provides reliable flow of data between two hosts on a network. It deals with functions such as dividing the data passed to it from the Application layer into sizes that are appropriate for the Network layer below it, acknowledging the received packets, and so on. On the other hand, UDP does not provide any reliability features. It just sends packets of data called *datagram* from one host to the other, and it relies on the application-level techniques to make arrangements for dealing with the lost packets.

Network Layer

The Network layer—also known as the Internet layer—is responsible for the movement of packets across the network. It takes care of the routing and delivery responsibility for the network packets. The Internet protocol works at the Network layer. The IP packets include a checksum feature that provides the assurance that a packet received has not been corrupted or modified in transit.

Link Layer

The Link layer, also known as the Data-Link layer or the Network Interface layer, generally consists of the device driver in the operating system and the corresponding network interface card in the system. This layer corresponds to the OSI reference model's Physical and Data-Link layers. When data is to be sent across the network, the network protocols will communicate with the device driver for the network interface card, which will in turn encapsulate the data in the right format and send it out to the physical medium for further transmission. Examples that fall under this category include device drivers and the network interface cards.

Check out this diagram, which compares the OSI reference model and the TCP/IP model.

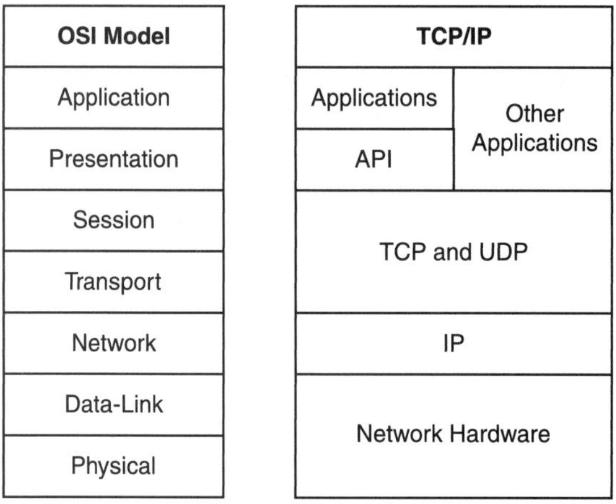

OSI Model	TCP/IP
Application	Applications / API — Other Applications
Presentation	
Session	TCP and UDP
Transport	
Network	IP
Data-Link	Network Hardware
Physical	

Figure 6.3   OSI Reference Model and TCP/IP Model

Best-Effort Delivery/Service

The *best-effort* delivery describes a network service in which the network does not provide full reliability or any special features that recover lost or corrupted packets during a communication process. It generally performs some type of error control (for example, discarding all frames that may have been corrupted during the communication process) but does not provide a guarantee for the data delivery. A best-effort service generally requires reliability features to be provided by a higher layer protocol.

A real-life example of a system that uses best-effort delivery is snail mail (or the postal service). You are not sure that a letter will reach its final destination. However, by paying some extra amount, you can obtain a delivery confirmation receipt.

In the TCP/IP protocol suite, TCP is responsible for providing guaranteed services while the IP provides the best-effort delivery. TCP performs the function of obtaining a delivery confirmation from the recipient and returning it to the sender. Because the Internet protocol provides the basic packet delivery services without any guarantee, it is called a best-effort delivery service.

Encapsulation

When an application sends data using TCP/IP, the data is sent down the protocol stack, passing through each layer of the stack, until it is sent as a stream of bits across the network medium. At each layer, additional layer-specific information is added by appending headers (and in some cases trailer information is also added) to the received data. Each layer on the sending system adds its own header information, and the receiving system reverses the process by examining the header message, stripping it of its header, and directing it to the appropriate layer. The implementation of the layered feature is performed by the encapsulation feature/process.

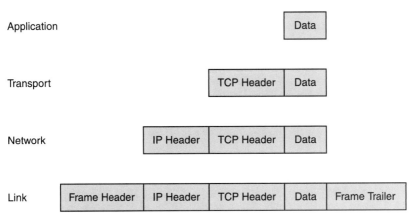

Figure 6.4 Encapsulation

Internet Protocol (IP)

IP (the Internet Protocol) provides a basic framework for the transport of traffic from a source system to a destination system on the Internet/intranet. The fact that all TCP, UDP, ICMP, and IGMP data packets are transmitted as an IP datagram makes the IP protocol the workhorse protocol of the TCP/IP protocol suite. IP is responsible for providing an unreliable, connectionless datagram delivery service. By the term unreliable, I mean that

there is no guarantee that an IP datagram will be successfully delivered to its final destination. IP provides a best-effort service. For example, when something goes wrong while
in transmission, such as an intermediate router generating some buffer issues, the IP has
a simple error handling algorithm to take care of the issue. It throws away the datagram
and generates an ICMP message back to the source system. The required reliability is
the responsibility of the upper layers of the TCP/IP model. A TCP/IP tutorial (RFC 1180—
TCP/IP Tutorial) can be found at http://www.faqs.org/rfcs/rfc1180.html.

The IP Header

The standard IP header is defined in RFC 791 and is available at http://www.faqs.org/rfcs/
rfc791.html. The normal size of the IP header is 20 bytes, unless options are present, in
which it might scale up to a maximum of 60 bytes. Embedded in the data portion of the
IP packet is the protocol-specific packet (such as a TCP or UDP packet) data.

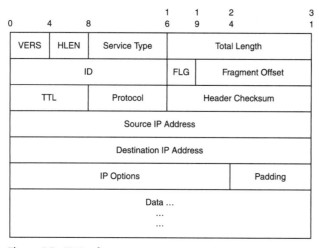

Figure 6.5   IP Header

The IP header diagram is a graphical representation of the IP packet. The most significant
bit is numbered 0 at the left of the diagram (see Figure 6.5), and the least significant bit of
a 32-bit value is numbered 31 on the right. The various IP header fields are as follows:

- **Version Number (VERS)**—This is a four-bit field that specifies the IP protocol
  version used. The value ranges from 0 to 15. The current version of the IP used
  is version 4, also referred to as IPv4. The next generation IP is IP version 6, also
  referred to as IPv6. For IPv4, the value of the version number field is 4.

- **Internet Header Length (IHL or HLEN)**—The header length is a four-bit field
  (whose value ranges from 0 to 15) that specifies the length of the header in 32-
  bit (four-byte) words. Because it's a 4-bit field, it limits the header to 60 bytes
  (15 times 4). Padding bytes are added to fill up the header to a multiple of 32
  bits. The normal value of this field (when no options are present) is 5.

- **Service Type**—The service type (also known as *Type of Service* or TOS) is an 8-bit field whose values range from 0 to 255. The TOS field is composed of a three-bit precedence field, four TOS bits, and an unused bit that must be 0. The four TOS bits are minimize delay, maximize throughput, maximize reliability, and minimize monetary cost. Out of these four bits, only one can be turned on. If all the four bits are 0, it implies a normal service. RFC 1340 specifies that these bits should be set by all the standard applications, and RFC 1349 contains some corrections to this RDC, and a more details description of the TOS feature. The new routing protocols such as OSPF and IS-IS are capable of making routing decisions based on this field.

The following figure shows the recommended values of the TOS field for commonly used applications.

Application	Minimize Delay	Maximize Throughput	Maximize Reliability	Minimize Cost	Hex Value
FTP					
Control	1	0	0	0	0 x 10
Data	0	1	0	0	0 x 08
Any Bulk Data	0	1	0	0	0 x 08
Telnet/Rlogin	1	0	0	0	0 x 10
TFTP	1	0	0	0	0 x 10
SMTP					
Command Phase	1	0	0	0	0 x 10
Data Phase	0	1	0	0	0 x 08
DNS					
UDP Query	1	0	0	0	0 x 10
TCP Query	0	0	0	0	0 x 00
Zone Transfer	0	1	0	0	0 x 08
ICMP					
Error	0	0	0	0	0 x 00
Query	0	0	0	0	0 x 00
Any IGP	0	0	1	0	0 x 04
SNMP	0	0	1	0	0 x 04
BOOTP	0	0	0	0	0 x 00
NNTP	0	0	0	1	0 x 02

Figure 6.6 Recommended Values for the TOS Field

- **Total Length**—A 16-bit field that specifies the total length of the IP datagram in bytes. Using this field and the Header Length field, you can determine where the data portion of the IP datagram starts and its total length. Because this is a 16-bit field, the maximum size of an IP datagram is 65535 bytes. If a packet is larger than the physical media can carry, the packet will be fragmented into multiple smaller packets that the media can support.

- **ID Field**—A 16-bit field that uniquely identifies each datagram sent by a host. It normally increments by one each time a datagram is sent. All fragments of an original packet will have the same ID value from the original packet to allow the fragments to be identified and reassembled into the original packet.

- **Flags**—The Flag field is a 3-bit field whose value can range from 0 to 7 and contains three control flags. Out of these three flags, two are used to manage fragmentation and the third one is reserved. The details are as follows:

  - **Reserved**—(should always be 0).

  - **DF**—Do not fragment bit (D), which can have the following values:

    Value set to 1—When set to 1, specifies that the datagram should not be fragmented.

    Value set to 0—When set to 0, specifies that the datagram may be fragmented during transport.

  - **MF**—More fragment bit (M), which can have the following values:

    Value set to 1—When set to 1, indicates that more fragments are yet to come in the fragmented message.

    Value set to 0—When set to 0, indicates that the last fragment in a message.

    Normal IP datagram packets will have these three bits set to 000.

- **Fragment Offset**—The fragment offset is a 13-bit field whose value ranges from 0 to 8191. It identifies where in the original datagram the fragment belongs. The fragment offset is measures in units of 8 octets (64 bits). The first fragment has offset 0.

- **Time-to-Live (TTL)**—The Time-to-Live, or TTL, field is an 8-bit field whose value ranges from 0 to 255. It sets the upper limit on the number of routers through which a datagram can pass. Each time a packet passes or hops through a router, the field is decremented by one. If the TTL value drops to zero, the packet is discarded, and an ICMP TTL exceeded message is sent back to the originating system. It limits the lifetime of the datagram and ensures that packets cannot persist on the Internet indefinitely in the event of a routing loop or similar network problems.

- **Protocol**—The Protocol field is an 8-bit field whose values can range from 0 to 255. This field indicates the type of transport protocol that is being used by the message being transmitted in the subject packet. The protocol numbers that appear in this field are found in the "/etc/protocols? file on a FreeBSD system. Please refer Appendix B for a complete listing of the protocol values used under this field. Some common values of interest are:
  - 1—ICMP
  - 2—IGMP
  - 6—TCP
  - 17—UDP
- **IP Header checksum**—The IP Header checksum is a 16-bit field whose value can range from 0 to 65,535. It is a checksum of the IP header and does not cover any data that follows the header. ICMP, IGMP, UDP, and TCP all have a checksum in their own headers to cover their header and data. The checksum is calculated by the computer using ones-compliment arithmetic. Because the header contents change whenever a packet passes from one router to the next, the checksum is calculated at each hop.
- **Source Address**—A 32-bit field that contains the source IP address of the packet.
- **Destination Address**—A 32-bit field that contains the destination IP address of the packet.
- **Options**—This is a 0 to 40-byte field that can have multiple optional features, including:
  - Security and handling restrictions
  - Record route
  - Timestamp
- **Padding**—The Internet header padding is used to ensure that the Internet header ends on a 32-bit boundary. A series of 8-bit bytes consisting of all 0s is used to pad the header up to the number of 32-bit words specified in the Internet Header Length field.
- **Data**—The data field contains the data portion of the IP datagram packet. The length of the data packet is the difference between the Total Length field and the IHL field.

Transmission Control Protocol (TCP)

The TCP protocol provides a very important service in the TCP/IP protocol suite, as it provides a standard general-purpose method for reliable delivery of data. Rather than developing their own transport protocols, applications can use TCP to provide reliable delivery of data. TCP provides end-to-end reliability between the application processes running on one computer system to another application process running on another computer system by adding services on top of IP. The Internet Protocol (IP) is connectionless and does not provide any guarantee on delivery of packets. TCP assumes that IP is inherently unreliable and adds services to ensure end-to-end delivery of data.

Some of the basic features of TCP are:

- Data transfer
- Reliability
- Connections
- Flow control
- Precedence and security
- Multiplexing

How TCP Works

There are four distinct elements that uniquely identify a TCP connection. They are:

- IP address of the sender
- IP address of the receiver
- TCP port of the sender
- TCP port of the receiver

TCP uses a 16-bit port number and the port numbers are ranged from 0 through 65536. These ports are basically divided into two ranges as follows:

- **Well known port numbers (0 to 1023)**—Used by well-known services and administered by IANA. These port numbers are also known as *registered port numbers.*
- **Ephemeral ports (1024 to 65535)**—Used by user programs to provide services or used as client ports for establishing connections. Also known as *transient port numbers.*

For a communication to be initiated/established, a listening process must be running on the receiving host to accept and respond to TCP connection requests. If the destination system receives a TCP packet for a port that is not listening, a TCP RST packet is sent back to the source by the destination host.

To establish a TCP session, the two computers participating in the session must first go through what is known as the *three-way handshake*. Typically, each time a TCP connection is being established or closed, a certain type of data packet exchange takes place. Before you learn more about the exact exchange that takes place, it is important to understand that TCP data packets can have a variety of different flags enabled, as explained in the following table.

Flag	Meaning
URG (urgent)	This flag tells the receiver that the data pointed at by the urgent pointer field is required urgently.
ACK (acknowledgment)	This flag is turned on whenever the sender wants to acknowledge the receipt of all data sent by the receiving end.
PSH (push)	This flag means that the data must be passed on to the application as soon as possible.
RST (reset)	If this flag is turned on in a packet being sent by system A to system B, it means that there has been a problem with the connection and A wants B to reset the connection.
SYN (synchronize)	If system A wants to establish a three-way TCP connection with system B, then it sends its own sequence number to the host (system B) requesting that a connection be established. Such a packet is known as the *synchronize sequence numbers* or *SYN packet*.
FIN (finish)	If data is being transferred from system A to system B, and system A has finished sending all data packets and wants to end the TCP/IP connection that it has established with B, it sends a packet with a FIN flag to system B.

There are two scenarios in which a three-way handshake takes place:

- Establishing a connection (an active open)
- Terminating a connection (an active close)

The steps in making a connection are as follows:

- Client: Sends a message with the SYN flag on.
- Server: Replies to the client with a message that has SYN and ACK flags on.
- Client: Replies to the server's SYN/ACK message with an ACK message.

During the three-way handshake process, various TCP/IP parameters are set that make sure that the two machines can participate in a TCP session. After the handshake is completed, a session is established and the machines can start transferring the Application layer data.

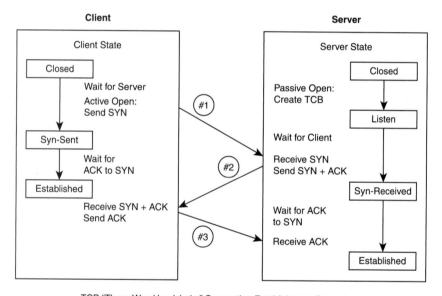

TCP "Three-Way Handshake" Connection Establishment Procedure

Figure 6.7   TCP Three-Way Handshake

When the client is finished with the communication, it will send a FIN/ACK packet, signaling that it wishes to close the connection. The server, upon receiving the initial FIN, sends an ACK acknowledging the FIN, and if the server does not have any more data to send, it sends a FIN packet to the client. When the client responds with an ACK of its own, the connection is considered closed. Either party can also abort the connection by sending a RST/ACK packet, which will cause the connection to be immediately closed.

TCP Header

The standard TCP header is defined in RFC 791 (http://www.faqs.org/rfcs/rfc791.html) and the TCP packet structure is illustrated in the following figure.

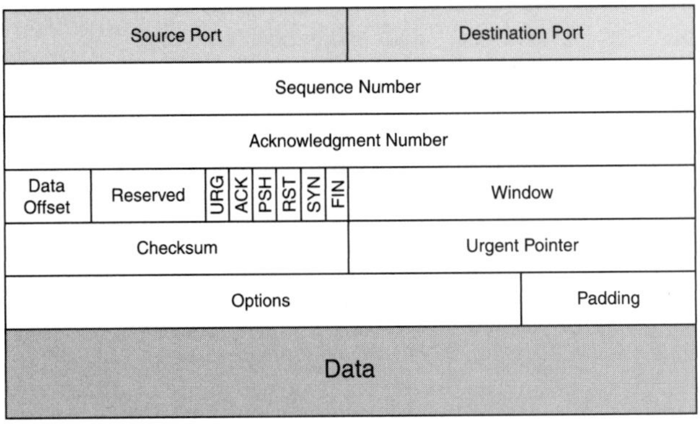

Figure 6.8   TCP Header

Like most TCP/IP protocols, the TCP header uses a 32-bit word format. The following section defines the individual fields in the TCP header:

- **Source port**—A 16-bit field whose value can range from 0 to 65535. This field determines the source port of the connection. When a connection is attempted or is being conducted, this field specifies which port the local machine is waiting to listen for responses from the destination machine.

- **Destination port**—A 16-bit field whose value can range from 0 to 65535. It identifies the destination port of the connection. When a user wants to connect to a service on a remote machine, the Application layer program specifies which port initial connections should use. When not a part of an initial connection, this specifies which port number is used for the remote machine as a packet is being sent out to its destination.

- **Sequence number**—A 32-bit field whose value can range from 0 to 2^{32-1} is the number of the first byte of data in the current message. If the SYN flag field is set to 1, this field defines the initial sequence number (ISN) to be used for that session, and the first data offset is ISN+1. A 32-bit value is used to avoid using old sequence numbers that already may have been assigned to data that is in transit on the network.

- **Acknowledgment number**—A 32-bit field whose value can range from 0 to 2^{32-1} and is used to indicate the sequence number of the next byte expected by the receiver. TCP acknowledgements are cumulative, which means that a single acknowledgement can be used to acknowledge a number of prior TCP message segments. In the first packet sent (the initial SYN), this field is undefined.

- **Data Offset**—The Data Offset field is a 4-bit field whose value can range from 0 to 15. This field indicates the number of 32-bit words in the TCP header. This field is needed because the TCP Options field could be variable in length. Without TCP options, the Data Offset field is five words (20 octets). Even if the TCP header includes an option, it is an integral number of 32 bits. The maximum size of a TCP header is thus 15 times 4, or 60 bytes. Values of 0 through 4 are invalid.

- **Reserved field**—The Reserved field is a 6-bit field reserved for future expansion and must be set to 0.

- **Flags**—A 6-bit field that contains the following six 1-bit flags having the following meanings:

  - The **ACK** flag indicates that the Acknowledgement Number field is valid.

  - The **SYN** flag is used to indicate the opening of a virtual-circuit connection.

  - The **FIN** flag is used to terminate the connection.

  - The **RST** bit is used to reset the virtual circuit due to unrecoverable errors. When an RST is received in a TCP segment, the receiver must respond by immediately terminating the connection. A reset causes both sides immediately to release the connection and all its resources. As a result, transfer of data ceases in both directions, which can result in the loss of data that is in transit. A TCP RST is not the normal way to close a TCP connection; it indicates an abnormal condition. To close a TCP connection normally, the FIN flag is used. The reasons for a reset include a host crash or delayed duplicate SYN packets.

  - When the **PSH** flag is set, it tells TCP immediately to deliver data for this message to the upper-layer process.

  - The **URG** flag is used to send out-of-band data without waiting for the receiver to process octets already in the stream.

- **Window field**—A 16-bit field whose values can range from 0 to 65535. This field indicates the amount of receive buffer space available. The Window field is used by the receiver of the communication to implement flow control. The receiving TCP reports a "window" to the sending TCP. This contains the number of octets—starting with the acknowledgement number—that the receiving TCP is currently prepared to receive.

- **Checksum**—A 16-bit field whose values can range from 0 to 65535. This value is 1s complement of the 1s complement sum of all the 16-bit words in the TCP packet. For detailed information on what *1s complement* means, please refer to the exhaustive Wikipedia article at http://en.wikipedia.org/wiki/Ones_complement#Ones.27_complement. A 96-bit pseudo header is prepended to the TCP header for checksum computation.

- **Urgent pointer**—A 16-bit field whose values can range from 0 to 65535. It points to the last byte of any "urgent" data that an application wants to transfer immediately to the receiving host, bypassing normal buffering. This field should have a value of 0 unless the Urgent flag is set.

- **Option**—The Option field is a multiple of eight bits in length and is used for various option capabilities that tune the behavior of the TCP communications. These options are added as necessary to bring the TCP header length to an even multiple of 32 bits. The Option field is included in the checksum.

- **Data**—The application data is placed here. The length of this field should match the total packet size specified in the IP header, minus the Internet header length, minus the TCP data offset.

User Datagram Protocol (UDP)

User Datagram Protocol (UDP) is a protocol that is used at the Transport layer for connectionless, nonguaranteed communication. Unlike TCP, UDP does not set up a connection and does not use acknowledgements. UDP is given the Internet protocol number of 17 and is defined in RFC 768 (www.faqs.org/rfcs/rfc768.html).

UDP uses 16-bit port numbers similar to TCP. When a UDP packet is sent to a port that's not listening, it will respond with an ICMP port unreachable message to the packet sender.

Common network applications that use UDP include the Domain Name System (DNS), streaming media applications, Voice over IP, Trivial File Transfer Protocol (TFTP), and online games.

Let's look at the UDP header format.

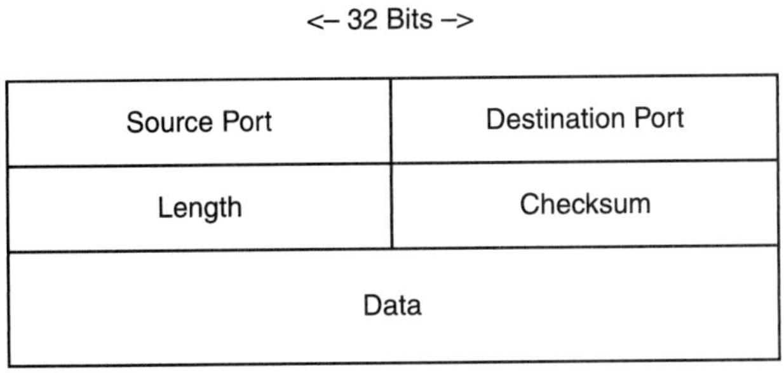

<- 32 Bits ->

Source Port	Destination Port
Length	Checksum
Data	

Figure 6.9   UDP Header

The UDP header consists of four 16-bit fields (4 times 16), which make a total of eight bytes in length. The UDP header comes immediately after the IP header. The details of the individual fields are as follows:

- **Source port**—A 16-bit field specifying the source port. Values can range from 0 to 65535.

- **Destination port**—A 16-bit field specifying the destination port. Values can range from 0 to 65535.

- **Length**—A 16-bit field whose values can range from 0 to 65535. It is the length of the UDP header and the UDP data in bytes. The minimum value for this field is eight bytes.

- **UDP checksum**—A 16-bit field whose values can range from 0 to 65535. The UDP checksum covers the UDP header and the UDP data. With UDP, the checksum is optional, whereas with TCP, it is mandatory.

Internet Control Message Protocol (ICMP)

ICMP, documented in RFC 792 (http://www.faqs.org/rfcs/rfc792.html), is a protocol tightly integrated with IP. It is used for sending error messages, performing diagnostics, and controlling the flow of data. Because ICMP uses IP, ICMP packet delivery is unreliable and hosts cannot count on receiving ICMP packets for any kind of network problem.

Some of the functions of ICMP are as follows:

- Announces network errors

- Announces network congestion

- Assists in troubleshooting

- Announces timeouts

The protocol identifier number assigned to ICMP in the standard IP packet is 1 and is documented in RFC 792. IP implementations are required to support ICMP, and it is considered an integral part of IP. To avoid the infinite looping of messages about messages, no ICMP messages are sent about ICMP messages. What this means is that you cannot generate an ICMP error message as a result of receiving an ICMP error message. Refer to RFC 1122 for more information (http://www.faqs.org/rfcs/rfc1122.html).

ICMP Packet Format

The ICMP packet format is as shown here.

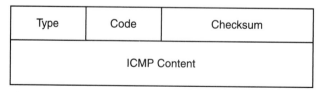

Figure 6.10   ICMP Packet Format

The various fields in the ICMP packet are as follows:

- **ICMP type**—An 8-bit field whose values can range from 0 to 255. This field encodes the type of ICMP message being sent. The various values are as follows:

Type	Description
0	Echo reply
1	Reserved
2	Reserved
3	Destination unreachable
4	Source quench
5	Redirect
6	Alternate host address
7	Unassigned
8	Echo request
9	Router advertisement
10	Router solicitation
11	Time exceeded
12	Parameter problem
13	Timestamp request
14	Timestamp reply
15	Information request
16	Information reply
17	Address mask request
18	Address mask reply
19	Reserved (for security)
20–29	Reserved (for robustness experiment)
30	Traceroute
31	Conversion error
32	Mobile host redirect
33	IPv6 where-are-you
34	IPv6 I-am-here
35	Mobile registration request
36	Mobile registration reply
37	Domain Name request
38	Domain Name reply
39	SKIP algorithm discovery protocol
40	Photuris, security failures
41	Experimental mobility protocols
42– 255	Reserved

- **ICMP code**—An 8-bit field that encodes a subcategory of the type. For a complete listing of the ICMP codes, visit http://www.iana.org/assignments/icmp-parameters.

- **ICMP checksum**—A 16-bit field checksum that covers the ICMP message. This is the 16-bit 1s complement of the 1s complement sum of the ICMP message starting with the Type field. The Checksum field should be cleared to 0 before generating the checksum.

- **ICMP message-specific data**—A variable length field that contains the data specific to the message type indicated by the Type and Code fields. All ICMP error messages will store the Internet header and at least the first eight bytes of the Internet data (which typically will be the protocol header). This information allows the receiving system to identify the hosts and port numbers to which the error message refers.

Address Resolution Protocol (ARP)

Two IP-enabled network device systems on the same subnet communicate using the low-level protocols and addressing mechanisms defined for the specific medium that is in use. The Address Resolution Protocol provides for a mechanism for IP-based devices to locate the hardware-specific addresses of other devices on the same subnet or local network. This service is mandatory in order for IP-enabled systems to communicate with each other.

ARP Packet Format

ARP is defined in RFC 826. According to this RFC, an ARP packet is made up of nine fields. The total size of the packet will vary according to the size of the physical addresses in use on the local network medium. ARP was designed to handle different types of media with varying hardware address lengths. An ARP packet format is shown in the following figure.

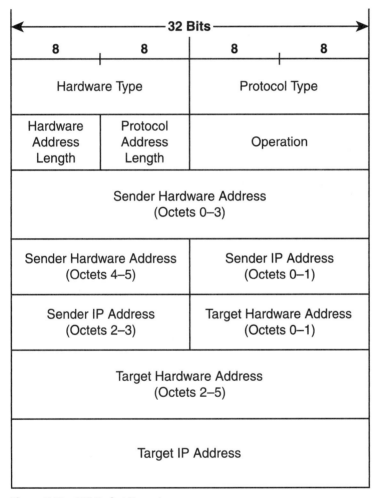

Figure 6.11   ARP Packet Format

The ARP packet contains the following fields:

- **Hardware type**—A 16-bit field whose values can range from 0 to 65535. This field identifies the hardware address type being requested, in decimal format. This field uses decimal codes to indicate the address type that is being requested. Some of the hardware types are as follows:

Number	Hardware Type
1	Ethernet (10MB)
2	Experimental Ethernet (3MB)
3	Amateur Radio AX.25
4	Proteon ProNET Token Ring
5	Chaos
6	IEEE 802 Networks
7	ARCNET
8	Hyperchannel
9	Lanstar
10	Autonet Short Address
11	LocalTalk
12	LocalNet (IBM PCNet or SYTEK LocalNET)
13	Ultra link
14	SMDS
15	Frame Relay
16	Asynchronous Transmission Mode (ATM)
17	HDLC
18	Fibre Channel
19	Asynchronous Transmission Mode (ATM)
20	Serial Line
21	Asynchronous Transmission Mode (ATM)
22	MIL-STD-188-220
23	Metricom
24	IEEE 1394.1995
25	MAPOS
26	Twinaxial
27	EUI-64
28	HIPARP
29	IP and ARP over ISO 7816-3
30	ARPSec
31	IPsec tunnel
32	InfiniBand (TM)
33	TIA-102 Project 25 Common Air Interface (CAI)

- **Protocol type**—A 16-bit field whose values can range from 0 to 255. It identifies the higher level protocol in use. For Ethernet networks, the value for IP is 0x0800 (in hexadecimal).
- **Hardware address length**—An 8-bit field whose values can range from 0 to 255. It specifies the length (in bytes) of the hardware addresses provided in the Source and Destination Hardware Address fields. Some of the most common hardware types and the sizes of their hard address (in bytes) are shown here:

Hardware Type	Size (Bytes)
Digital-Intel-Xerox (DIX) Ethernet	6
IEEE 802.3 Ethernet	6
IEEE 802.5 Token Ring	6
ARCnet	1
FDDI	6
Frame Relay	2, 3, or 4
SMDS	8

- **Protocol address length**—An 8-bit field whose values can range from 0 to 255. It specifies the length (in bytes) of the higher level protocols address found in the Source and Destination Protocol Address fields. For IPv4, this value is always 4.
- **Operation code**—A 16-bit field whose values can range from 0 to 65535. It identifies the purpose of the ARP packet. Some of the common values are as follows:

Message Type	Description
1	ARP Request
2	ARP Response
3	Reverse ARP Request
4	Reverse ARP Response
8	Inverse ARP Request
9	Inverse ARP Response

- **Source hardware address**—A variable length field that identifies the hardware address of the system issuing the ARP packet. The packet may be a request packet or a response packet. The length of the field depends on the value in the Hardware Address Length field.

- **Source protocol address**—A variable length field that identifies the higher-level address of the system issuing the ARP packet. The packet may be a request packet or a response packet. The length of the field depends on the value in the Protocol Address Length field.

- **Destination hardware address**—A variable length field that identifies the hardware address of the ARP packet's destination, which could be a broadcast (as used in requests) or a specific system (as used in responses). The length of the field depends on the value in the Hardware Address Length field.

- **Destination protocol address**—A variable length field that identifies the higher level protocol address of the ARP packet's destination. The packet may be a request packet or a response packet. The length of the field depends on the value in the Protocol Address Length field.

- **Data**—This section contains any additional data that the subject protocol requires as part of its operational requirements.

Fragmentation and Path MTU Discovery

A discussion on TCP/IP and IDS is not complete without talking about the theory of fragmentation. *Fragmentation* occurs when an IP datagram traveling on a network has to traverse a network with a maximum transmission unit that is smaller than the size of the datagram. For example, the Maximum Transmission Unit (MTU) for an IP datagram for Ethernet is 1,500 bytes. If a datagram is larger than 1,500 bytes and needs to traverse an Ethernet network, it needs to be fragmented by a router that is directing it to the Ethernet network.

Why should you think about fragmentation? Even though fragmentation is a normal network event, malicious hackers can exploit this feature to craft fragments with the intention of avoiding detection by routers and intrusion-detection systems that cannot deal with fragmentation.

Three fields in the IP header are used to support the fragmentation of packets:

- IP Identification (ID field)
- Fragmentation offset
- Flags

Path MTU Discovery is the process that determines the MTU between two hosts (assuming that the route does not change) so that packets can be sent without going through fragmentation. You can find more information on the process of Path MTU discovery in the RFC 1191 (http:// www.faqs.org/rfcs/rfc1191.html).

Summary

This chapter covered the foundation blocks of the TCP/IP stack and some of the major protocols associated with it. This chapter is only the tip of the iceberg; the full-feature list associated with various protocols is beyond the scope of this book. RFCs are typically reliable sources for understanding the various protocols more deeply. Without proper understanding of the protocols used in a network, an IDS/security administrator cannot effectively operate the IDS and the network security tools available in his or her security arsenal.

CHAPTER **7**

Microsoft Internet Security and Acceleration Server 2004 (ISA Server 2004)

Attack him where he is unprepared; appear where you are not expected.
—Sun Tzu, Author of *The Art of War*

Introduction

Microsoft Internet Security and Acceleration Server 2004 (ISA Server) is Microsoft's integrated security gateway that helps protect the IT environment from Internet-based threats. Some of the features of the ISA Server include:

- Firewall
- Policy-based administration
- Virtual Private Network (VPN) support
- Dynamic IP filtering
- Intrusion detection
- Web cache
- Reports
- Gatekeeper H.323
- Client deployment

Because this book deals with intrusion detection, this chapter concentrates on the intrusion detection and intrusion prevention features of the ISA Server.

ISA Server 2004 is capable of performing:

- Common attack detection and prevention
- DNS attack detection and prevention
- Various IP options and IP fragment filtering

Installing Microsoft ISA Server 2004 on a Microsoft Windows Server 2003

For this book, we will be performing a clean installation on a multi-homed machine. The following steps illustrate how to install the ISA Server software on a dual-homed (two Ethernet cards) Windows Server 2003 machine. This is a newly installed machine that has only the Windows Server 2003 OS installed. The IP addressing information is configured on each of the Ethernet interfaces.

1. Insert the ISA Server 2004 installation CD into the CD-ROM.

2. From the dialog box shown here, click on Install ISA Server 2004 option/link.

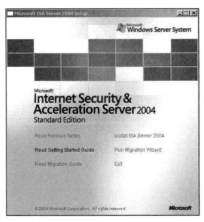

Figure 7.1 First Screen of the ISA Server Installation Wizard Allows Users to Read the Documentation Material

The installation preparation will begin, as shown.

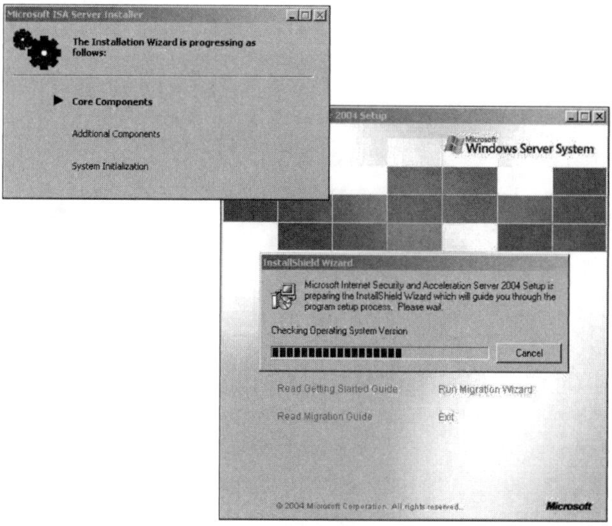

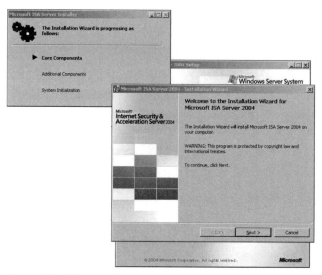

Figure 7.2   Clicking Install ISA Server 2004 Starts the Installation Process

3. Click Next on the Welcome to the Installation Wizard for Microsoft ISA Server 2004 page.

Figure 7.3   Welcome Screen of the Installation Wizard

4. Read the license agreement and select I Accept the Terms in the License Agreement if they are acceptable to you. Click Next.

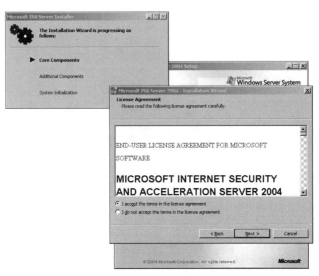

Figure 7.4   The License Agreement Screen of the Installation Wizard

5. On the Customer Information page, enter your name and the name of your organization in the User Name and Organization text boxes. Enter your serial number in the Product Serial Number text box. Click Next to continue to the next screen.

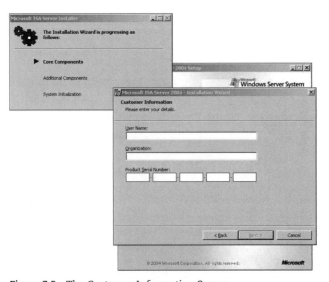

Figure 7.5   The Customer Information Screen

The Setup Type screen allows for several installation options: Typical, Complete, and Custom. A Typical installation includes all ISA options except the Firewall Client Installation Share and the Message Screener. A Complete installation includes all options. A Custom installation allows for the exclusion or inclusion of multiple ISA components.

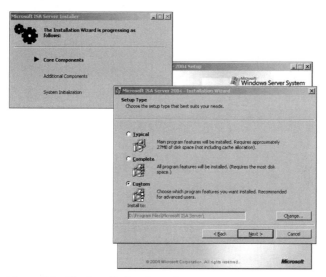

Figure 7.6   The Installation Setup Type

6. On the Setup Type page, select Custom. If you do not want to install the ISA Server 2004 software on the C: drive, click Change to change the location of the program files on the hard disk.

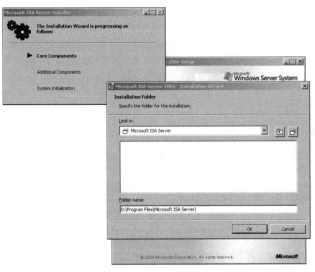

Figure 7.7 The Installation Folder Screen

7. After changing the installation path (if required), click OK to return to the Setup Type screen. Click Next to proceed to the Custom Setup screen.

8. On the Custom Setup page, choose which components to install. By default, when you select Custom, the Firewall Services, ISA Server Management, and Advanced Logging features are installed.

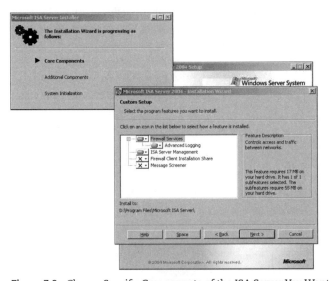

Figure 7.8 Choose Specific Components of the ISA Server You Want to Install

9. To add or remove components, click on its down-arrow key and adjust as needed. After you've checked all the features you want, click Next to continue.

Figure 7.9   It's Easy to Select or Deselect Specific Components of the ISA Server

10. After you choose the features you want, click Next to continue.

11. The Internal Network screen allows you to specify which network belongs to the internal network range. For configuring, click on the Add button.

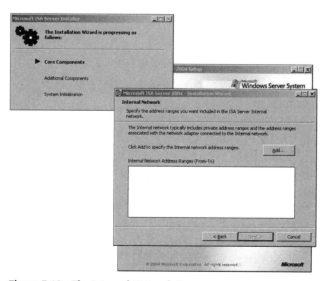

Figure 7.10   The Internal Network Range

12. Enter the range or ranges of your internal IP addresses in the From and To fields. Click on the Add button to move the entered range into the Internal Network Address Ranges field.

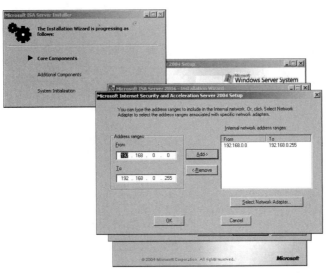

Figure 7.11   A Range of 198.168.0.0 to 192.168.0.255 Has Been Specified as the Internal Network Range

13. Additionally, you can click the Select Network Adapter button to select the suitable options for your internal network adapter. Click OK to return to the previous screen.

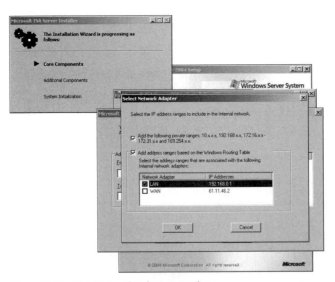

Figure 7.12   The Network Adapter Settings

14. The installation will return to the Internal Network screen. Review the internal network ranges and then click Next to continue.

Figure 7.13   Review the Internal Network Ranges Here

15. The Firewall Client Connection Settings window appears. If you want to allow computers running earlier versions of the Firewall client software to connect to the ISA Server 2004, check the box labeled Allow Computers Running Earlier Versions of Firewall Client Software to Connect. Click Next.

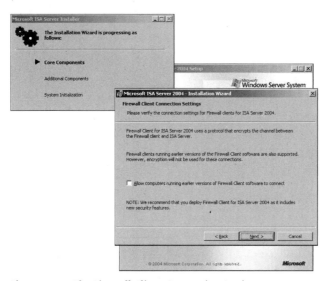

Figure 7.14   The Firewall Client Connection Settings

16. The next screen informs you that during the installation, some services will be restarted or disabled. Click Next to proceed.

Figure 7.15   Review the Information Displayed

17. The Ready to Install the Program screen appears. Click on the Install button to start the installation.

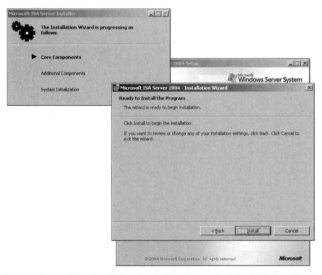

Figure 7.16   The Final Screen Before the Actual Installation Procedure Starts

The installation proceeds, as shown here.

Figure 7.17   The Actual Installation Has Now Begun

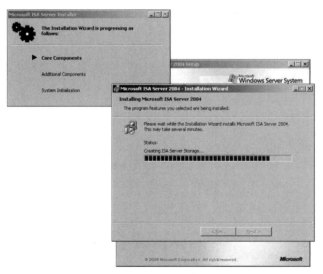

Figure 7.18   Creating ISA Server Storage

Once the installation of core components is over, the additional components will be installed.

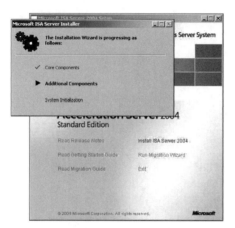

Figure 7.19   Additional Components Are Now Being Installed

18. Once the additional components are installed, the Installation Wizard Completed screen will appear. Click on Finish to complete the installation.

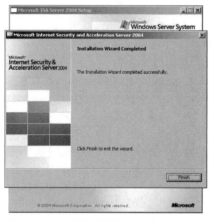

Figure 7.20   Click Finish to Exit the Installation Wizard

19. The installation program will prompt for a reboot. Click on Yes to proceed with the reboot.

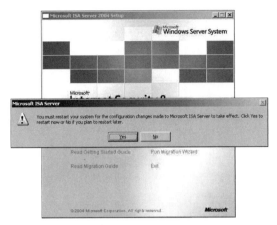

Figure 7.21   You Must Reboot to Complete the Installation Process

Enabling Intrusion Detection in ISA Server 2004

By default, intrusion detection is not enabled in Microsoft ISA Server 2004. To enable intrusion detection and DNS attack detection, follow these steps:

1. Open Microsoft Internet Security and Acceleration Server 2004 management console.

2. Expand your server name (in this case, the server name is PROXY).

3. Expand the Configuration node.

4. Click on the General node and click on Enable Intrusion Detection and DNS Attack Detection. See the next figure.

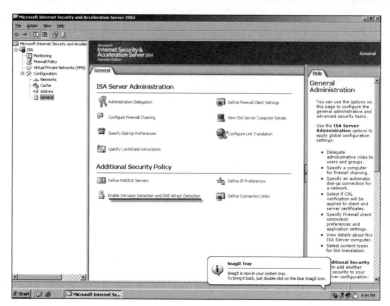

Figure 7.22   Click the Enable Intrusion Detection and DNS Attack Detection Link

This will bring up the Intrusion Detection window with the Common Attacks tab Selected, as shown.

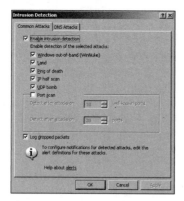

Figure 7.23   Select the Various Settings That You Want to Configure

5. On the Common Attacks tab, make sure that the Enable Intrusion Detection box is checked. ISA Server provides detection of the following types of attacks:

- Windows out-of-band (WinNuke)
- LAND
- Ping of death
- IP half scan
- UDP bomb
- Port scan
- DNS host name overflow (DNS Attack)
- DNS length overflow (DNS Attack)
- DNS zone transfer (DNS Attack)

6. If the Port Scan option is checked under the Common Attacks tab, you have the option to configure the number of attacks after which the detection is triggered. Refer to the next figure.

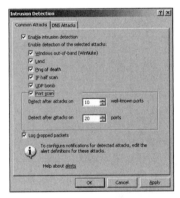

Figure 7.24   You May Choose from Intrusion Detection, Log Dropped Packets, and Other Options

7. The Log Dropped Packets option is enabled by default. This option creates a log entry of all the packets that are dropped by the ISA Server. To disable the login of dropped packets, uncheck this option.

Windows Out-of-Band (WinNuke)

The Windows out-of-band attack, also known as Windows OOB bug or WinNuke, exploits a known vulnerability in Microsoft network products.

How WinNuke Works

The attacker establishes a TCP/IP connection with the target IP address using port 139. Port 139 is used for NetBIOS. Once the connection is established, data is sent using the MSG_OOB (or Urgent) flag in the packet header. This flag instructs the computer's Winsock to send data, called *out-of-band data*. The out-of-band data is a logically independent transmission channel associated with each pair of connected stream sockets Out-of-band data is delivered to the user independently of normal data.

Upon receipt, the targeted Windows server expects a pointer to the location in the packet where the Urgent data ends, with normal data following. However, the out-of-band pointer in the packet created by the attacker points to the end of the frame with no data following. The target machine does not know how to handle this particular situation and will cease communicating with the network. Services will be denied to any users who subsequently try to communicate with the target machine. To reestablish the network communication or to bring back the target server to an operational state, a reboot is required.

Windows 95, Windows NT 3.51, and Windows NT 4.0 are vulnerable to the WinNuke exploit. The later versions of windows are not vulnerable to WinNuke. Microsoft ISA Server 2004 can detect any attempt to launch an out-of-band attack on its protected network.

LAND Attack

A *LAND attack* is a remote denial-of-service (DoS) attack caused by sending a spoofed TCP SYN packet to a machine with the source host/port the same as the destination host/port. The reason a LAND attack works is because it causes the machine to reply to itself continuously.

Ping of Death

A *ping of death* (abbreviated POD) is a type of attack on a computer that involves sending a ping request that is larger than 65536 bytes, which is the maximum size that IP allows. Although a ping larger than 65536 bytes is too large to fit in one packet that can be transmitted, TCP/IP allows a packet to be fragmented, essentially splitting the packet into smaller segments that are later reassembled. Attackers took advantage of this flaw by fragmenting packets that, when they are received, total more than the allowed number of bytes. This causes a buffer overload on the operating system at the receiving end, thus crashing the system.

This exploit has affected a wide variety of systems, including UNIX, Linux, Mac, Windows, printers, and routers. However, almost all of the new generation OSes have been fixed, so this bug is mostly historical.

TCP "IP Half Scans"

The Transmission Control Protocol (TCP) level of the TCP/IP transport protocol is connection-oriented. A connection-oriented protocol requires that, before any data can be transmitted, a reliable connection be obtained and acknowledged. TCP level data transmissions, connection establishment, and connection termination maintain specific control parameters that govern the entire process. The control bits used are as follows:

- URG: Urgent pointer field significant
- ACK: Acknowledgement field significant
- PSH: Push function
- RST: Reset the connection
- SYN: Synchronize sequence numbers
- FIN: No more data from sender

To establish a TCP session, the two computers participating in the session must first go through what is known as the *three-way handshake*. There are two scenarios where a three-way handshake will take place:

- Establishing a connection (an active open)
- Terminating a connection (an active close)

The steps in the connection establishment are as follows:

- Client: Sends a message with the SYN flag on.
- Server: Replies to the client with a message that has SYN and ACK flags on.
- Client: Replies to the server's SYN/ACK message with an ACK message.

During the three-way handshake process, various TCP/IP parameters are set that make sure that the two machines can participate in a TCP session. After the handshake is completed, a session is established and the machines can start transferring the Application layer data.

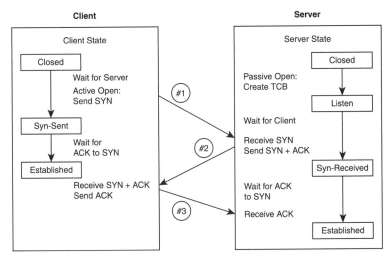

TCP "Three-Way Handshake" Connection Establishment Procedure

Figure 7.25   The TCP Three-Way Handshake Connection Establishment Procedure

This session establishment feature of TCP can be used to detect open ports on a system. Putting it in simple terms, if you want to know which TCP ports are open on a particular system, you can generate a three-way handshake on all TCP ports at the destination computer. However, this approach has the following two disadvantages:

- It is more time consuming as it requires a three-step process.
- It is more prone to be detected as a full connection is established.

The alternative is to eliminate the final ACK message sent by the target/client to the originator/attacker. This kind of scanning is known as *TCP/IP half scans*. In this kind of technique, only the first two steps of the classic three-way TCP/IP handshake take place. As soon as the client sends back a SYN/ACK message (in Step 2), your job as an attacker is done because this reply contains all the information that you need.

- Check for the application listening at that port.
- Ensure that no application listens at that port.
- Reply with an ICMP destination unreachable packet.

For a large number of UDP packets, the victimized system will be forced into sending many ICMP packets, eventually leading it to being unreachable by other clients. To complicate the issues, the attacker may also spoof the IP address of the UDP packets, ensuring that the excessive ICMP return packets do not reach the attacker's location, and making the attacker's network location(s) harder to determine.

UDP Bomb

The *UDP bomb attack,* also known as the *UDP flood attack,* is a denial-of-service (DoS) attack using the User Datagram Protocol (UDP), a session-less computer networking protocol. A UDP bomb attack can be initiated by sending a large number of UDP packets to random ports on a remote host. As a result, the distant host will crash, hang, or reboot.

Port Scanning

Port scanning is defined as the art of finding out the weakness of a computer or network by scanning or probing system ports via requests for information. IT professionals can use it as a genuine tool to discover and correct security holes. However, attackers can also use it maliciously to detect and exploit system weaknesses.

Detection and Prevention of DNS Attacks

The DNS filter of the ISA firewall protects the DNS servers that are published by the ISA Server using server-publishing rules. To access/configure the DNS filter, go to the DNS Attacks tab under the Intrusion Detection window. Refer to the following figure.

Figure 7.26   The DNS Filter Settings

By checking the Enable Detection and Filtering of DNS Attacks option, you ensure that the ISA Server will filter the incoming traffic for the following:

- DNS host name overflow
- DNS length overflow
- DNS zone transfers

DNS Hostname Overflow

The DNS hostname overflow is a kind of DNS denial-of-service attack. A DNS hostname overflow occurs when a DNS response for a hostname exceeds a certain fixed length (255 bytes). Applications that do not check the length of the hostnames may return overflow internal buffers when copying this hostname, allowing a remote attacker to execute arbitrary commands on a targeted computer.

DNS Length Overflow

The DNS responses for Internet Protocol (IP) addresses contain a Length field, which should be four bytes.

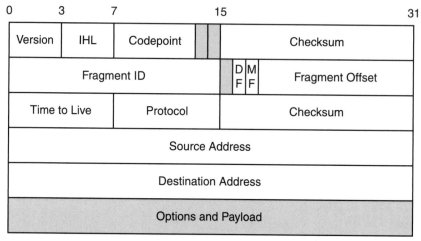

Figure 7.27   An IP Data Packet

By formatting a DNS response value, some applications that execute DNS lookups will overflow internal buffers, allowing a remote attacker to execute arbitrary commands on a targeted computer.

DNS Zone Transfer

Domain Names System (DNS) is a vital and critical component of the Internet. DNS zone transfer is a type of DNS transaction that's used to replicate DNS data from one DNS server to another. In other words, a DNS zone transfer intrusion occurs when a client system uses a DNS client application to transfer zones from an internal DNS server. There are two types of zone transfers, full and incremental. The zone transfer operates on top of the TCP, and takes the form of a client-server transaction.

Summary

When configured and enabled, ISA Server will identify any attack targeted against your network and will perform a set of manually configured alerts based on the scenario. Microsoft ISA Server compares the network traffic and the generated log entries to well-known attack methods in its database and generates the trigger alerts. Actions such as connection termination or service termination can also be initiated based on the triggers. Finally, with the add-on feature of ISA Server, you can add more feature-rich intrusion detection add-ons that enable you to customize the system for your business requirements.

8

Testing an ISA Server Installation

It is a matter of life and death, a road either to safety or to ruin. Hence it is a subject of inquiry which can on no account be neglected.
—Sun Tzu, Author of *The Art of War*

Okay, so you have successfully installed and configured the ISA Server 2004 for intrusion detection (and prevention). So what's next?

After the installation is over, the first thing you should do is check/audit the installation. You need to make sure that the ISA Server is doing what it is supposed to be doing. By auditing the security infrastructure, you will have a clear vision about your real attack surface.

Notes

Covering all the intrusion detection capabilities of ISA Server is beyond the scope of this book. For the purpose of this book, I will be covering an instance of a port scan and the related alerts and log files generated. For more comprehensive information on the ISA server, I highly recommend the book titled *Configuring ISA Server 2004* written by Dr. Tom Shinder. You may also visit the Web sites http://www.microsoft.com/isaserver/default.mspx and http://www.isaserver.org/ for more information on the ISA Server.

This section covers the following aspects:

- How to test an ISA Server for port scans
- How the ISA Server reacts to a port scan

Before you begin, make sure that you are not performing the following labs in a live production environment, as doing so may have varying consequences on network performance. If you are performing the lab session on a network, obtain permission from the Sys/Network Admin or from the concerned authorities, as port scanning is not allowed on many networks.

Launching the First Phase

The first thing that hackers do when they want to attack a system is find out all the information about that target system. The results of a port-scanning attempt are valuable sources of information for attackers.

Network Setup for the Lab

In order to carry out a port scan in this example, you will be using two systems connected through a switch. The network diagram is in the following figure.

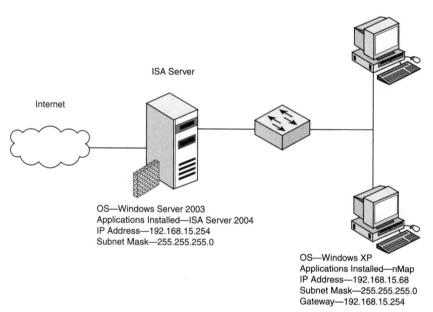

ISA Server

Internet

OS—Windows Server 2003
Applications Installed—ISA Server 2004
IP Address—192.168.15.254
Subnet Mask—255.255.255.0

OS—Windows XP
Applications Installed—nMap
IP Address—192.168.15.68
Subnet Mask—255.255.255.0
Gateway—192.168.15.254

Figure 8.1   The Network Setup for the Port-Scanning Test

The configuration details are as follows.

ISA Server:

- OS: Windows Server 2003
- Applications installed: ISA Server 2004
- IP address: 192.168.15.254
- Subnet mask: 255.255.255.0

Client machine:

- OS: Windows XP
- Applications installed: nMap
- IP address: 192.168.15.68
- Subnet mask: 255.255.255.0
- Gateway: 192.168.15.254

Port Scanning the ISA Server

This example uses the nMap tool from the client machine (192.168.15.68) to port scan the ISA Server (192.168.15.254). You can get a copy of the nMap tool from http://insecure.org/nmap/download.html.

To start the port scan, enter the following command from the command prompt and press Enter:

```
nMap -v -sT 192.168.15.254.
```

The output of the command is shown here:

```
C:\Documents and Settings\vikas>nmap -v -sT 192.168.0.1


Starting Nmap 4.20 ( http://insecure.org ) at
   2007-05-05 07:27 Eastern Daylight Time
Initiating ARP Ping Scan at 07:27
Scanning 192.168.0.1 [1 port]
Completed ARP Ping Scan at 07:27, 0.09s elapsed (1 total hosts)
mass_dns: warning: Unable to determine any DNS servers.
   Reverse DNS is disabled.
 Try using --system-dns or specify valid servers with --dns_servers
Initiating Connect() Scan at 07:27
Scanning 192.168.0.1 [1697 ports]
Discovered open port 8080/tcp on 192.168.0.1
Connect() Scan Timing: About 39.19% done; ETC: 07:28 (0:00:46 remaining)
```

```
Discovered open port 139/tcp on 192.168.0.1
Discovered open port 445/tcp on 192.168.0.1
Completed Connect() Scan at 07:29, 85.27s elapsed (1697 total ports)
Host 192.168.0.1 appears to be up ... good.
Interesting ports on 192.168.0.1:
Not shown: 1694 filtered ports
PORT       STATE SERVICE
139/tcp   open   netbios-ssn
445/tcp   open   microsoft-ds
8080/tcp open   http-proxy
MAC Address: 00:E0:4D:05:52:B3 (Internet Initiative Japan)


Nmap finished: 1 IP address (1 host up) scanned in 86.078 seconds
                Raw packets sent: 1 (42B) | Rcvd: 1 (42B)


C:\Documents and Settings\vikas>
```

The following figure shows the output.

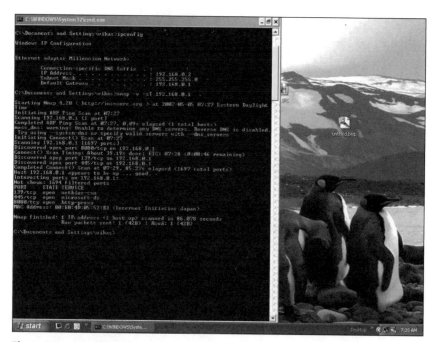

Figure 8.2 nMap Output

The Other Side of the Story

Now let's see what is happening at the other side—the ISA Server:

1. Open the Microsoft Internet Security and Acceleration Server 2004 management console by clicking Start>All Programs>Microsoft ISA Server>ISA Server Management.

2. Expand your server name (in this case, the server name is PROXY).

3. Click on the Monitoring node.

4. On the middle pane, click on the Alerts tab to open the Alert window.

    The number of connections that nMap establishes to scan the firewall generates an ISA log alert, as shown here.

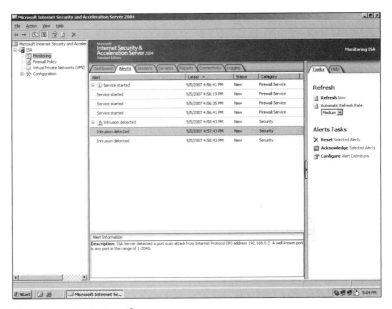

Figure 8.3 An ISA Log Alert

This alert is also written to the event log, which you can access as follows:

1. Right-click on My Computer and select Manage.

2. Under System Tools, expand the Event Viewer node.

3. Click on the Application node to view the Application event logs (see Figure 8.4).

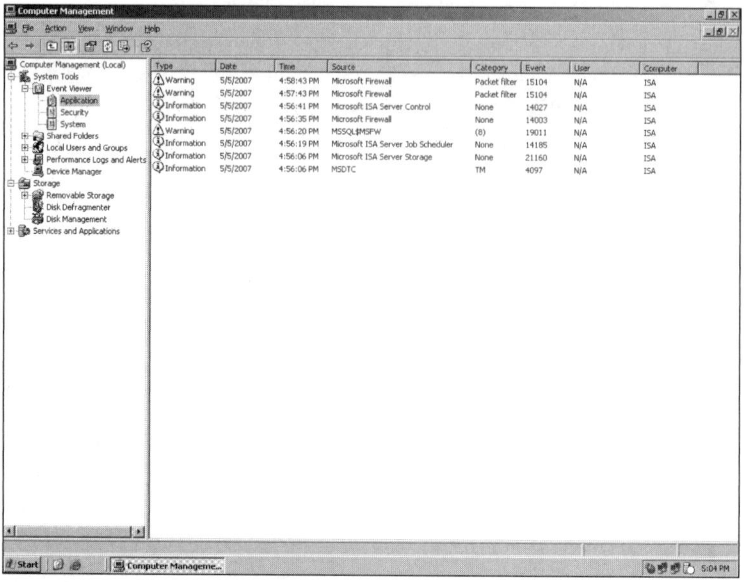

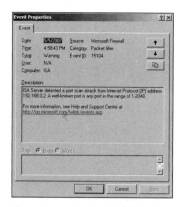

Figure 8.4   The Application Event Log

As shown, the ISA Server (shown as Microsoft Firewall in the Application event log) has generated a Warning log. You can view more details about the Warning log by opening (double-clicking) the event log entry. Refer to Figure 8.5.

Figure 8.5   Viewing the Warning Log Entry in More Detail

When the ISA Server denies a packet, it drops the packet and the connection. The port scanners don't know if the port is closed or filtered.

Tip

Another technique some use is fragmented packets that scan the targets. However, because the ISA firewall only runs on Windows servers, Windows by default discards all fragmented traffic. A scan with fragmented packets will produce no results in this scenario.

Summary

In this chapter, you learned how to perform a very simple port scan to make sure that your ISA Server is capable of detecting port scans as configured. The lab exercise performed is only the tip of the iceberg. There are various scenarios and port-scanning techniques that can be performed and evaluated using the setup used in this chapter. The best resource to find out more information about different port-scanning techniques is on the nMap Web site. As discussed earlier in this book, nMap is by the far the most powerful and effective network reconnaissance tool available. The Web site contains documentation and other related information on different port-scanning techniques.

CHAPTER **9**

TCPdump and WinDump

If he is taking his ease, give him no rest. If his forces are united, separate them.
—Sun Tzu, Author of *The Art of War*

TCPdump, and its Windows cousin WinDump, is a popular and widely used network security tool that can give you some insight into the traffic activity that occurs on a given network. TCPdump is popularly considered the first intrusion-detection system. Almost all of the current IDS systems support TCPdump format files, and it is highly useful when employing multiple IDS technologies.

TCPdump, the command-line network analyzer for UNIX/Linux-based systems, gathers data from the network, deciphers the bits, and displays the output in its native format. Most operating systems require root/administrator level privileges to successfully run TCPdump. The reason behind this is that to read packets from the network requires access to system devices that are accessible only to root/administrator level users.

WinDump

WinDump is the Windows version of TCPdump. WinDump is fully compatible with TCPdump and can be used to watch, diagnose, and save to disk network traffic based on various complex rules. It can run under Windows 95, 98, ME, NT, 2000, XP, 2003, and Vista.

WinDump captures using the WinPcap library and drivers, which can be downloaded freely from http://www.winpcap.org. WinDump supports 802.11b/g wireless capture and troubleshooting through the CACE technologies AirPcap adapter. WinDump is free and is released under a BSD-style license.

Using TCPdump/WinDump

TCPdump was originally developed by the Network Research Group at Lawrence Berkeley National Laboratory (LBNL) (see http://ee.lbl.gov/), and it is currently maintained by and is available at http://www.tcpdump.org.

By default, TCPdump now comes pre-installed with almost all flavors of Linux distributions. The chances are very rare that you will have to manually install TCPdump on a Linux system. The case is different with Windows machines, where you have to use Win-Dump. WinDump can be downloaded from http://www.winpcap.org/windump/.

> **Notes**
>
> libpcap (for Linux-based systems) or WinPcap (for Windows-based systems) is required for TCPdump/WinDump to function. More information on WinPcap/libpcap and their installation processes can be found in Chapter 5 of this book.

Downloading and Installing WinDump

The WinDump home page is at http://www.winpcap.org/windump/default.htm. The Win-Dump source files can be downloaded from http://www.winpcap.org/windump/install/.

The step-by-step instructions for installing WinDump are as follows:

1. Point your browser to http://www.winpcap.org/windump/install/.

2. Click on the link WinDump.exe to download the WinDump Installer. The latest WinDump version is 3.9.5. The file is 556KB.

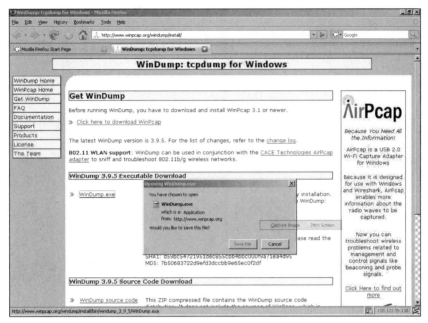

Figure 9.1   The WinDump Download Process

For the purposes of this book, I have downloaded the .exe file to C:\.

1. Open the command prompt and navigate to C:\.

2. Type **windump** without any parameter to run WinDump. The output will be similar to the following:

```
C:\>windump

windump: listening on \Device\NPF_{A819BAEF-346E-4A04-872E-
8C546D37825E}

12:37:23.144749 IP L203.1045 > 255.255.255.255.1211:
UDP, length 90

12:37:23.553659 IP system.mydomain.com.123 > DC.123: NTPv3,
    symmetric active, length 68

12:37:23.554539 IP DC.123 > system.mydomain.com.123: NTPv3,
    Server, length 68

12:37:23.815943 IP system.mydomain.com.137 > L203.137:
UDP, length 50

12:37:23.816885 IP L203.137 > system.mydomain.com.137:
UDP, length 193

12:37:23.818770 IP system.mydomain.com.137 > DC.137:
UDP, length 50
```

```
12:37:23.818935 IP DC.137 > system.mydomain.com.137:
UDP, length 265

12:37:28.802520 IP L204.1036 > 255.255.255.255.1211:
UDP, length 90

12:37:28.821600 arp who-has L204 tell system.mydomain.com

12:37:28.821757 arp reply L204 is-at 00:08:02:db:5e:cd
(oui Unknown)

12:37:28.821764 IP system.mydomain.com.137 > L204.137:
UDP, length 50

12:37:28.822136 IP L204.137 > system.mydomain.com.137:
UDP, length 193

12:37:32.514975 arp who-has M117 tell PROXY

12:37:32.823370 arp who-has M117 tell system.mydomain.com

12:37:32.823613 arp reply M117 is-at 00:16:76:86:f6:d2
(oui Unknown)

12:37:32.823619 IP system.mydomain.com.137 > M117.137:
UDP, length 50

12:37:32.823916 IP M117.137 > system.mydomain.com.137:
UDP, length 193

12:37:32.825279 IP system.mydomain.com.137 > PROXY.137: UDP,
length 50

12:37:32.825581 IP PROXY.137 > system.mydomain.com.137: UDP,
length 247

12:37:38.085757 IP L204.137 > 192.168.15.255.137: UDP, length 50

12:37:38.086407 arp who-has L204 tell L202


21 packets captured
23 packets received by filter
0 packets dropped by kernel
```

Running TCPdump for the First Time

You run TCPdump by issuing the command - *tcpdump*. By default, it reads all the traffic from the default network interface and throws all the output to the console. A sample output of TCPdump is shown here:

```
[root@localhost ~]# tcpdump


tcpdump: verbose output suppressed, use -v or -vv for full
protocol decode
```

```
listening on eth0, link-type EN10MB (Ethernet), capture size 96 bytes

15:29:09.546452 IP 192.168.15.66.1036 > 255.255.255.255.1211:
    UDP, length 90

15:29:09.547055 IP 192.168.15.100.32769 > 192.168.15.2.domain:
    60202+ PTR? 255.255.255.255.in-addr.arpa. (46)

15:29:09.547236 IP 192.168.15.2.domain > 192.168.15.100.32769:
    60202 NXDomain* 0/1/0 (128)

15:29:09.547374 IP 192.168.15.100.32769 > 192.168.15.2.domain:
    53319+ PTR? 66.15.168.192.in-addr.arpa. (44)

15:29:09.547514 IP 192.168.15.2.domain > 192.168.15.100.32769:
    53319 NXDomain 0/1/0 (121)

15:29:09.547674 IP 192.168.15.100.32769 > 192.168.15.2.domain:
    26281+ PTR? 2.15.168.192.in-addr.arpa. (43)

15:29:09.547807 IP 192.168.15.2.domain > 192.168.15.100.32769:
    26281 NXDomain 0/1/0 (120)

15:29:09.547910 IP 192.168.15.100.32769 > 192.168.15.2.domain:
    29553+ PTR? 100.15.168.192.in-addr.arpa. (45)

15:29:09.548042 IP 192.168.15.2.domain > 192.168.15.100.32769:
    29553 NXDomain 0/1/0 (122)


9 packets captured

9 packets received by filter

0 packets dropped by kernel

[root@localhost ~]#
```

You can control the behavior and output of the TCPdump to fit to your own requirements. You do this by means of the command-line options and filters available for TCPdump.

TCPdump Filters

By default, TCPdump collects all the data from the network interface card. What if you want to collect only UDP traffic? This is where the TCPdump filters come into play. TCPdump has a filter that enables you to specify the records that you are interested in collecting. To collect only UDP records, issue the command *tcpdump udp*. The filter in this example is *udp*.

```
[root@localhost ~]# tcpdump udp

tcpdump: verbose output suppressed, use -v or -vv for full
protocol decode
listening on eth0, link-type EN10MB (Ethernet), capture size 96 bytes
15:56:20.830276 IP 192.168.15.3.netbios-ns > 192.168.15.255.
netbios-ns:
    NBT UDP PACKET(137): QUERY; REQUEST; BROADCAST
15:56:20.830882 IP 192.168.15.100.32769 > 192.168.15.2.domain:
    6363+ PTR? 255.15.168.192.in-addr.arpa. (45)
15:56:20.831069 IP 192.168.15.2.domain > 192.168.15.100.32769:
    6363 NXDomain 0/1/0 (122)
15:56:20.831199 IP 192.168.15.100.32769 > 192.168.15.2.domain:
    10626+ PTR? 3.15.168.192.in-addr.arpa. (43)
15:56:21.129732 IP 192.168.15.2.domain > 192.168.15.100.32769:
    10626 NXDomain*- 0/1/0 (120)
15:56:21.129975 IP 192.168.15.100.32769 > 192.168.15.2.domain:
    53430+ PTR? 2.15.168.192.in-addr.arpa. (43)
15:56:21.130118 IP 192.168.15.2.domain > 192.168.15.100.32769:
    53430 NXDomain 0/1/0 (120)
15:56:21.130223 IP 192.168.15.100.32769 > 192.168.15.2.domain:
    2276+ PTR? 100.15.168.192.in-addr.arpa. (45)
15:56:21.435251 IP 192.168.15.2.domain > 192.168.15.100.32769:
    2276 NXDomain*- 0/1/0 (122)


9 packets captured
9 packets received by filter
0 packets dropped by kernel
[root@localhost ~]#
```

Reading and Writing to Files Using TCPdump

By default, TCPdump dumps all the collected output to the console. If you want to collect all the data and use it for future analysis, you can collect it in a binary format (also known as raw format) and then write it to a file on your storage media. To collect data in raw output mode, use the command *tcpdump -w filename*, where *filename* is the name of the file to which the records will be written in binary format.

```
[root@localhost tmp]# tcpdump -w file1.dump -v
tcpdump: listening on eth0, link-type EN10MB (Ethernet), capture size 96
bytes
13 packets captured
2 packets received by filter
0 packets dropped by kernel
```

To read from a raw output file, the command-line option *-r* is used. The command is *tcpdump -r filename*. This option reads input to TCPdump from *filename* rather than from the default network interface card.

```
[root@localhost tmp]# tcpdump -r file1.dump
reading from file file1.dump, link-type EN10MB (Ethernet)
16:49:56.874578 IP 216-239-53-83.google.com.http > 192.168.15.100.37811:
    P 318256797:318256830(33) ack 1446071525 win 17520 <nop,nop,timestamp
    270903 4632740>
16:49:56.874596 IP 192.168.15.100.37811 > 216-239-53-83.google.com.http:
    . ack 33 win 1996 <nop,nop,timestamp 4662761 270903>
16:49:56.874720 IP 192.168.15.100.37811 > 216-239-53-83.google.com.http:
    F 1:1(0) ack 33 win 1996 <nop,nop,timestamp 4662762 270903>
16:49:56.874842 IP 216-239-53-83.google.com.http > 192.168.15.100.37811:
    F 33:33(0) ack 1 win 17520 <nop,nop,timestamp 270903 4632740>
16:49:56.874861 IP 192.168.15.100.37811 > 216-239-53-83.google.com.http:
    . ack 34 win 1996 <nop,nop,timestamp 4662762 270903>
16:49:56.875328 IP 216-239-53-83.google.com.http > 192.168.15.100.37811:
    . ack 2 win 17520 <nop,nop,timestamp 270903 4662762>
16:49:56.881691 IP 192.168.15.100.37814 > 216-239-53-83.google.com.http:
    S 1475593059:1475593059(0) win 5840 <mss 1460,sackOK,timestamp
    4662769 0,nop,wscale 2>
16:49:56.882674 IP 216-239-53-83.google.com.http > 192.168.15.100.37814:
    S 3311015842:3311015842(0) ack 1475593060 win 16384
    <mss 1460,nop,wscale 0,nop,nop,timestamp 0 0,nop,nop,sackOK>
16:49:56.882713 IP 192.168.15.100.37814 > 216-239-53-83.google.com.http:
    . ack 1 win 1460 <nop,nop,timestamp 4662770 0>
```

```
16:49:56.882762 IP 192.168.15.100.37814 > 216-239-53-83.google.com.http:
   P 1:1431(1430) ack 1 win 1460 <nop,nop,timestamp 4662770 0>
16:49:57.023479 IP 216-239-53-83.google.com.http > 192.168.15.100.37814:
   . ack 1431 win 16090 <nop,nop,timestamp 270905 4662769>
16:49:59.051495 IP 192.168.15.66.netbios-ns > 192.168.15.255.netbios-ns:
   NBT UDP PACKET(137): QUERY; REQUEST; BROADCAST
16:49:59.052421 arp who-has 192.168.15.66 tell 192.168.15.58
[root@localhost tmp]#
```

Changing the Default Value of Bytes Collected by TCPdump

The number of bytes collected by TCPdump plays a major role when you're analyzing the packet contents. TCPdump, by default, does not collect the entire datagram. There are three major reasons behind this:

- The amount of storage space required for saving the packets captured is prohibitive.

- The performance issues are prohibitive, as it will require more memory and associated hardware.

- The users/administrators are generally interested only in the header portion of the datagram.

The snapshot length, also known as the *snaplen*, determines the exact number of bytes collected. The default TCPdump snapshot length is 68 bytes if TCPdump is not built with IPv6 support. If TCPdump is built with IPv6 support, the default snapshot length is 96 bytes. So when you are trying to save the packets to a file using the *-w* option of TCPdump, only the first 68 or 96 bytes of the packet (depending on the default) are saved in the capture.

Do these 68 bytes of data suffice? Let's analyze it with the knowledge you learned in Chapter 6 of this book. The following figure shows the breakdown of a sample packet.

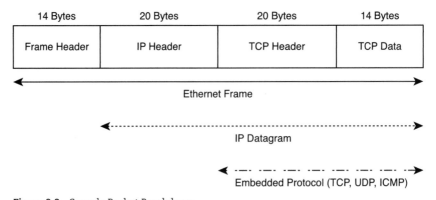

Figure 9.2   Sample Packet Breakdown

The first thing to remember here is that the header length can be different for different packets depending upon the protocol involved and the header options set.

- The first portion of the packet is the link layer header. In normal cases, it will be an Ethernet frame header, occupying 14 bytes for the link layer header and containing information like the source and destination MAC addresses.

- The next header is the IP datagram header. The minimum size of an IP header is 20 bytes if no IP options are set.

- The next layer of encapsulated protocol header size (TCP, UDP, ICMP, and so on) can range from 8 bytes to more than 20 bytes for TCP headers with various options set.

- The data or payload of the packet comes after these header packets. The default length of TCPdump *snaplen* allows only 14 bytes of the TCP data to be collected.

To change the default snaplen, use the *tcpdump -s length* option, in which *length* is the desired number of bytes to be collected. If you are planning to capture an entire Ethernet frame (excluding the four bytes of trailer), use the command *tcpdump -s 1514*. This captures the 14-byte Ethernet frame header and the maximum transmission unit length for Ethernet of 1500 bytes (14 + 1500 = 1514).

A Quick Byte for Ethereal Users

If you are using Ethereal for a network capture and do not turn on the Limit Each Packet to {N} Bytes option ("N" defaults to 68), the entire packet will be saved in the capture file. See the following figure.

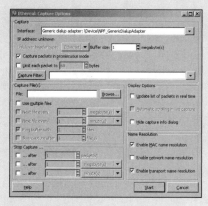

Figure 9.3   Ethereal Capture Options

You can access the Ethereal Capture Options by going to the Capture menu and selecting the Options menu.

TCPdump Output Format

Understanding the TCPdump output is mandatory for any IDS/security administrator. Without understanding the output format, an administrator will find it very difficult to manage and analyze the data collected. Let's analyze a sample TCP record.

```
11:15:32.068903 IP 192.168.15.100. 59351 >
fedora.redhat.com.http: S 3142808255:3142808255(0)
win 5840 <mss 1460,sackOK,timestamp 344527 0,nop,wscale 2>
```

- **11:15:32.068903**—This is the timestamp in the format of two digits for hours, two digits for minutes, two digits for seconds, and six digits for fractional parts of a second.

- **IP 192.168.15.100**—This is the source IP address. If name resolution happens, you will see the hostname here.

- **59351**—This is the source port number, or port service.

- **>**—This is the marker to indicate a directional flow going from the source to the destination.

- **fedora.redhat.com**—This is the destination hostname.

- **http**—This is the place for the destination service or port number.

- **S**—This is the TCP flag. The S represents the SYN flag, which indicates a request to start a TCP connection.

- **3142808255:3142808255(0)**—This is the beginning TCP sequence number. After the colon is the ending TCP sequence number (data bytes).

Notes

If you look at the TCP sequence number described here (3142808255:3142808255(0)), you can see that the beginning and ending sequence numbers are the same. TCP uses sequence numbers to order the data received in various packets. For establishing a session, the beginning sequence number represents the initial sequence number (ISN), selected as a unique number to mark the first byte of data. The ending sequence number is calculated as the beginning sequence number plus the number of data bytes sent within the TCP segment. This is a session establishment packet and the number of data bytes sent for a session establishment request is usually 0. This is why the numbers are the same. This brings me to an important point—normal session establishments do not send data.

- **win 5840**—This is the receiving buffer size (in bytes) of 192.168.15.100 for this connection.

- **<mss 1460,sackOK,timestamp 344527 0,nop,wscale 2>**—These are TCP options. Options are enclosed in angle brackets (<>).

As discussed earlier, TCP connections have one or more flags set. These flags are used to indicate the function(s) of the connection. The following table shows the TCP flags and their representation in TCPdump.

TCP Flag	Flag Representation in TCPdump
SYN	S
ACK	Ack
FIN	F
RESET	R
PUSH	P
URGENT	Urg
Placeholder	.

Most of the UDP records will have the word *udp* in the TCPdump output. ICMP records are easily identifiable, as the word *icmp* appears in all the ICMP record output.

More on Absolute and Relative Sequence Numbers with TCPdump

Continuing with the topic of absolute and relative sequence numbers, because the sequence numbers are big in size and length, it will be very difficult to track those in a normal scenario. TCPdump makes analyzing the sequence numbers an easy task with the help of a concept called *sequence numbers*. TCPdump changes the absolute ISN to relative sequence numbers after the two communicating hosts exchange their ISNs. If you want to view the sequence numbers in their raw form instead of as relative sequence numbers, use the TCPdump option *–S*. A sample packet capture with the TCPdump *–S* option is shown next (see the bold numbers, which are the sequence numbers).

```
[root@localhost ~]# tcpdump tcp -S
tcpdump: verbose output suppressed, use -v or -vv for full protocol decode
listening on eth0, link-type EN10MB (Ethernet), capture size 96 bytes
19:36:02.115348 IP 192.168.15.100.54110 > 64.233.189.104.http:
 S 3464921837:3464 921837(0) win 5840 <mss 1460,sackOK,timestamp
```

```
6689488 0,nop,wscale 2>
19:36:02.115999 IP 64.233.189.104.http > 192.168.15.100.54110:
 S 944633344:944633344(0) ack 3464921838 win 16384
 <mss 1460,nop,wscale 0,nop,nop,timestamp 0 0,no p,nop,sackOK>
19:36:02.116068 IP 192.168.15.100.54110 > 64.233.189.104.http:
. ack 944633345 w in 1460 <nop,nop,timestamp 6689489 0>
19:36:02.116191 IP 192.168.15.100.54110 > 64.233.189.104.http:
 P 3464921838:3464922333(495) ack 944633345 win 1460
<nop,nop,timestamp 6689489 0>
19:36:02.314005 IP 64.233.189.104.http > 192.168.15.100.54110:
. ack 3464922333 win 17025 <nop,nop,timestamp 370313 6689489>
19:36:02.418958 IP 64.233.189.104.http > 192.168.15.100.54110:
 P 944633345:944633818(473) ack 3464922333 win 17025
 <nop,nop,timestamp 370313 6689489>
19:36:02.418993 IP 192.168.15.100.54110 > 64.233.189.104.http: .
 ack 944633818 w in 1728 <nop,nop,timestamp 6689792 370313>
19:36:02.420830 IP 192.168.15.100.54111 > 64.233.189.104.http: S
3467667122:3467667122(0) win 5840 <mss 1460,sackOK,timestamp
 6689794 0,nop,wscale 2>
19:36:02.421871 IP 64.233.189.104.http > 192.168.15.100.54111: S
3729653044:3729653044(0) ack 3467667123 win 16384
 <mss 1460,nop,wscale 0,nop,nop,timestamp 0 0, nop,nop,sackOK>
19:36:02.421911 IP 192.168.15.100.54111 > 64.233.189.104.http:
. ack 3729653045 win 1460 <nop,nop,timestamp 6689795 0>
19:36:02.421966 IP 192.168.15.100.54111 > 64.233.189.104.http: P
3467667123:3467667615(492) ack 3729653045 win 1460
 <nop,nop,timestamp  6689795 0> 19:36:02.532762
IP 64.233.189.104.http > 192.168.15.100.54111:
. ack 3467667615 win 17028 <nop,nop,timestamp 370315 6689795>
19:36:02.734420 IP 64.233.189.104.http > 192.168.15.100.54111:
. 3729653045:3729654493(1448) ack 3467667615 win 17028
<nop,nop,timestamp 370317 6689795>
19:36:02.734466 IP 192.168.15.100.54111 > 64.233.189.104.http:
. ack 3729654493 win 2184 <nop,nop,timestamp 6690107 370317>
19:36:02.734541 IP 64.233.189.104.http > 192.168.15.100.54111:
. 3729654493:3729655941(1448) ack 3467667615 win 17028
 <nop,nop,timestamp 370317 6689795>
19:36:02.734567 IP 192.168.15.100.54111 >
 64.233.189.104.http: . ack 3729655941 win 2908
<nop,nop,timestamp 6690108 370317>
19:36:02.734808 IP 64.233.189.104.http > 192.168.15.100.54111:
 P 3729655941:3729657153(1212) ack 3467667615 win 17028
 <nop,nop,timestamp 370317 6690107>
19:36:02.734833 IP 192.168.15.100.54111 > 64.233.189.104.http:
. ack 3729657153 win 3632 <nop,nop,timestamp 6690108 370317>

18 packets captured
18 packets received by filter
0 packets dropped by kernel

[root@localhost ~]#
```

Changing the Capture Interface in TCPdump

By default, TCPdump is configured to set the lowest number interface as the active one, excluding the loop back interface. For example, if you have two network interface cards eth0 and eth1, TCPdump by default listens on eth0. If you have to change the default interface, use the *-i* option of TCPdump. For example, to change the default interface to ppp0, you would issue the following command:

```
tcpdump -i ppp0
```

The Hexadecimal Feature of TCPdump

TCPdump can dump all the captured data in a hexadecimal format. The command is to access this feature is:

```
tcpdump -x
```

This is a very useful feature for those who want to perform a deep-level packet analysis of all the fields. The default display does not show all the fields of the capture data. An example of a field whose data is not displayed is the length of the IP header. A sample capture packet follows:

```
[root@localhost ~]# tcpdump -x
tcpdump: verbose output suppressed, use -v or -vv for full
protocol decode
listening on eth0, link-type EN10MB (Ethernet), capture size 96 bytes
20:02:42.213745 IP 192.168.15.100.60400 > 64.233.189.104.http: P
  826889392:826889910(518) ack 2307392020 win 3632 <nop,nop,timestamp
  8289830 386124>
        0x0000:   4500 023a 77bd 4000 4006 f2a2 c0a8 0f64
                  E..:w.@.@......d
        0x0010:   40e9 bd68 ebf0 0050 3149 54b0 8988 0214
                  @..h...P1IT.....
        0x0020:   8018 0e30 ff0d 0000 0101 080a 007e 7e26
                  ...0.........~~&
        0x0030:   0005 e44c 4745 5420 2f20 4854 5450 2f31
                  ...LGET./.HTTP/1
        0x0040:   2e31 0d0a 486f 7374 3a20 7777 772e 676f
                  .1..Host:.www.go
        0x0050:   6f67                                     og
20:02:42.214587 IP 192.168.15.100.32774 > 192.168.15.2.domain:
                  6511+ PTR? 104.189.233.64.in-addr.arpa. (45)
        0x0000:   4500 0049 7e27 4000 4011 1cc6 c0a8 0f64
                  E..I~'@.@......d
        0x0010:   c0a8 0f02 8006 0035 0035 9da3 196f 0100
                  .......5.5...o..
        0x0020:   0001 0000 0000 0000 0331 3034 0331 3839
                  .........104.189
```

```
0x0030:   0332 3333 0236 3407 696e 2d61 6464 7204
          .233.64.in-addr.
0x0040:   6172 7061 0000 0c00 01                        arpa.....
          20:02:42.214774 IP 192.168.15.2.domain >
          192.168.15.100.32774:
          6511 NXDomain 0/1/0 (105)
0x0000:   4500 0085 fd9a 0000 8011 9d16 c0a8 0f02
          E..............
0x0010:   c0a8 0f64 0035 8006 0071 a8d2 196f 8183
          ...d.5...q...o..
0x0020:   0001 0000 0001 0000 0331 3034 0331 3839
          .........104.189
0x0030:   0332 3333 0236 3407 696e 2d61 6464 7204
          .233.64.in-addr.
0x0040:   6172 7061 0000 0c00 01c0 1000 0600 0100
          arpa............
0x0050:   002a                                          .*
```

```
3 packets captured
3 packets received by filter
0 packets dropped by kernel
[root@localhost ~]
```

TCPdump Options

The various TCPdump options (information from TCPdump man pages) are listed in the following table:

Option	Description
-a	Attempt to convert network and broadcast addresses to names.
-c	Exit after receiving *count* packets.
-d	Dump the compiled packet-matching code in a human readable form to standard output and stop.
-dd	Dump packet-matching code as a C program fragment.
-ddd	Dump packet-matching code as decimal numbers (preceded with a *count*).
-e	Print the link-level header on each dump line.

Option	Description
-f	Print foreign Internet addresses numerically rather than symbolically (this option is intended-ed to get around serious brain damage in Sun's *yp* server; usually it hangs forever when trans-lating nonlocal Internet numbers).
-F	Use *file* as input for the filter expression. An additional expression given on the command line is ignored.
-i	Listen on interface. If unspecified, TCPdump searches the system interface list for the lowest numbered, configured up interface (ex-cluding loop-back). Ties are broken by choosing the earliest match.
-l	Make *stdout* line buffered. Useful if you want to see the data while capturing it. For example: `tcpdump -l	tee dat'` or `tcpdump -l > dat & tail -f dat`.
-n	Don't convert addresses (that is, host address-es, port numbers, and so on) to names.
-N	Don't print domain name qualification of host names. For example, if you give this flag then TCPdump will print `nic` instead of `nic.ddn.mil`.
-O	Don't run the packet-matching code optimizer. This is useful only if you suspect a bug in the optimizer.
-p	Don't put the interface into promiscuous mode. Note that the interface might be in pro-miscuous mode for some other reason; hence, -p cannot be used as an abbreviation for ether host {local-hw- addr} or ether broadcast.
-q	Quick (quiet?) output. Print less protocol infor-mation so output lines are shorter.
-r	Read packets from *file* (which was created with the -w option). Standard input is used if *file* is -.

Option	Description
-s	Snarf snaplen bytes of data from each packet rather than the default of 68 (with SunOS's NIT, the minimum is actually 96). 68 bytes is adequate for IP, ICMP, TCP, and UDP but may truncate protocol information from name server and NFS packets. Packets truncated because of a limited snapshot are indicated in the output with *[|proto]'*, where *proto* is the name of the protocol level at which the truncation has occurred. Note that taking larger snapshots both increases the amount of time it takes to process packets and, effectively, decreases the amount of packet buffering. This may cause packets to be lost. You should limit snaplen to the smallest number that will capture the protocol information you're interested in.
-T	Force packets selected by "expression" to be interpreted by the specified type. Currently known types are rpc (Remote Procedure Call), rtp (Real-Time Applications protocol), rtcp (Real-Time Applications control protocol), vat (Visual Audio Tool), and wb (distributed White Board).
-S	Print absolute, rather than relative, TCP sequence numbers.
-t	Don't print a timestamp on each dump line.
-tt	Print an unformatted timestamp on each dump line.
-v	(Slightly more) verbose output. For example, the time-to-live and type of service information in an IP packet is printed.
-vv	Even more verbose output. For example, additional fields are printed from NFS reply packets.
-w	Write the raw packets to *file* rather than parsing and printing them out. They can later be printed with the -r option. Standard output is used if file is -.
-x	Print each packet (minus its link level header) in hex. The smaller of the entire packet or *snaplen* bytes will be printed.

Expressions in TCPdump

The TCPdump expressions can be used to extract packets matching certain character-istics. TCPdump uses the Berkeley Packet Filtering (BPF) language to carry out packet matching using expressions that match bytes within the packet. The TCPdump expres-sions include the normal arithmetic and logical operators (which are similar to the ones used in C language) and packet bytes. A packet that matches the expression is processed by the BPF application. The packets that do not match the expression pattern are not dis-played or processed.

TCPdump allows the users to selectively look at the packet data at the bit or byte level for a given protocol. The format for the selection is:

proto[expr:size]

where *proto* can be one of the following:

- fddi
- ip
- arp
- rarp
- tcp
- udp
- icmp

These represent the protocol layers for the index operation. The byte offset, which is rela-tive to the indicated protocol layer, is represented by *expr*. The *size* field in the expression format is optional and indicates the number of bytes in the *subject* field. The values can be 1, 2, or 4. The default value is 1.

The format of the numeric values used in BPF expressions are similar to the ones used in C language. For example:

- To represent a hexadecimal (base-16) value, 0x is used. For example, 0xabcd.
- To represent an octal (base-8) value, 0 is used. For example, 01234.

Additionally, the following operators can be used in constructing the TCPdump expressions:

- Arithmetic and Boolean operators such as +, −, *, /, &, and |.
- Logical operators such as && (represents "and") and || (represents "or").
- Relational operators such as <, >, <=, >=, and =.
- Bit-shift operators such as >> and <<.
- The negation operator – (!).
- Parentheses ( ).

Consider this simple example:

```
tcp[2:2] = 80
```

In this example, the expression looks for a TCP packet with a destination port set to 80. In the expression, *tcp* indicates that the expression is looking for TCP packets. The first 2 indicates the byte count from the beginning of the protocol header (in this case, it is TCP). The second 2 indicates the number of bytes. So, to sum up, the expression is looking for TCP packets whose third byte (remember the counting starts from 0, that is why it's 2 in the expression) and fourth bytes (total two bytes) are set to 80. Remember, bytes two and three of the TCP header indicate the destination port.

Summary

A properly crafted TCPdump packet filter and expression can be used as an IDS. This chapter covered TCPdump and WinDump and their basic operations. It also covered various TCPdump switches and discussed how to craft TCPdump expressions using the Berkeley Packet Filtering (BPF) language. The other important point to note here is that almost all IDSs can examine and store the TCPdump traffic format. All these features make TCPdump a powerful security tool in the arsenal of a security administrator.

## CHAPTER 10

Using Snort

Attack him where he is unprepared, appear where you are not expected.
—Sun Tzu, Author of *The Art of War*

Snort is a very flexible network intrusion-detection system that has a large set of pre-configured rules. Snort also allows you to write your own ruleset. There are several mailing lists on the Internet (including ones at snort.org, antionline.com, packetstormsecurity.org, and www.securityfocus.com) where people share new Snort rules that can counter the latest attacks.

Snort is a modern security application that can perform the following three functions:

- It can serve as a packet sniffer.
- It can work as a packet logger.
- It can work as a network-based intrusion-detection system (NIDS).

Currently, Snort is released for the following operating systems (x86-architecture): Linux, Free BSD, NetBSD, OpenBSD, and Windows. Other systems supported include Spart-architecture, Solaris, MacOS X and MkLinux, and PA-RISC HP-UX. The source code for Snort is available under GPL license, and the same can be used to port the code to other operating systems.

The Snort system requirements are as follows:

- **Network Interface Card**—A minimum of one NIC card is required. However, it is strongly recommended that you have two NICs on the system on which Snort is installed. The first NIC should be configured without an IP address to silently listen to the network traffic. The second NIC should be used for managing the sensor, sending alerts, and for handling other normal TCP/IP activity.

- **Consideration for a switched network**—If Snort is operating on a switched network, make sure the switch port to which the Snort system is connected is set to spanning mode. This ensures that all traffic sent out from any other port on this switch is also sent to the spanning port.

How Snort Works

Snort is a very popular intrusion-detection and prevention tool that I recommend for all readers. In this section, you learn how to best install, configure, and use Snort.

Packet Decoder/Packet Capture Library

The first component that comes into the show is the packet decoder. The packet capture library is a distinct piece of software that takes Snort network packets from the network card. On Linux and UNIX systems, Snort uses libpcap. On Windows systems, Snort uses WinPcap. Snort uses an ordered set of customizable behaviors to determine which traffic matches its rules and should be alerted on. The incoming data is decoded first by the packet decoder. The packet decoder determines which protocol is in use for a given packet and matches the data against allowable behavior for packets of that protocol.

The Preprocessor

The data is then sent through any preprocessors that are enabled in the snort.conf file. The preprocessors are Snort plug-ins that parse incoming data. Data is passed to the preprocessor after it has been parsed by the packet decoder. If Snort is run without a preprocessor specified in the snort.conf configuration file, it will display each individual packet as it arrives.

The Detection Engine

The detection engine takes data from the packet decoder and preprocessors (if any are enabled) and compares that data against the rules configured in the snort.conf configuration file.

The Alerting and Logging Components

After the rules have been matched against the data, the alerting and logging components come into the picture. Any matches found are then sent to the alerting and logging component, which will be passed through the output plug-ins. Snort's logging mechanism is responsible for archiving the packets that triggered the Snort rules. The alerting mechanism notifies the analyst that a rule has been fired. Similar to the preprocessors, these functions are set in the snort.conf configuration file. This is the file where you can specify which alerting and logging components are enabled. The various options available for sending/logging the alerts are as follows:

- Record/log the alerts to a log file.
- Send the alert through SMB pop-up window to a Windows workstation.
- Send the alerts through UNIX sockets.
- SNMP traps (enable a client system within a network to notify the management system of important events through unsolicited SNMP messages).

- Store the alerts in a SQL database (for example, MySQL or PostgreSQL).

- Page the alerts using third-party tool integration.

- Send the alerts to a cell phone via SMS text messages (requires third-party tool integration as well).

Output Plug-Ins

The *output* plug-in is the means by which Snort gets the intrusion data to the user/administrator. The purpose of the *output* plug-in is to dump alerting data to another resource or file. Multiple *output* plug-ins can be activated to perform different functions. Following is the section of the snort.conf configuration file that deals with the *output* plug-in:

```
# alert_syslog: log alerts to syslog
# ----------------------------------
# Use one or more syslog facilities as arguments.  Win32 can also optionally
# specify a particular hostname/port.  Under Win32, the default hostname is
# '127.0.0.1', and the default port is 514.
#
# [Unix flavors should use this format...]
# output alert_syslog: LOG_AUTH LOG_ALERT
#
# [Win32 can use any of these formats...]
# output alert_syslog: LOG_AUTH LOG_ALERT
# output alert_syslog: host=hostname, LOG_AUTH LOG_ALERT
# output alert_syslog: host=hostname:port, LOG_AUTH LOG_ALERT
```

As is evident from these configuration lines, the output plug-in can be configured for UNIX-based systems and for Windows-based systems. The line output alert_syslog: LOG_AUTH LOG_ALERT specifies that Snort will be using the *alert_syslog* output plug-in to log the authentication information and alerts to the syslog facility on the local machine. If you want to log the information to a syslog daemon running on a different machine on the network, you can configure the IP address and the port number of the remote server.

Installing Snort on Windows

This section covers the step-by-step installation of Snort on a Windows machine. The installation is performed in two steps, as follows:

- Installation of WinPcap

- Installation of Snort

Installation of WinPcap

You can download WinPcap from http://www.winpcap.org/install/default.htm. The official home page for WinPcap describes it as:

- WinPcap is the industry-standard tool for link-layer network access in a Windows environment. It allows applications to capture and transmit network packets bypassing the protocol stack, and has the additional useful features, including kernel-level packet filtering, a network statistics engine, and support for remote packet capture.

- WinPcap consists of a driver that extends the operating system to provide low-level network access, and a library that is used to easily access the low-level network layers. This library also contains the Windows version of the well-known libpcap UNIX API.

The detailed steps are as follows:

1. Point your browser to http://www.winpcap.org/install/default.htm.

2. Click on the link WinPcap auto-installer (driver + DLLs) to download the file. The latest stable version of WinPcap is version 3.1. (Refer to the following screenshot.)

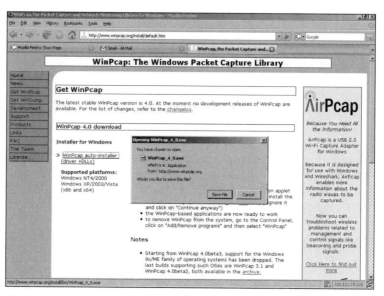

Figure 10.1   The WinPcap Download

3. After saving/downloading the file called WinPcap_3_1.exe to your local machine, double-click on the file to start the WinPcap installation. The installer will load into memory, as shown in the following figure.

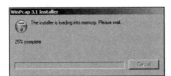

Figure 10.2 WinPcap 3.1 Installer

4. After the memory loading, the WinPcap 3.1 Installer will start. Click Next to proceed to the license agreement.

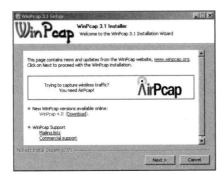

Figure 10.3 WinPcap 3.1 Setup

5. After reviewing the license agreement, you can proceed to the installation by clicking I Agree.

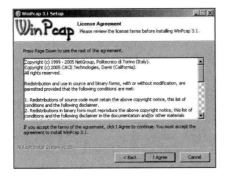

Figure 10.4 WinPcap License Agreement

The WinPcap installation will start, as shown in the following figure.

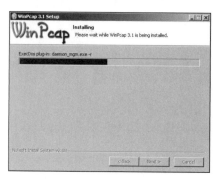

Figure 10.5   WinPcap 3.1 Installation

6. Once the installation is complete, you are greeted with the Completing the WinPcap 3.1 Setup Wizard window, indicating that WinPcap 3.1 has been successfully installed on the computer.

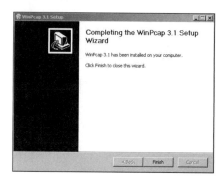

Figure 10.6   WinPcap 3.1 Setup Complete Window

7. Make sure that installation is complete by going to the Start menu and choosing Programs or All Programs, depending on your Windows version. Make sure that a new folder named WinPcap is created under (All) Programs, as shown in the following figure.

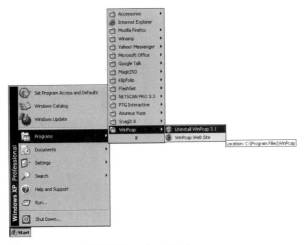

Figure 10.7   Verify WinPcap Installation

Installation of Snort

The Snort home page is at http://www.snort.org/. You can download the Snort files from the following two locations:

- Binary: http://www.snort.org/dl/
- Windows setup files: http://www.snort.org/dl/binaries/win32/

The step-by-step instructions for installing Snort are as follows:

1. Point your browser to http://www.snort.org/dl/binaries/win32/.

2. Click on the link Snort_2_6_1_1_Installer.exe to download the Snort installer. The latest stable version of Snort is version 2.6.1.1 (Refer to the following screenshot.)

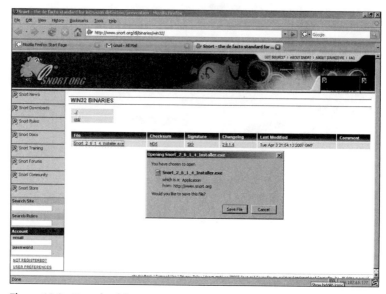

Figure 10.8   Download Snort

3. After saving/downloading the file Snort_2_6_1_1_Installer.exe to the local machine, double-click on the file to start the Snort installation. You are greeted with the license agreement. After reviewing the license agreement, you can proceed to the installation by clicking I Agree.

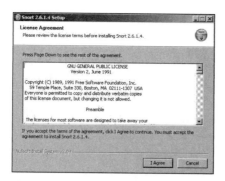

Figure 10.9   Snort License Agreement

4. The Installation Options window appears. By default, Windows' version of Snort supports logging of data to MySQL and ODBC databases. In the Installation Options window, you can select from the following three options:

> I do not plan to log to a database, or I am planning to log to one of the databases listed above.

> I need support for logging to Microsoft SQL Server. Note that the SQL Server client software must already be installed on this computer.

> I need support for logging to Oracle. Note that the Oracle client software must already be installed on this computer.

Because you are going for a simple installation in this example, select the first option "I do not plan to log to a database, or I am planning to log to one of the databases listed above" and then click the Next button to proceed to the next step.

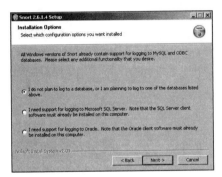

Figure 10.10   Snort Installation Options

5. In the next window—Choose Components—you have to choose the features of Snort that you want to install. The various components are:

- Snort
- Dynamic modules
- Documentation
- Schemas

The total space required for installing all the components is around 7.7MB. Keep the default selection (select all) and click Next to proceed to the next window.

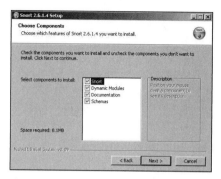

Figure 10.11   Snort Installation: Choose Components

6. In the next window—Choose Install Location—accept the default installation location of C:\Snort. Click Next to proceed.

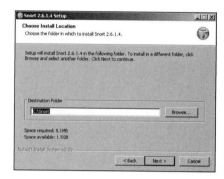

Figure 10.12   Snort Installation: Choose Install Location

The installation will start/progress, as shown here.

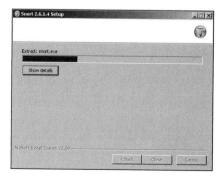

Figure 10.13   Snort Installation: Setup Progress

Once the installation is completed, the details will be shown, as shown here.

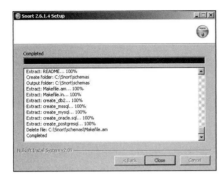

Figure 10.14   Snort Installation: Setup Completed

7. Once you click the Close button, the installation process will display a message stating that Snort requires WinPcap to be installed on the machine. In this case, you have already installed WinPcap. See the following figure.

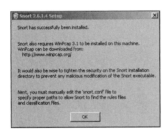

Figure 10.15   Snort Installation Message

Your Snort installation is complete now.

Testing a Snort Installation

To make sure that Snort is installed and working, follow these steps:

1. Open a command prompt (go to Start, Run and then type **cmd**).

2. Navigate to the bin folder under the Snort installation location; in the case here, you would navigate to C:\Snort\bin by issuing the following command:

```
cd c:\Snort\bin
```

3. Type **snort** and press Enter. Because Snort does not find any options/parameters, it will exist with an error (Uh, you need to tell me to do something...), as shown here:

```
C:\>cd Snort


C:\Snort>cd bin


C:\Snort\bin>snort
***
*** interface device lookup found: \
***


   ,,_     -*> Snort! <*-
  o"  )~   Version 2.4.3-ODBC-MySQL-FlexRESP-WIN32 (Build 26)
   ''''    By Martin Roesch & The Snort Team: http://www.snort.org/
team.html
          (C) Copyright 1998-2005 Sourcefire Inc., et al.
 NOTE: Snort's default output has changed in version 2.4.1!
       The default logging mode is now PCAP, use "-K ascii" to activate
       the old default logging mode.


USAGE: snort [-options] <filter options>
       snort /SERVICE /INSTALL [-options] <filter options>
       snort /SERVICE /UNINSTALL
       snort /SERVICE /SHOW
Options:
         -A        Set alert mode: fast, full, console,
                      or none  (alert file alerts only)
         -b        Log packets in tcpdump format (much faster!)
        -c <rules> Use Rules File <rules>
         -C        Print out payloads with character data only (no hex)
         -d        Dump the Application Layer
         -e        Display the second layer header info
         -E        Log alert messages to NT Eventlog. (Win32 only)
         -f        Turn off fflush() calls after binary log writes
        -F <bpf>   Read BPF filters from file <bpf>
        -G <0xid>  Log Identifier (to uniquely id events for multiple
                   snorts)
```

```
-h <hn>    Home network = <hn>
-i <if>    Listen on interface <if>
-I         Add Interface name to alert output
-k <mode>  Checksum mode (all,noip,notcp,noudp,noicmp,none)
-K <mode>  Logging mode (pcap[default],ascii,none)
-l <ld>    Log to directory <ld>
-L <file>  Log to this tcpdump file
-n <cnt>   Exit after receiving <cnt> packets
-N         Turn off logging (alerts still work)
-o         Change the rule testing order to Pass|Alert|Log
-O         Obfuscate the logged IP addresses
-p         Disable promiscuous mode sniffing
-P <snap>  Set explicit snaplen of packet (default: 1514)
-q         Quiet. Don't show banner and status report
-r <tf>    Read and process tcpdump file <tf>
-R <id>    Include 'id' in snort_intf<id>.pid file name
-s         Log alert messages to syslog
-S <n=v>   Set rules file variable n equal to value v
-T         Test and report on the current Snort configuration
-U         Use UTC for timestamps
-v         Be verbose
-V         Show version number
-W         Lists available interfaces. (Win32 only)
-w         Dump 802.11 management and control frames
-X         Dump the raw packet data starting at the link layer
-y         Include year in timestamp in the alert and log files
-Z         Set the performonitor preprocessor file path and name
-z         Set assurance mode, match on established sessions
           (for TCP)
-?         Show this information
<Filter Options> are standard BPF options, as seen in TCPDump


Uh, you need to tell me to do something...


: No such file or directory


C:\Snort\bin>
```

Using Snort as a Packet Sniffer and Logger

As discussed earlier, Snort can also be used as a packet sniffer and logger. This section discusses the various sniffer and logging features of Snort. Snort can be run from the command line as a packet sniffer, in order to view the live network traffic passing through. Additionally, this traffic can be logged in three ways:

- Log the traffic to a database like MySQL.
- Log the traffic in ASCII text output.
- Log the traffic in TCPdump binary format.

Snort can be run as a packet sniffer using the following command:

```
snort -dev
```

where:

d is used to show the application layer data in the packet.

e is used to display the link layer data in the packet.

v is used for running in verbose mode.

An example is shown here:

```
root@1[knoppix]# snort -dev
Running in packet dump mode

Initializing Network Interface eth0

        --= Initializing Snort =--
Initializing Output Plugins!
Decoding Ethernet on interface eth0

        --= Initialization Complete =--

   ,,_       -*> Snort! <*-
  o"  )~   Version 2.3.2 (Build 12)
   ''''      By Martin Roesch & The Snort Team: http://www.snort.org/team.html
            (C) Copyright 1998-2004 Sourcefire Inc., et al.

12/26-11:49:52.508462 0:13:20:CA:DE:19 -> 0:12:17:3B:E1:AE type:0x800 len:0x4A
192.168.15.100:1024 -> 203.197.12.42:53 UDP TTL:32 TOS:0x0 ID:54924 IpLen:20
DgmLen:60 DF
Len: 32
B8 91 01 00 00 01 00 00 00 00 00 00 03 77 77 77  .............www
06 67 6F 6F 67 6C 65 03 63 6F 6D 00 00 01 00 01  .google.com.....

=+=+=+=+=+=+=+=+=+=+=+=+=+=+=+=+=+=+=+=+=+=+=+=+=+=+=+=+=+=+=+=+

12/26-11:49:52.598475 0:12:17:3B:E1:AE -> 0:13:20:CA:DE:19 type:0x800 len:0x13E
```

```
203.197.12.42:53 -> 192.168.15.100:1024 UDP TTL:249 TOS:0x0 ID:36400 IpLen:20
DgmLen:304 DF
Len: 276
B8 91 81 80 00 01 00 03 00 07 00 05 03 77 77 77   ............www
06 67 6F 6F 67 6C 65 03 63 6F 6D 00 00 01 00 01   .google.com.....
C0 0C 00 05 00 01 00 09 2D 6B 00 08 03 77 77 77   ........-k...www
01 6C C0 10 C0 2C 00 01 00 01 00 00 01 20 00 04   .l...,....... ..
48 0E CB 68 C0 2C 00 01 00 01 00 00 01 20 00 04   H..h.,....... ..
48 0E CB 63 C0 30 00 02 00 01 00 01 44 5F 00 04   H..c.0......D_..
01 63 C0 30 C0 30 00 02 00 01 00 01 44 5F 00 04   .c.0.0......D_..
01 64 C0 30 C0 30 00 02 00 01 00 01 44 5F 00 04   .d.0.0......D_..
01 65 C0 30 C0 30 00 02 00 01 00 01 44 5F 00 04   .e.0.0......D_..
01 66 C0 30 C0 30 00 02 00 01 00 01 44 5F 00 04   .f.0.0......D_..
01 67 C0 30 C0 30 00 02 00 01 00 01 44 5F 00 04   .g.0.0......D_..
01 61 C0 30 C0 30 00 02 00 01 00 01 44 5F 00 04   .a.0.0......D_..
01 62 C0 30 C0 B0 00 01 00 01 00 01 48 C8 00 04   .b.0........H...
D8 EF 35 09 C0 60 00 01 00 01 00 01 48 B0 00 04   ..5..`......H...
40 E9 A1 09 C0 80 00 01 00 01 00 01 48 C8 00 04   @...........H...
D1 55 89 09 C0 90 00 01 00 01 00 01 48 C8 00 04   .U..........H...
48 0E EB 09 C0 A0 00 01 00 01 00 01 48 BB 00 04   H...........H...
40 E9 A7 09                                       @...

=+=+=+=+=+=+=+=+=+=+=+=+=+=+=+=+=+=+=+=+=+=+=+=+=+=+=+=+=+=+=+=+

12/26-11:49:52.598784 0:13:20:CA:DE:19 -> 0:12:17:3B:E1:AE type:0x800 len:0x4A
192.168.15.100:1789 -> 72.14.203.104:80 TCP TTL:32 TOS:0x0 ID:34163 IpLen:20
DgmLen:60 DF
******S* Seq: 0xB4005381  Ack: 0x0  Win: 0x16D0  TcpLen: 40
TCP Options (5) => MSS: 1460 SackOK TS: 4294891250 0 NOP WS: 2

=+=+=+=+=+=+=+=+=+=+=+=+=+=+=+=+=+=+=+=+=+=+=+=+=+=+=+=+=+=+=+=+

12/26-11:49:52.956423 0:12:17:3B:E1:AE -> 0:13:20:CA:DE:19 type:0x800 len:0x3C
72.14.203.104:80 -> 192.168.15.100:1789 TCP TTL:242 TOS:0x0 ID:46222 IpLen:20
DgmLen:44
***A**S* Seq: 0x6AF61189  Ack: 0xB4005382  Win: 0x1FFE  TcpLen: 24
TCP Options (1) => MSS: 1460

=+=+=+=+=+=+=+=+=+=+=+=+=+=+=+=+=+=+=+=+=+=+=+=+=+=+=+=+=+=+=+=+
```

If you want to stop Snort from sniffing packets, press Ctrl+C. Snort will stop sniffing the data packets and will display the summary of all the traffic it has detected. A sample output is shown here:

```
===================

Snort received 12 packets
    Analyzed: 12(100.000%)
    Dropped: 0(0.000%)
```

```
===========================================================
Breakdown by protocol:
      TCP: 8          (66.667%)
      UDP: 4          (33.333%)
     ICMP: 0          (0.000%)
      ARP: 0          (0.000%)
    EAPOL: 0          (0.000%)
     IPv6: 0          (0.000%)
      IPX: 0          (0.000%)
    OTHER: 0          (0.000%)
  DISCARD: 0          (0.000%)
===========================================================
Action Stats:
ALERTS: 0
LOGGED: 0
PASSED: 0
===========================================================
Snort exiting
root@1[knoppix]# snort -dev
```

Configuring Snort IDS

The first thing you need to do after you complete the Snort installation is customize Snort to your needs. The snort.conf file is the first file to begin with. Snort stores its primary configuration in snort.conf, which is in the *%systemdrive%\snort\etc* directory by default (in the case here, it's c:\Snort\etc).

The snort.conf file contains the configuration settings that Snort uses every time it is invoked. To start with, navigate to the C:\Snort\etc directory and open the snort.conf file with any text editor.

Notes

Check out Appendix C for a full listing of the snort. conf file. Getting familiarized with the snort.conf file will help you more easily manage and troubleshoot your Snort installation.

For Snort to distinguish between the traffic coming into your network and the traffic going out of your network, you have to tell Snort the hosts and IP addresses in your network. For this, you need to change the *var HOME_NET* variable in the snort.conf file. This variable represents the internal network address of your LAN. Find the line

```
var HOME_NET any
```

and replace *any* with your IP address range. In an unaltered snort.conf file, this variable (*var HOME_NET any*) can be found on line 45. In most cases, this value will be an entire subnet or list of subnets, but it can also be in the form of a single IP address. For this book, I use the subnet of the internal network card, which is 192.168.15.0/24, which means that the address space of 192.168.15.0–192.168.15.254 will be represented, using a subnet mask of 255.255.255.0. So the changed line will be:

```
var HOME_NET 192.168.15.0/24
```

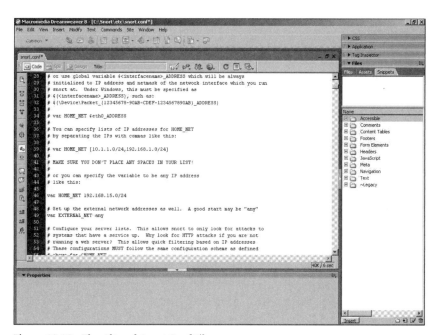

Figure 10.16   The Altered Snort.Conf File

The next variable in limelight is *var EXTERNAL_NET*. This variable can be found on line number 49 of the snort.conf file. This variable represents the subnet your external network adapter is answering requests or listening on. For the purpose of this book, we will leave this variable unchanged as:

```
var EXTERNAL_NET any
```

This tells Snort to listen for all addresses on the external network. For the purposes of this book, leave the default configuration *any* unchanged.

Lines 93 to 103 of the snort.conf file contain the following code:

```
## var HTTP_PORTS 80
## include somefile.rules
## var HTTP_PORTS 8080
## include somefile.rules
var HTTP_PORTS 80


# Ports you want to look for SHELLCODE on.
var SHELLCODE_PORTS !80


# Ports you do oracle attacks on
var ORACLE_PORTS 1521
```

These configuration variables indicate the specific ports on which Snort should watch for attacks.

The other important areas of the configuration file are the preprocessors, the *output* plug-in, and the ruleset sections. As discussed earlier, the preprocessors are Snort plug-ins that perform the parsing of incoming data. In the default snort.conf file, the preprocessor configuration starts on line 220. The first few lines are shown here:

```
####################################################
# Step #3: Configure preprocessors
#
# General configuration for preprocessors is of
# the form
# preprocessor <name_of_processor>: <configuration_options>
```

The *output* plug-in is the means by which Snort gets the intrusion data to the user/administrator. The purpose of the *output* plug-in is to dump alerting data to another resource or file. In the default snort.conf file, the *output* plug-in configuration starts on line 797. The first few lines are shown here:

```
##########################################################################
# Step #4: Configure output plugins
#
# Uncomment and configure the output plugins you decide to use.  General
# configuration for output plugins is of the form:
```

```
#
# output <name_of_plugin>: <configuration_options>
#
# alert_syslog: log alerts to syslog
# -----------------------------------
```

The Snort's ruleset defines the patterns and criteria it implements to look for potentially malicious traffic on the network. Without an effective ruleset, Snort is just another sniffer. In the default snort.conf file, the ruleset configuration starts on line 929. The first few lines are shown here:

```
###############################################################################
# Step #6: Customize your rule set
#
# Up to date snort rules are available at http://www.snort.org
#
# The snort web site has documentation about how to write
# your own custom snort rules.


#=========================================
# Include all relevant rulesets here
#
# The following rulesets are disabled by default:
#
#   web-attacks, backdoor, shellcode, policy, porn, info, icmp-info,
virus,
#   chat, multimedia, and p2p
#
# These rules are either site policy specific or require tuning in
# order to not generate false positive alerts in most environments.
#
# Please read the specific include file for more information and
# README.alert_order for how rule ordering affects how alerts are triggered.
#=========================================

include $RULE_PATH/local.rules
include $RULE_PATH/bad-traffic.rules
```

Once these settings have been made, you can verify Snort's functioning by running it in verbose mode. The command and the result of running in verbose mode is as shown here:

```
C:\Snort\bin>snort -v
Running in packet dump mode


          --■ Initializing Snort ■--
Initializing Output Plugins!
Var '\Device\NPF_{2D395F78-38FD-4F7A-AC25-CA5FA3BBB9DA}_ADDRESS' defined,
value
len = 25 chars, value = 1*.2*.3**.0/255.255.255.0
Verifying Preprocessor Configurations!
***
*** interface device lookup found: \
***


Initializing Network Interface \Device\NPF_GenericDialupAdapter
Decoding Ethernet on interface \Device\NPF_GenericDialupAdapter


          --■ Initialization Complete ■--


   ,,_      -*> Snort! <*-
  o"  )~    Version 2.6.1.2-ODBC-MySQL-FlexRESP-WIN32 (Build 34)
   ''''     By Martin Roesch & The Snort Team: http://www.snort.org/team.
html
          (C) Copyright 1998-2006 Sourcefire Inc., et al.


Not Using PCAP_FRAMES
*** Caught Int-Signal



===============================================================


Snort received 0 packets
    Analyzed: 0(0.000%)
    Dropped: 0(0.000%)
    Outstanding: 0(0.000%)
```

```
==================================================================
Breakdown by protocol:
      TCP: 0            (0.000%)
      UDP: 0            (0.000%)
     ICMP: 0            (0.000%)
      ARP: 0            (0.000%)
    EAPOL: 0            (0.000%)
     IPv6: 0            (0.000%)
  ETHLOOP: 0            (0.000%)
      IPX: 0            (0.000%)
     FRAG: 0            (0.000%)
    OTHER: 0            (0.000%)
  DISCARD: 0            (0.000%)
==================================================================
Action Stats:
ALERTS: 0
LOGGED: 0
PASSED: 0
==================================================================
Snort exiting

C:\Snort\bin>
```

The following table lists the various command-line options for Snort.

Command-Line Option	Definition
--A <alert>	Set <alert> mode to fast, full, console, or none. The full mode carries out the normal style alerts to the alert file. The fast mode writes the timestamp, message, IPs, and ports to the file and none turns off alerting.
--b	This option is used to log packets in TCPdump format. Logging is very fast, and you can use the TCPdump program later to display the data.

Command-Line Option	Definition
--c <cf>	One of the most commonly used option switches. This option is used to specify the location of the snort.conf file. When specified, Snort does not look into default locations of the configuration file snort.conf. For example, if the snort.conf file is located in the /etc directory, you can use the option as c /etc/snort.conf on the command line while starting Snort.
--C	This option prints the payloads with character data only, no hexdump.
--d	This option when used dumps the application layer data.
--D	This option runs Snort in daemon mode. The alerts are sent to /var/log/snort/alert unless otherwise specified.
--e	Display the second layer (Layer 2) header info.
--E	Log alert messages to NT Eventlog. This option is applicable to a Windows installation only.
--f	Turn off fflush<> calls after binary log writes.
--F <bpf>	Reads BPF filters from file <bpf>.
--g <gname>	Run snort as group ID <gname> after initialization. This option allows snort to drop root privileges after it has completed its initialization phase and is considered a security measure.
-G <0xid>	Log identifier used to uniquely ID events for multiple snorts.
-h <hn>	Set the home network to <hn>.
--i <if>	This option configures Snort to sniff on network interface <if>.
--I	Add the interface name to alert outputs.
--k <checksum mode>	Set <checksum mode> to all, noip, notcp, noudp, noicmp, or none. Configuring this option changes the checksum verification subsystem of Snort to optimize for maximum performance.
--K <mode>	Set the logging mode to pcap (which is the default), ascii, or none.
--l <ld>	Log packets to directory <ld>.
--L <file>	Log to tcpdump file <file>.
--m <mask>	Set the umask for all of Snort's output files to the indicated mask.

Command-Line Option	Definition
`--M <wkstn>`	Send WinPopup messages to the list of workstations contained in the `<wkstn>` file.
`--n <num>`	Exit after processing `<num>` packets.
`--N`	Turn off logging (alerts still work).
`--o`	Change the rule testing order to Pass | Alert | Log.
`--O`	Obfuscate the logged IP addresses when in ASCII packet dump mode. This option switch changes the IP addresses that get printed to the screen/log file to *xxx.xxx.xxx.xxx*.
`--p`	Disable promiscuous mode sniffing.
`--P <snaplen>`	Set the snaplen of Snort to `<snaplen>`. The default is 1514.
`--q`	Quiet mode. Do not show banner and status report.
`--r  <tf>`	Read and process the tcpdump file `<tf>`.
`--R <id>`	Include *id* in the `snort_intf<id.pid` filename.
`--s`	Log alert messages to syslog.
`--S <n-=v>`	Set variable name *n* to value *v*.
`--t <chroot>`	Changes Snort's root directory to `<chroot>` after initialization.
`--T`	Test and report on the current Snort configuration.
`--u <uname>`	Change the UID Snort runs under to `<uname>` after initialization.
`--U`	Use UTC for timestamps.
`--v`	Runs in verbose mode. Prints packets out to the console.
`--V`	Display the version number.
`--w`	Dump 802.11 management and control frames.
`--W`	List available interfaces (Win32 only).
`--X`	Dump the raw packet data starting at the link layer.
`--y`	Include year in timestamp in the alert and log files.
`--z`	Set the assurance mode for Snort alerts.
`--Z <file>`	Set the performonitor preprocessor file path and name.
`--?`	Show the help and usage summary associated with Snort.

Fooling an IDS

There are two approaches to fooling a network-based intrusion-detection system:

- The first option is to suffocate the NIDS with a huge amount of data so that the NIDS gets choked. This approach tries to bury the administrator in a pile of alert logs so big that he/she never sees the real attack. Tools that can be used under this scenario—Stick, Snot, and nMap (decoy scan).

- The second option is to design the attack in such a way that it won't match the signatures or algorithms that the IDS is preconfigured with. Tools used—nMap (Stealth scans), Fragrouter, and Whisker.

Summary

This chapter introduced the open source intrusion-detection system—Snort—and covered the various ways to download and install it on a Windows system. It also looked at the functioning of Snort as a packet-capturing and sniffer system. Finally, the chapter covered the basic operations of Snort and the basic configuration needed to get it up and running. Don't forget to check out Appendix C for a full listing of the snort.conf file. Getting familiarized with the snort.conf file will help you more easily manage and troubleshoot your Snort installation.

APPENDIX **A**

List of IDSs and IPSs

The following is the list of available commercial and open source intrusion-detection and prevention systems, sorted alphabetically.

- ActiveScout by ForeScout Technologies:
  http://www.forescout.com/index.php?url=products&section=activescout
- AirDefense Guard by AirDefense, Inc.: http://www.airdefense.net
- AirMagnet by AirMagnet, Inc.: http://airmagnet.com/
- Autonomous Agents for Intrusion Detection (AAFID) by CERIAS/Purdue University:
  http://www.cerias.purdue.edu/about/projects/aafid/
- Barbedwire IDS Softblade by BarbedWire Technologies:
  http://www.barbedwiretech.com/products/softblades.htm
- Blink Endpoint Intrusion Prevention by eEYE Digital Security:
  http://www.eeye.com/html/Products/Blink/index.html
- BlueSecure Centralized Intrusion Protection System by BlueSocket, Inc.:
  http://www.bluesocket.com/products/centralized_intrusion.html
- BlueSecure Distributed Intrusion Protection System by BlueSocket, Inc.:
  http://www.bluesocket.com/products/intrusionprotection.html
- Bro by Lawrence Berkeley National Laboratory: http://www.bro-ids.org/
- Cambia CM by Cambia Security, Inc.:
  http://www.intrusec.com/Product.About.asp
- Chkrootkit by several authors: http://www.chkrootkit.org/
- Cisco Intrusion Prevention System by Cisco Systems:
  http://www.cisco.com/en/US/products/sw/secursw/ps2113/index.html

- Cisco Security Agent by Cisco Systems: http://www.cisco.com/en/US/products/sw/secursw/ps5057/index.html
- DShield by Euclidian Consulting: http://www.dshield.org/
- Data Sentinel by Ionx: http://www.ionx.co.uk/html/products/data_sentinel/index.php
- DeepNines BBX Intrusion Prevention (IPS) by DeepNines Technologies: http://www.deepnines.com/ips.php
- Emerald by SRI: http://www.sdl.sri.com/projects/emerald/
- Enterasys Dragon Intrusion Defense System by Enterasys Networks: http://www.enterasys.com/products/advanced-security-apps/dragon-intrusion-detection-protection.aspx.
- eTrust Intrusion Detection by Computer Associates: http://www3.ca.com/Solutions/Product.asp?ID=163
- FTester Firewall and IDS Testing Tool by Inverse Path Ltd.: http://dev.inversepath.com/trac/ftester
- FireProof by Radware Ltd.: http://www.radware.com/content/products/fp/default.asp
- Firestorm NIDS by Gianni Tedesco: http://www.scaramanga.co.uk/firestorm/
- G-Server by Gilian Technologies Inc.: http://www.gilian.com/3gserver.shtml
- GFI LANGuard S.E.L.M. by GFI Software Ltd.: http://www.gfi.com/lanselm/
- Hogwash by Jason Larsen: http://hogwash.sourceforge.net/oldindex.html
- ipAngel by AmbironTrustWave: http://www.atwcorp.com/ips.php
- ISS Proventia Enterprise Protection by Internet Security Systems (ISS): http://www.iss.net/products/index.html
- ISS RealSecure by Internet Security Systems (ISS): http://www.iss.net/products/index.html
- Intrusion Alert by Unified Access: http://www.uac.com/Products/intrusion_alert.html
- Intrusion Detection Appliance by Intrusion Inc.: http://www.intrusion.com/products/
- Intrusion and Detection Platform by Netscreen: http://www.netscreen.com/products/datasheets/ds_ns_idp.jsp
- Juniper Networks Intrusion Detection & Prevention (IDP) by Juniper Networks: http://www.juniper.net/products/intrusion/
- KFSensor by Keyfocus: http://www.keyfocus.net/kfsensor/

- Mazu Profiler by Mazu Networks, Inc.:
  http://www.mazunetworks.com/products/mazu-profiler.php

- McAfee Host Intrusion Prevention for Desktops and Servers:
  http://www.mcafee.com/us/enterprise/products/host_intrusion_prevention/
  host_intrusion_prevention_desktop_server.html

- McAfee IntruShield Network Intrusion Prevention by Network Associates:
  http://www.mcafee.com/us/smb/products/network_intrusion_prevention/index.html

- ModSecurity by Ivan Ristic: http://www.modsecurity.org/

- NETSTAT by University of California:
  http://www.cs.ucsb.edu/~rsg/STAT/projects.html

- NFR Sentivist Intrusion Prevention System (IPS) by NFR Security:
  http://www.nfr.com/solutions/sentivist-ips.php

- NetBait by NetBait Inc.: http://www.netbaitinc.com/

- Next Generation Intrusion Detection Expert System (NIDES) by SRI:
  http://www.sdl.sri.com/projects/nides/

- Nitro Security IPS by Nitro Security:
  http://www.nitrosecurity.com/products/index.asp

- nPatrol by nSecure: http://www.nsecure.net/

- Prelude IDS by Yoann Vandoorselaere et al.: http://www.prelude-ids.org/

- PureSecure by DeMarc Security: http://www.demarc.com/products/

- RFprotect Wireless Intrusion Protection System by Network Chemistry:
  http://www.networkchemistry.com/products/

- Radware Fireproof by Radware Ltd.:
  http://www.radware.com/content/products/fp/default.asp

- STAT Neutralizer by Harris Corp.:
  http://www.statonline.harris.com/solutions/intrusion_prevention/index.asp

- Shadow IDS by the CIDER Project: http://www.nswc.navy.mil/ISSEC/CID/

- Shoki IDS by Stephen P. Berry: http://shoki.sourceforge.net/

- Siren by Penta Security: http://www.pentasecurity.com/english/productmain_1.html

- Snort IDS by Marty Roesch: http://www.snort.org/

- snort_inline by Rob McMillen: http://snort-inline.sourceforge.net/

- Snort-Wireless by Andrew Lockhart: http://snort-wireless.org/

- Sourcefire IMS by Sourcefire Inc.: http://www.sourcefire.com/

- StealthWatch by Lancope:
  http://www.lancope.com/XFRM.asp?RTN=Data/Home&XML=products.
  xml&XSL=products.xsl

- Strata Guard IDS/IPS by StillSecure:
  http://www.stillsecure.com/strataguard/index.php

- Symantec Intrusion Protection by Symantec:
  http://www.symantec.com/Products/enterprise?c=prodcat&refId=1005

- Systrace by Niels Provos: http://www.citi.umich.edu/u/provos/systrace/

- TippingPoint Intrusion Prevention System by 3COM/TippingPoint Technologies:
  http://www.tippingpoint.com/products_ips.html

- Tivoli Access Manager for Operating Systems by IBM:
  http://www-3.ibm.com/software/tivoli/products/access-mgr-operating-sys/

- Toplayer Attack Mitigator IPS by Top Layer Networks:
  http://www.toplayer.com/content/products/intrusion_detection/attack_mitigator.jsp

- Toplayer IDS Balancer by Top Layer Networks:
  http://www.toplayer.com/content/products/intrusion_detection/ids_balancer.jsp

- XSGuard IPS by XSGuard Systems B.V.: http://www.xsguard.nl/

APPENDIX **B**

Protocol Names and Values in the IP Header

Each data packet being sent across a network contains information about its protocol in the IP header. The following table lists all the possible protocol information the IP header can contain.

Value	Protocol
0	HOPOPT, IPv6 Hop-by-Hop Option
1	ICMP, Internet Control Message Protocol
2	IGAP, IGMP for user Authentication Protocol IGMP, Internet Group Management Protocol RGMP, Router-port Group Management Protocol
3	GGP, Gateway to Gateway Protocol
4	IP in IP Encapsulation
5	ST, Internet Stream Protocol
6	TCP, Transmission Control Protocol
7	UCL, CBT
8	EGP, Exterior Gateway Protocol
9	IGRP, Interior Gateway Routing Protocol
10	BBN RCC Monitoring

Value	Protocol
11	NVP, Network Voice Protocol
12	PUP (PARC Universal Packet)
13	ARGUS
14	EMCON, Emission Control Protocol
15	XNET, Cross Net Debugger
16	Chaos
17	UDP, User Datagram Protocol
18	TMux, Transport Multiplexing Protocol
19	DCN Measurement Subsystems
20	HMP, Host Monitoring Protocol
21	Packet Radio Measurement
22	XEROX NS IDP
23	Trunk-1
24	Trunk-2
25	Leaf-1
26	Leaf-2
27	RDP, Reliable Data Protocol
28	IRTP, Internet Reliable Transaction Protocol
29	ISO Transport Protocol Class 4
30	NETBLT, Network Block Transfer
31	MFE Network Services Protocol
32	MERIT Internodal Protocol
33	SEP, Sequential Exchange Protocol DCCP, Datagram Congestion Control Protocol
34	Third-Party Connect Protocol
35	IDPR, Inter-Domain Policy Routing Protocol
36	XTP, Xpress Transfer Protocol
37	Datagram Delivery Protocol
38	IDPR, Control Message Transport Protocol

Value	Protocol
39	TP++ Transport Protocol
40	IL Transport Protocol
41	IPv6 over IPv4
42	SDRP, Source Demand Routing Protocol
43	IPv6 Routing Header
44	IPv6 Fragment Header
45	IDRP, Inter-Domain Routing Protocol
46	RSVP, Reservation Protocol
47	GRE, General Routing Encapsulation
48	MHRP, Mobile Host Routing Protocol
49	BNA
50	ESP, Encapsulating Security Payload
51	AH, Authentication Header
52	Integrated Net Layer Security TUBA
53	IP with Encryption
54	NARP, NBMA Address Resolution Protocol
55	Minimal Encapsulation Protocol
56	TLSP, Transport Layer Security Protocol Using Kryptonet Key Management
57	SKIP (Simple Key Management Protocol for IP)
58	ICMPv6, Internet Control Message Protocol for IPv6 MLD, Multicast Listener Discovery
59	IPv6 No Next Header
60	IPv6 Destination Options
61	Any Host Internal Protocol
62	CFTP
63	Any Local Network
64	SATNET and Backroom EXPAK
65	Kryptolan

Value	Protocol
66	MIT Remote Virtual Disk Protocol
67	Internet Pluribus Packet Core
68	Any Distributed File System
69	SATNET Monitoring
70	VISA Protocol
71	Internet Packet Core Utility
72	Computer Protocol Network Executive
73	Computer Protocol Heart Beat
74	Wang Span Network
75	Packet Video Protocol
76	Backroom SATNET Monitoring
77	SUN ND PROTOCOL—Temporary
78	WIDEBAND Monitoring
79	WIDEBAND EXPAK
80	ISO-IP Protocol
81	VMTP, Versatile Message Transaction Protocol
82	SECURE-VMTP
83	VINES Protocol
84	TTP (Time Triggered Protocol)
85	NSFNET-IGP
86	Dissimilar Gateway Protocol
87	TCF Protocol
88	EIGRP (Enhanced Interior Gateway Routing Protocol)
89	OSPF, Open Shortest Path First Routing Protocol MOSPF, Multicast Open Shortest Path First
90	Sprite RPC Protocol
91	Locus Address Resolution Protocol
92	MTP, Multicast Transport Protocol

Value	Protocol
93	AX25 Frames Protocol
94	IP-within-IP Encapsulation Protocol
95	Mobile Internetworking Control Protocol
96	Semaphore Communications Sec. Pro.
97	EtherIP
98	Encapsulation Header
99	Any Private Encryption Scheme
100	GMTP
101	IFMP, Ipsilon Flow Management Protocol
102	PNNI over IP
103	PIM, Protocol Independent Multicast
104	ARIS (Aggregate Route Based IP Switching Protocol)
105	SCPS (Space Communications Protocol Standards)
106	QNX
107	Active Networks
108	IPPCP, IP Payload Compression Protocol
109	SNP, Sitara Networks Protocol
110	Compaq Peer Protocol
111	IPX in IP
112	VRRP, Virtual Router Redundancy Protocol
113	PGM, Pragmatic General Multicast
114	Any 0-hop Protocol
115	L2TP, Level 2 Tunneling Protocol
116	DDX, D-II Data Exchange
117	IATP, Interactive Agent Transfer Protocol
118	ST, Schedule Transfer
119	SRP, SpectraLink Radio Protocol

Value	Protocol
120	UTI (Universal Transport Interface)
121	SMP, Simple Message Protocol
122	SM (Sparse Mode Protocol)
123	PTP, Performance Transparency Protocol
124	ISIS over IPv4
125	FIRE
126	CRTP, Combat Radio Transport Protocol
127	CRUDP, Combat Radio User Datagram
128	SSCOPMCE
129	IPLT (IPDS MES Physical Layer Tester Protocol)
130	SPS, Secure Packet Shield
131	PIPE, Private IP Encapsulation within IP
132	SCTP, Stream Control Transmission Protocol
133	Fiber Channel
134	RSVP-E2E-IGNORE
135	Mobility Header
136	UDP-Lite, Lightweight User Datagram Protocol
137	MPLS in IP
138–252	Unassigned
253–254	Experimentation and Testing
255	Reserved

A P P E N D I X **C**

Default Snort Configuration File (snort.conf)

This appendix contains the default Snort configuration file contents.

```
#----------------------------------------------------
#   http://www.snort.org      Snort 2.1.2 Ruleset
#      Contact: snort-sigs@lists.sourceforge.net
#----------------------------------------------------
#  $ Id: snort.conf,v 1.333.2.3 2004/02/25 16:52:51 jh8 Exp  $
#
#########################################################
# This file contains a sample Snort configuration.
# You can take the following steps to create your own custom configuration:
#
#  1) Set the network variables for your network
#  2) Configure preprocessors
#  3) Configure output plugins
#  4) Customize your rule-set
#
#########################################################
# Step #1: Set the network variables:
#
```

```
# You must change the following variables to reflect your local network.
# The variable is currently set up for an RFC 1918 address space.
#
# You can specify it explicitly as:
#
# var HOME_NET 10.1.1.0/24
#
# or use global variable $<interfacename>_ADDRESS which will be always
# initialized to IP address and netmask of the network interface which
# you run snort at.  Under Windows, this must be specified as
# $(<interfacename>_ADDRESS), such as:
# $(\Device\Packet_{12345678-90AB-CDEF-1234567890AB}_ADDRESS)
#
# var HOME_NET $eth0_ADDRESS
#
# You can specify lists of IP addresses for HOME_NET
# by separating the IPs with commas like this:
#
# var HOME_NET [10.1.1.0/24,192.168.1.0/24]
#
# MAKE SURE YOU DON'T PLACE ANY SPACES IN YOUR LIST!
#
# or you can specify the variable to be any IP address
# like this:

var HOME_NET any

# Set up the external network addresses as well.  A good start may be "any"
var EXTERNAL_NET any

# Configure your server lists.  This allows Snort to only look for attacks
# to systems that have a service up.  Why look for HTTP attacks if you are
# not running a web server?  This allows quick filtering based on IP
# addresses. These configurations MUST follow the same configuration
# scheme as defined above for $HOME_NET.
```

```
# List of DNS servers on your network
var DNS_SERVERS $HOME_NET

# List of SMTP servers on your network
var SMTP_SERVERS $HOME_NET

# List of web servers on your network
var HTTP_SERVERS $HOME_NET

# List of sql servers on your network
var SQL_SERVERS $HOME_NET

# List of telnet servers on your network
var TELNET_SERVERS $HOME_NET

# List of snmp servers on your network
var SNMP_SERVERS $HOME_NET

# Configure your service ports.  This allows Snort to look for attacks
# destined to a specific application only on the ports that
# application runs on.  For example, if you run a web server on
# port 8081, set your HTTP_PORTS variable like this:
#
# var HTTP_PORTS 8081
#
# Port lists must either be continuous [eg 80:8080], or a
# single port [eg 80]. We will be adding support for a real list
# of ports in the future.

# Ports you run web servers on
#
# Please note:  [80,8080] does not work.
# If you wish to define multiple HTTP ports,
#
## var HTTP_PORTS 80
## include somefile.rules
```

```
## var HTTP_PORTS 8080
## include somefile.rules
var HTTP_PORTS 80

# Ports you want to look for SHELLCODE on.
var SHELLCODE_PORTS !80

# Ports you do oracle attacks on
var ORACLE_PORTS 1521

# other variables
#
# AIM servers.  AOL has a habit of adding new AIM servers, so instead of
# modifying the signatures when they do, we add them to this
# list of servers.
var AIM_SERVERS # [64.12.24.0/24,64.12.25.0/24,64.12.26.14/24,64.12.28.0/
24,64.12.29.0/
24,64.12.161.0/24,64.12.163.0/24,205.188.5.0/24,205.188.9.0/24]

# Path to your rules files (this can be a relative path)
var RULE_PATH ../rules

# Configure the Snort decoder
# ==============================
#
# Snort's decoder will alert on lots of things such as header
# truncation or options of unusual length or
# infrequently used tcp options.
#
# Stop generic decode events:
#
# config disable_decode_alerts
#
# Stop Alerts on experimental TCP options
#
# config disable_tcpopt_experimental_alerts
```

```
#
# Stop Alerts on obsolete TCP options
#
# config disable_tcpopt_obsolete_alerts
#
# Stop Alerts on T/TCP alerts
#
# In Snort 2.0.1 and above, this only alerts when a TCP option
# is detected that shows T/TCP being actively used on the network.
# If this is normal behavior for your network,
# disable the next option.
#
# config disable_tcpopt_ttcp_alerts
#
# Stop Alerts on all other TCPOption type events:
#
# config disable_tcpopt_alerts
#
# Stop Alerts on invalid ip options
#
# config disable_ipopt_alerts

# Configure the detection engine
# ================================
#
# Use a different pattern matcher in case you have a
# machine with very limited resources:
#
# config detection: search-method lowmem


##################################################
# Step #2: Configure preprocessors
#
# General configuration for preprocessors is of
# the form
# preprocessor <name_of_processor>: <configuration_options>
```

```
# Configure Flow tracking module
# -------------------------------
#
# The Flow tracking module is meant to start unifying the state-keeping
# mechanisms of Snort into a single place. Right now, only
# a portscan detector is implemented, but in the long term,
# many of the stateful subsystems of Snort will be migrated over
# to becoming flow plugins. This must be enabled for flow-portscan
# to work correctly.
#
# See README.flow for additional information
#
preprocessor flow: stats_interval 0 hash 2

# frag2: IP defragmentation support
# -------------------------------
# This preprocessor performs IP defragmentation.  This plugin will also detect
# people launching fragmentation attacks (usually DoS) against hosts.  No
# arguments loads the default configuration of the preprocessor, which is a 60
# second timeout and a 4MB fragment buffer.

# The following (comma delimited) options are available for frag2
#    timeout [seconds] - sets the number of [seconds] that an unfinished
#                         fragment will be kept around waiting for completion;
#                         if this time expires the fragment will be flushed.
#    memcap [bytes] - limit frag2 memory usage to [number] bytes
#                         (default:  4194304)
#
#    min_ttl [number] - minimum ttl to accept
#
#    ttl_limit [number] - difference of ttl to accept without alerting
#                         will cause false positives with router flap
#
# Frag2 uses Generator ID 113 and uses the following SIDS
# for that GID:
#  SID     Event description
```

```
# -----    -------------------
#   1      Oversized fragment (reassembled frag > 64k bytes)
#   2      Teardrop-type attack


preprocessor frag2

# stream4: stateful inspection/stream reassembly for Snort
#-----------------------------------------------------------------------
# Use in concert with the -z [all|est] command line switch to defeat stick/snot
# against TCP rules.  Also performs full TCP stream reassembly, stateful
# inspection of TCP streams, etc.  Can statefully detect various portscan
# types, fingerprinting, ECN, etc.

# stateful inspection directive
# no arguments loads the defaults (timeout 30, memcap 8388608)
# options (options are comma delimited):
#   detect_scans - stream4 will detect stealth portscans and generate alerts
#                  when it sees them when this option is set.
#   detect_state_problems - detect TCP state problems; this tends to be very
#                           noisy because there are a lot of crappy ip stack
#                           implementations out there.
#
#   disable_evasion_alerts - turn off the possibly noisy mitigation of
#                            overlapping sequences.
#
#
#   min_ttl [number]       - set a minimum ttl that Snort will accept to
#                            stream reassembly.
#
#   ttl_limit [number]     - differential of the initial ttl on a session versus
#                            the normal that someone may be playing games.
#                            Routing flap may cause lots of false positives.
#
#   keepstats [machine|binary] - keep session statistics, add "machine" to
#                            get them in a flat format for machine reading, add
#                            "binary" to get them in a unified binary output
```

```
#                          format.
#   noinspect - turn off stateful inspection only.
#   timeout [number] - set the session timeout counter to [number] seconds;
#                      default is 30 seconds.
#   memcap [number] - limit stream4 memory usage to [number] bytes.
#   log_flushed_streams - if an event is detected on a stream, this option will
#                         cause all packets that are stored in the stream4
#                         packet buffers to be flushed to disk.  This only
#                         works when logging in pcap mode!
#
# Stream4 uses Generator ID 111 and uses the following SIDS
# for that GID:
#  SID     Event description
# -----    --------------------
#   1       Stealth activity
#   2       Evasive RST packet
#   3       Evasive TCP packet retransmission
#   4       TCP Window violation
#   5       Data on SYN packet
#   6       Stealth scan: full XMAS
#   7       Stealth scan: SYN-ACK-PSH-URG
#   8       Stealth scan: FIN scan
#   9       Stealth scan: NULL scan
#   10      Stealth scan: NMAP XMAS scan
#   11      Stealth scan: Vecna scan
#   12      Stealth scan: NMAP fingerprint scan stateful detect
#   13      Stealth scan: SYN-FIN scan
#   14      TCP forward overlap


preprocessor stream4: disable_evasion_alerts


# tcp stream reassembly directive
# no arguments loads the default configuration
#   Only reassemble the client,
#   Only reassemble the default list of ports (See below),
#   Give alerts for "bad" streams
```

```
#
# Available options (comma delimited):
#   clientonly - reassemble traffic for the client side of a connection only
#   serveronly - reassemble traffic for the server side of a connection only
#   both - reassemble both sides of a session
#   noalerts - turn off alerts from the stream reassembly stage of stream4
#   ports [list] - use the space separated list of ports in [list], "all"
#                  will turn on reassembly for all ports, "default" will turn
#                  on reassembly for ports 21, 23, 25, 53, 80, 143, 110, 111
#                  and 513.

preprocessor stream4_reassemble

# http_inspect: normalize and detect HTTP traffic and protocol anomalies
#
# Lots of options available here. See doc/README.http_inspect.
# unicode.map should be wherever your snort.conf lives, or given
# a full path to where Snort can find it.
preprocessor http_inspect: global \
    iis_unicode_map unicode.map 1252

preprocessor http_inspect_server: server default \
    profile all ports { 80 8080 8180 } oversize_dir_length 500

#
#  Example unique server configuration
#
#preprocessor http_inspect_server: server 1.1.1.1 \
#   ports { 80 3128 8080 } \
#   flow_depth 0 \
#   ascii no \
#   double_decode yes \
#   non_rfc_char { 0x00 } \
#   chunk_length 500000 \
#   non_strict \
#   oversize_dir_length 300 \
```

```
#     no_alerts


# rpc_decode: normalize RPC traffic
# ---------------------------------
# RPC may be sent in alternate encodings besides the usual 4-byte encoding
# that is used by default. This plugin takes the port numbers that RPC
# services are running on as arguments - it is assumed that the given ports
# are actually running this type of service. If not, change the ports or turn
# it off.
# The RPC decode preprocessor uses generator ID 106.
#
# arguments: space separated list
# alert_fragments - alert on any rpc fragmented TCP data
# no_alert_multiple_requests - don't alert when >1 rpc query is in a packet
# no_alert_large_fragments - don't alert when the fragmented
#                             sizes exceed the current packet size
# no_alert_incomplete - don't alert when a single segment
#                             exceeds the current packet size

preprocessor rpc_decode: 111 32771


# bo: Back Orifice detector
# -------------------------
# Detects Back Orifice traffic on the network.  Takes no arguments in 2.0.
#
# The Back Orifice detector uses Generator ID 105 and uses the
# following SIDS for that GID:
#  SID     Event description
# -----    -------------------
#   1       Back Orifice traffic detected

preprocessor bo


# telnet_decode: Telnet negotiation string normalizer
# ---------------------------------------------------
```

```
# This preprocessor "normalizes" telnet negotiation strings from telnet and ftp
# traffic.  It works in much the same way as the http_decode preprocessor,
# searching for traffic that breaks up the normal data stream of a protocol and
# replacing it with a normalized representation of that traffic so that the
# "content" pattern matching keyword can work without requiring modifications.
# This preprocessor requires no arguments.
# Portscan uses Generator ID 109 and does not generate any SID currently.


preprocessor telnet_decode


# Flow-Portscan: detect a variety of portscans
# ----------------------------------------
# Note:  The Flow preprocessor (above) must first be enabled for Flow-Portscan to
# work.
#
# This module detects portscans based off of flow creation in the flow
# preprocessors.  The goal is to catch one->many hosts and one->many
# portsscans.
#
# Flow-Portscan has numerous options available; please read
# README.flow-portscan for help configuring this option.


# Flow-Portscan uses Generator ID 121 and uses the following SIDS for that GID:
#  SID    Event description
# -----    -------------------
#  1      flow-portscan: Fixed Scale Scanner Limit Exceeded
#  2      flow-portscan: Sliding Scale Scanner Limit Exceeded
#  3      flow-portscan: Fixed Scale Talker Limit Exceeded
#  4      flow-portscan: Sliding Scale Talker Limit Exceeded


# preprocessor flow-portscan: \
#       talker-sliding-scale-factor 0.50 \
#       talker-fixed-threshold 30 \
#       talker-sliding-threshold 30 \
#       talker-sliding-window 20 \
#       talker-fixed-window 30 \
```

```
#        scoreboard-rows-talker 30000 \
#        server-watchnet [10.2.0.0/30] \
#        server-ignore-limit 200 \
#        server-rows 65535 \
#        server-learning-time 14400 \
#        server-scanner-limit 4 \
#        scanner-sliding-window 20 \
#        scanner-sliding-scale-factor 0.50 \
#        scanner-fixed-threshold 15 \
#        scanner-sliding-threshold 40 \
#        scanner-fixed-window 15 \
#        scoreboard-rows-scanner 30000 \
#        src-ignore-net [192.168.1.1/32,192.168.0.0/24] \
#        dst-ignore-net [10.0.0.0/30] \
#        alert-mode once \
#        output-mode msg \
#        tcp-penalties on

# arpspoof
#-----------------------------------------
# Experimental ARP detection code from Jeff Nathan, detects ARP attacks,
# unicast ARP requests, and specific ARP mapping monitoring.  To make use of
# this preprocessor you must specify the IP and hardware address of hosts on
# the same layer 2 segment as you specify one host IP MAC combo per line.
# Also takes a "-unicast" option to turn on unicast ARP request detection.
# Arpspoof uses Generator ID 112 and uses the following SIDS for that GID:

# SID    Event description
# -----  -------------------
# 1      Unicast ARP request
# 2      Etherframe ARP mismatch (src)
# 3      Etherframe ARP mismatch (dst)
# 4      ARP cache overwrite attack

#preprocessor arpspoof
```

```
#preprocessor arpspoof_detect_host: 192.168.40.1 f0:0f:00:f0:0f:00


# Performance Statistics
# ---------------------
# Documentation for this is provided in the Snort Manual.  You should read it.
# It is included in the release distribution as doc/snort_manual.pdf
#
# preprocessor perfmonitor: time 300 file /var/snort/snort.stats pktcnt 10000


#######################################################################
# Step #3: Configure output plugins
#
# Uncomment and configure the output plugins you decide to use.  General
# configuration for output plugins is of the form:
#
# output <name_of_plugin>: <configuration_options>
#
# alert_syslog: log alerts to syslog
# ----------------------------------
# Use one or more syslog facilities as arguments.  Win32 can also optionally
# specify a particular hostname/port.  Under Win32, the default hostname is
# '127.0.0.1', and the default port is 514.
#
# [UNIX flavours should use this format...]
# output alert_syslog: LOG_AUTH LOG_ALERT
#
# [Win32 can use any of these formats...]
# output alert_syslog: LOG_AUTH LOG_ALERT
# output alert_syslog: host=hostname, LOG_AUTH LOG_ALERT
# output alert_syslog: host=hostname:port, LOG_AUTH LOG_ALERT


# log_tcpdump: log packets in binary tcpdump format
# -------------------------------------------------
# The only argument is the output file name.
#
```

```
# output log_tcpdump: tcpdump.log


# database: log to a variety of databases
# ---------------------------------------
# See the README.database file for more information about configuring
# and using this plugin.
#
# output database: log, mysql, user=root password=test dbname=db host=localhost
# output database: alert, postgresql, user=snort dbname=snort
# output database: log, odbc, user=snort dbname=snort
# output database: log, mssql, dbname=snort user=snort password=test
# output database: log, oracle, dbname=snort user=snort password=test


# unified: Snort unified binary format alerting and logging
# --------------------------------------------------------------
# The unified output plugin provides two new formats for logging and generating
# alerts from Snort, the "unified" format.  The unified format is a straight
# binary format for logging data out of Snort that is designed to be fast and
# efficient.  Used with barnyard (the new alert/log processor), most of the
# overhead for logging and alerting to various slow storage mechanisms such as
# databases or the network can now be avoided.
#
# Check out the spo_unified.h file for the data formats.
#
# Two arguments are supported.
#    filename - base filename to write to (current time_t is appended)
#    limit    - maximum size of spool file in MB (default: 128)
#
# output alert_unified: filename snort.alert, limit 128
# output log_unified: filename snort.log, limit 128


# You can optionally define new rule types and associate one or more output
# plugins specifically to that type.
#
# This example will create a type that will log to just tcpdump.
# ruletype suspicious
```

```
# {
#    type log
#    output log_tcpdump: suspicious.log
# }
#
# EXAMPLE RULE FOR SUSPICIOUS RULETYPE:
# suspicious tcp $HOME_NET any -> $HOME_NET 6667 (msg:"Internal IRC Server";)
#
# This example will create a rule type that will log to syslog and a mysql
# database:
# ruletype redalert
# {
#    type alert
#    output alert_syslog: LOG_AUTH LOG_ALERT
#    output database: log, mysql, user=snort dbname=snort host=localhost
# }
#
# EXAMPLE RULE FOR REDALERT RULETYPE:
# redalert tcp $HOME_NET any -> $EXTERNAL_NET 31337 \
#    (msg:"Someone is being LEET"; flags:A+;)

#
# Include classification & priority settings
#

include classification.config

#
# Include reference systems
#

include reference.config

###################################################################
# Step #4: Customize your ruleset
#
```

```
# Up-to-date Snort rules are available at http://www.snort.org.
#
# The Snort web site has documentation about how to write your own custom Snort
# rules.
#
# The rules included with this distribution generate alerts based on
# suspicious activity. Depending on your network environment, your security
# policies, and what you consider to be suspicious, some of these rules may
# either generate false positives or may be detecting activity you consider to
# be acceptable; therefore, you are encouraged to comment out rules that are
# not applicable in your environment.
#
# The following individuals contributed many of rules in this distribution.
#
# Credits:
#    Ron Gula <rgula@securitywizards.com> of Network Security Wizards
#    Max Vision <vision@whitehats.com>
#    Martin Markgraf <martin@mail.du.gtn.com>
#    Fyodor Yarochkin <fygrave@tigerteam.net>
#    Nick Rogness <nick@rapidnet.com>
#    Jim Forster <jforster@rapidnet.com>
#    Scott McIntyre <scott@whoi.edu>
#    Tom Vandepoel <Tom.Vandepoel@ubizen.com>
#    Brian Caswell <bmc@snort.org>
#    Zeno <admin@cgisecurity.com>
#    Ryan Russell <ryan@securityfocus.com>




#==========================================
# Include all relevant rulesets here.
#
# The following rulesets are disabled by default:
#
#    web-attacks, backdoor, shellcode, policy, porn, info, icmp-info, virus,
#    chat, multimedia, and p2p
```

```
#
# These rules are either site policy specific or require tuning in
# order not to generate false positive alerts in most environments.
#
# Please read the specific include file for more information and
# README.alert_order for how rule ordering affects how alerts are triggered.
#==========================================

include $RULE_PATH/local.rules
include $RULE_PATH/bad-traffic.rules
include $RULE_PATH/exploit.rules
include $RULE_PATH/scan.rules
include $RULE_PATH/finger.rules
include $RULE_PATH/ftp.rules
include $RULE_PATH/telnet.rules
include $RULE_PATH/rpc.rules
include $RULE_PATH/rservices.rules
include $RULE_PATH/dos.rules
include $RULE_PATH/ddos.rules
include $RULE_PATH/dns.rules
include $RULE_PATH/tftp.rules

include $RULE_PATH/web-cgi.rules
include $RULE_PATH/web-coldfusion.rules
include $RULE_PATH/web-iis.rules
include $RULE_PATH/web-frontpage.rules
include $RULE_PATH/web-misc.rules
include $RULE_PATH/web-client.rules
include $RULE_PATH/web-php.rules

include $RULE_PATH/sql.rules
include $RULE_PATH/x11.rules
include $RULE_PATH/icmp.rules
include $RULE_PATH/netbios.rules
include $RULE_PATH/misc.rules
include $RULE_PATH/attack-responses.rules
```

```
include $RULE_PATH/oracle.rules
include $RULE_PATH/mysql.rules
include $RULE_PATH/snmp.rules

include $RULE_PATH/smtp.rules
include $RULE_PATH/imap.rules
include $RULE_PATH/pop2.rules
include $RULE_PATH/pop3.rules

include $RULE_PATH/nntp.rules
include $RULE_PATH/other-ids.rules
# include $RULE_PATH/web-attacks.rules
# include $RULE_PATH/backdoor.rules
# include $RULE_PATH/shellcode.rules
# include $RULE_PATH/policy.rules
# include $RULE_PATH/porn.rules
# include $RULE_PATH/info.rules
# include $RULE_PATH/icmp-info.rules
# include $RULE_PATH/virus.rules
# include $RULE_PATH/chat.rules
# include $RULE_PATH/multimedia.rules
# include $RULE_PATH/p2p.rules
include $RULE_PATH/experimental.rules

# Include any thresholding or suppression commands. See threshold.conf
# in the <snort src>/etc directory for details. Commands don't
# necessarily need to be contained in this conf, but a separate conf
# makes it easier to maintain them.
# Uncomment if needed.
# include threshold.conf
```

One-Way Cable for IDS Deployment

This document was originally written by Patrick Gray in 2002, which can be found at http://www.sentinelsecurity.net/whitepapers/OneWayCable-original.pdf.

This appendix is copied from http://www.sentinelsecurity.net/whitepapers/onewaycable.pdf under the terms of the GNU Free Documentation License.

Why the One-Way Cable?

When deploying network intrusion-detection systems (NIDS), it's vital to keep these systems invisible to users and abusers of the network(s) they monitor.

By using a one-way cable, it is not physically possible (without firmware modification) to send packets in both directions down the wire, usually out from the NIDS. Yet the cable still allows the interface to monitor all packets coming in the other direction. This is a very effective way to achieve the main goal of network intrusion detection—to be undetected, yet be able to directly monitor network traffic. Consider these benefits:

- **Connection speed**—Using the method described later in this document, it is possible for a 100Mbit network card to maintain 100Mbps half-duplex network connectivity, with no errors.

- **Connection options**—Admins commonly use 100Mbps hubs with one-way cable setups, as it allows them to not only sniff at 100Mbps half duplex, but to also have a one-way cable back into the sniffing hub.

  This allows packet flow in the other direction, which you can use for active-response techniques, including TCP resets and ICMP responses.

Creating a One-Way Cable

There are a few papers online that detail how to make a one-way cable by introducing a high-pass filter (capacitor) in-line with the transmit pair. That method is supposed to introduce CRC errors to the transmit pair; however, this method produced some very weird results when tested at 100Mbps.

The following wiring diagram (Figure A.1) is what this example used to create the one-way Ethernet cable.

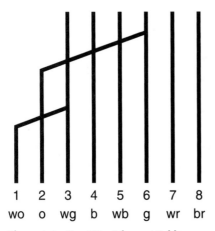

1	2	3	4	5	6	7	8
wo	o	wg	b	wb	g	wr	br

Figure A.1   One-Way Ethernet Cable

If the cable modification shown in the figure is made flawlessly, there should be no transmission problems or packet loss. However, if the wiring modification is imperfect, there will be problems, mainly poor electromagnetic performance, which results in packet loss.

Follow these step-by-step instructions to set up a one-way cable:

1. Measure out the length of cable you want to use and cut, freeing it from the reel (this is important, as you need to remove a twisted pair from the entire length of the cable).
2. Strip one end as you would normally, to attach an RJ45 head.

3. Untwist and separate the wires into the correct order (shown in Figure A.2).

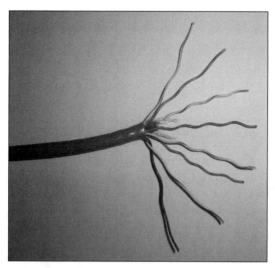

Figure A.2   Separate the Cables

Notes

The correct order for the wires comes from the standard EIA/TIA T568B: http://www.faqs.org/faqs/LANs/cabling-faq/index.html.

4. Group wires 1 and 3, and then 2 and 6, as per wiring diagram in Figure A.3.

Figure A.3   Group the Cables

5. Using a sharp knife, cut the plastic covering off the wires you need to join too, being careful not to damage the wires.

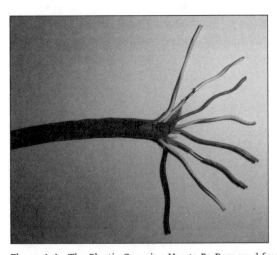

Figure A.4   The Plastic Covering Has to Be Removed from the Wires

6. Now, completely remove the orange and white/orange twisted pair from the entire length of the cable. This helps reduce unwanted transmission line effects, which can introduce errors.

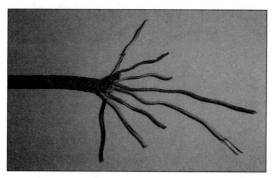

Figure A.5   The Orange and White/Orange Twisted Pair Has Been Removed

7. Cut a short length (5 cm/2.5 inches) of the freshly removed orange and white/orange wire pair and untwist.

8. Solder the removed wires, as per Figure A.6 (wire 1 to wire 3 and wire 2 to wire 6).

Figure A.6   Wire 1 Has to Be Soldered to Wire 3, and Wire 2 Has to Be Soldered to Wire 6

9. Prepare the wires to slide into an RJ45 head, being careful to keep the solder/bare wire apart.

At this point, you could/should insulate the bare wire/solder section with electrical tape. (This has been skipped so it is easier to see exactly what's happening).

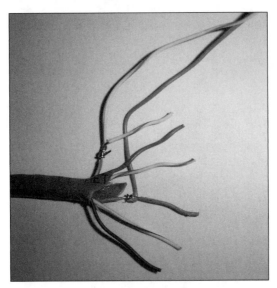

Figure A.7   The Bare Wire Has to Be Insulated

10. Ensuring you have the correct wire order, slide the wires carefully into the RJ45 head.

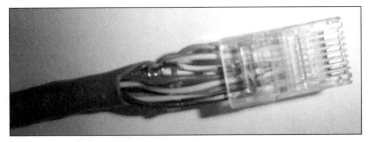

Figure A.8   The Wires Are Carefully Slid into the RJ45 Head

11. Crimp and cable-test. Figure A.9 shows the modified/soldered end (which shows all eight wires).

Figure A.9 The Modified/Soldered End (All Eight Wires)

Figure A.10 shows the other end (which shows only the six wired wires).

Figure A.10 Only Six Wires are Wired in the Unmodified End

12. Label the ends. The modified head, with all eight wires, should go into the *sniffing* device, be it a 100Mbit hub, a mirror/span port, or a proper network tap. The unmodified head, with only six wires, should go into the *sniffer* device; that is, the NIDS system.

Incorrect cabling will lead to link failure—nothing more—so use the LEDs, that's what they're there for.

You should now have a 100% effective and very cheap 100Mbit half-duplex network tap.

APPENDIX **E**

Trojan Port Numbers

This appendix contains an exhaustive list of popular Trojans and the respective default port numbers they usually run on.

Port	Trojan	Port	Trojan
2	Death	7000	Remote Grab, Kazimas, SubSeven
21	Back Construction, Blade Runner, Doly Trojan, Fore, FTP Trojan, Invisible FTP, Larva, Net Administrator, Senna Spy FTP Server, WebEx, WinCrash, Motiv, MBT	7001	Freak88
23	Tiny Telnet Server, Truva Atl	7215	SubSeven
25	Aji, Antigen, Email Password Sender, Gip, Happy 99, I Love You, Kuang 2, Magic Horse, Moscow Email Trojan, Naebi, NewApt, ProMail Trojan, Shtrilitz, Stealth, Tapiras, Terminator, WinPC, WinSpy	7300	NetMonitor

Port	Trojan	Port	Trojan
31	Agent 31, Hackers Paradise, Masters Paradise	7301	NetMonitor
41	DeepThroat	7306	NetMonitor
48	DRAT	7307	NetMonitor
50	DRAT	7308	NetMonitor
59	DMSetup	7424	Host Control
79	Firehotcker	7424 (UDP)	Host Control
80	Back End, Executor, Hooker, RingZero	7789	Back Door Setup, ICKiller
99	Hidden	7983	Mstream
110	ProMail Trojan	8080	RingZero
113	Invisible Identd Deamon, Kazimas	8787	Back Orifice 2000
119	Happy 99	8897	HackOffice
121	JammerKillah	8988	BacHack
123	Net Controller	8989	Rcon
133	Farnaz, 146 Infector	9000	Netministrator
146 (UDP)	Infector	9325 (UDP)	Mstream
170	A Trojan	9400	InCommand
421	TCP wrappers	9872	al of Doom
456	Hackers Paradise	9873	al of Doom
531	Rasmin	9874	al of Doom
555	Ini Killer, NeTAdministrator, Phase Zero, Stealth Spy	9875	al of Doom
606	Secret Service	9876	Cyber Attacker, RUX
666	Attack FTP, Back Construction, NokNok, Cain and Abel, Satanz Backdoor, ServeU	9878	TransScout
667	SniperNet	9989	iNiKiller
669	DP Trojan	9999	The Prayer
692	GayOL	10067 (UDP)	al of Doom
777	Aim Spy	10085	Syphillis

Port	Trojan	Port	Trojan
808	WinHole	10086	Syphillis
911	Dark Shadow	10101	BrainSpy
999	DeepThroat, WinSatan	10167 (UDP)	al of Doom
1000	Der Spacher 3	10528	Host Control
1001	Der Spacher 3, Le Guardien, Silencer, WebEx	10520	Acid Shivers
1010	Doly Trojan	10607	Coma
1011	Doly Trojan	10666 (UDP)	Ambush
1012	Doly Trojan	11000	Senna Spy
1015	Doly Trojan	11050	Host Control
1016	Doly Trojan	11051	Host Control
1020	Vampire	11223	Progenic Trojan, Secret Agent
1024	NetSpy	12076	Gjamer
1042	Bla	12223	Hack'99 KeyLogger
1045	Rasmin	12345	GabanBus, My Pics, NetBus, Pie Bill Gates, Whack Job, Xbill
1050	MiniCommand	12346	GabanBus, NetBus, Xbill
1080	WinHole	12349	BioNet
1081	WinHole	12361	Whack-a-Mole
1082	WinHole	12362	Whack-a-Mole
1083	WinHole	12623 (UDP)	DUN Control
1090	Xtreme	12624	Buttman
1095	RAT	12631	WhackJob
1097	RAT	12754	Mstream
1098	RAT	13000	Senna Spy
1099	BFevolution, RAT	13010	Hacker Brazil
1170	Psyber Stream Server, Streaming Audio Trojan, Voice	15092	Host Control
1200 (UDP)	NoBackO	15104	Mstream
1201 (UDP)	NoBackO	16660	Stacheldracht

Port	Trojan	Port	Trojan
1207	SoftWAR	16484	Mosucker
1212	Kaos	16772	ICQ Revenge
1225	Scarab	16969	Priority
1234	Ultors Trojan	17166	Mosaic
1243	BackDoorG, SubSeven, SubSeven Apocalypse, Tiles	17300	Kuang2 The Virus
1245	VooDoo Doll	17777	Nephron
1255	Scarab	18753 (UDP)	Shaft
1256	Project nEXT	19864	ICQ Revenge
1269	Mavericks Matrix	20001	Millennium
1313	NETrojan	20002	AcidkoR
1338	Millenium Worm	20034	NetBus 2 Pro, NetRex, Whack Job
1349 (UDP)	BO DLL	20203	Chupacabra
1492	FTP99CMP	20331	Bla
1509	Psyber Streaming Server	20432	Shaft
1524	Trinoo	20432 (UDP)	Shaft
1600	Shivka Burka	21544	GirlFriend, Kidterror, Schwindler, WinSp00fer
1777	Scarab	22222	Prosiak
1807	SpySender	23023	Logged
1966	Fake FTP	23432	Asylum
1969	OpC BO	23456	Evil FTP, Ugly FTP, Whack Job
1981	Shockrave	23476	Donald Dick
1999	BackDoor, TransScout	23476 (UDP)	Donald Dick
2000	Der Spaeher 3, Insane Network, TransScout	23477	Donald Dick
2001	Der Spaeher 3, TransScout, Trojan Cow	26274 (UDP)	Delta Source
2002	TransScout	26681	Spy Voice
2003	TransScout	27374	SubSeven

Port	Trojan	Port	Trojan
2004	TransScout	27444 (UDP)	Trinoo
2005	TransScout	27573	SubSeven
2023	Ripper	27665	Trinoo
2080	WinHole	29104	Host Control
2115	Bugs	29891 (UDP)	The Unexplained
2140	Deep Throat, The Invasor	30001	TerrOr32
2155	Illusion Mailer	30029	AOL Trojan
2283	HVL Rat5	30100	NetSphere
2300	Xplorer	30101	NetSphere
2565	Striker	30102	NetSphere
2583	WinCrash	30103	NetSphere
2600	Digital RootBeer	30103 (UDP)	NetSphere
2716	The Prayer	30129	Masters Paradise
2773	SubSeven	30133	NetSphere
2801	Phineas Phucker	30303	Sockets de Troie
3000	Remote Shutdown	30947	Intruse
3024	WinCrash	30999	Kuang2
3128	RingZero	31335 (UDP)	Trinoo
3129	Masters Paradise	31336	Bo Whack, ButtFunnel
3150	Deep Throat, The Invasor	31337	Baron Night, BO client, BO2, Bo Facil
3456	Terror Trojan	31337 (UDP)	BackFire, Back Orifice, DeepBO, Freak
3459	Eclipse 2000, Sanctuary	31338	NetSpy DK, ButtFunnel
3700	al of Doom	31338 (UDP)	Back Orifice, DeepBO
3791	Eclypse	31339	NetSpy DK
3801 (UDP)	Eclypse	31666	BOWhack
4000	Skydance	31785	Hack'a'Tack
4092	WinCrash	31787	Hack'a'Tack
4242	Virtual Hacking Machine	31788	Hack'a'Tack

Port	Trojan	Port	Trojan
4321	BoBo	31789 (UDP)	Hack'a'Tack
4444	Prosiak, Swift Remote	31791 (UDP)	Hack'a'Tack
4567	File Nail	31792	Hack'a'Tack
4590	ICQTrojan	32100	Peanut Brittle, Project nEXT
5000	Bubbel, Back Door Setup, Sockets de Troie	32418	Acid Battery
5001	Back Door Setup, Sockets de Troie	33333	Blakharaz, Prosiak
5010	Solo	33577	PsychWard
5011	One of the Last Trojans (OOTLT)	33777	PsychWard
5031	NetMetropolitan	33911	Spirit 2001a
5031	NetMetropolitan	34324	BigGluck, TN
5321	Firehotcker	34555 (UDP)	Trinoo (Windows)
5343	wCrat	35555 (UDP)	Trinoo (Windows)
5400	Blade Runner, Back Construction	37651	YAT
5401	Blade Runner, Back Construction	40412	The Spy
5402	Blade Runner, Back Construction	40421	Agent 40421, Masters Paradise
5550	Xtcp	40422	Masters Paradise
5512	Illusion Mailer	40423	Masters Paradise
5555	ServeMe	40426	Masters Paradise
5556	BO Facil	41666	Remote Boot
5557	BO Facil	41666 (UDP)	Remote Boot
5569	Robo Hack	44444	Prosiak
5637	PC Crasher	47262 (UDP)	Delta Source
5638	PC Crasher	50505	Sockets de Troie
5742	WinCrash	50766	Fore, Schwindler
5882 (UDP)	Y3K RAT	51996	Cafeini
5888	Y3K RAT	52317	Acid Battery 2000

Port	Trojan	Port	Trojan
6000	The Thing	53001	Remote Windows Shutdown
6006	The Thing	54283	SubSeven
6272	Secret Service	54320	Back Orifice 2000
6400	The Thing	54321	School Bus
6667	Schedule Agent	54321 (UDP)	Back Orifice 2000
6669	Host Control, Vampyre	57341	NetRaider
6670	DeepThroat, BackWeb Server, WinNuke eXtreame	58339	ButtFunnel
6711	SubSeven	60000	Deep Throat
6712	Funny Trojan, SubSeven	60068	Xzip 6000068
6713	SubSeven	60411	Connection
6723	Mstream	61348	Bunker Hill
6771	DeepThroat	61466	Telecommando
6776	2000 Cracks, BackDoor G, SubSeven	61603	Bunker Hill
6838 (UDP)	Mstream	63485	Bunker Hill
6912	Shit Heep (not 69123!)	65000	Devil, Stacheldracht
6939	Indoctrination	65432	The Traitor
6969	GateCrasher, Priority, IRC 3, NetController	65432 (UDP)	The Traitor
6970	GateCrasher	65535	RC

APPENDIX F

Data Hiding and Data Carving: The Crux of Digital Investigation

Consider this real-life case. It was about 11:30 at night when I received a call from some officials. I was asked to come to the police station immediately. When I got there, I saw a young boy sitting and a computer system being placed in front of him. The officials were trying to get any information about possible video clips being hidden somewhere in the computer. The boy was denying the presence of any clips in the computer.

I was informed that several people were allegedly involved in selling clips and videos with adult content that were made locally by superimposing local faces on the images. This had resulted in harassment of local girls. An operation was thus started to grab such people. The boy that I was looking at was suspected of being part of the operation.

The police officials, not having been trained in computer forensics, were not able to find anything in the computer system. Yet they were pretty sure the information was some-where on the computer.

I immediately switched off the computer system and started the imaging process wherein an image was obtained from the hard drive of the suspected system. The first thing that I did was simply load the image as a drive and browse it. Well, I found what police officials were looking for:

- A "Control Panel" situated on drive D (the mounted image?)
- A "Recycle Bin" on the drive D (the mounted image?)

The suspicion rose. After a few minutes of work, I found an entire drive filled with porn clips. The case took a move in the right direction.

This turned out to be a very typical way of hiding data.

Techniques of data hiding and protection: This is what you'll read about in this appendix. The data-hiding techniques discussed here are not comprehensive, as new techniques keep on evolving. This appendix covers the most common techniques used on the Microsoft Windows platform.

Hiding Files and Folders: The Operating System Way

Every popular operating system to the best of my knowledge provides some means of hiding its files or folders. In Windows, the *attrib* command sets the parameter. The eleventh byte of the directory entry sets the File attributes. These attributes can be set using the Command in Windows called *attrib*. For more details, just go to the command prompt and type **attrib /?** and you will see the way in which you can set or remove an attribute. The other way to set an attribute is by right-clicking on the file or folder to be hidden and then clicking Properties. At the window that appears, you can set three out of the four attributes—Read-Only, Hidden, and Archive.

The Hidden attribute is one that is very often used to hide a file or folder. For those who use the Windows system GUI, it's important to configure your system to display these hidden files and folders. To do this on a Windows XP system, go to Tools in the Explorer menu and click Folder Options. Select the Tab View and select the option called Show Hidden Files and Folders. This will show any hidden files and folders in a lighter color.

There are two other attributes that most people are ignorant about, at least in part.

The System Attribute

This attribute is designed to identify system files so that they are dealt with in a special manner and are not deleted accidentally.

There is no way to set this attribute in the File Property window, but you can set them with the help of the *attrib* command.

The command line to do so is:

```
attrib +H +S <file/folder>
```

This command sets the Hidden and System attributes simultaneously. This will hide the file in such a fashion that even if you set the settings to Show Hidden Files and Folders, it won't get displayed. In case you set only the System attribute, it will still be visible in Explorer.

Before setting this attribute, you need to clear all other attributes.

To make Windows display the files and folders with the System attributes set, you need to uncheck the option called Hide Protected Operating System Files in the Folder > View Box option.

As a forensic investigator, you should always have this setting for the View option.

DOS Command to View All the Files

The DOS command to view all the files and folders is the *dir* command. This command by default doesn't show the hidden and system files. To view them, you need to add the */a* switch. Thus, the following command will show an entire directory with all files and folders:

```
Dir /a
```

Important switches for the *dir* command include:

- */q* shows the owner of the file.
- */t* shows the modified time of the files and folders. (This switch can be additionally modified with C for creation time, L for last access time, and W for last written time—last time it was modified.)
- */x* shows the short name format along with the long name format.

As a forensic investigator, I suggest you use a > (redirector) to redirect the output to a text file for later analysis. Be sure that the output file is located on the investigator's hard drive and not the image or evidence drive. The command can be something like

```
Dir /a > c:\directory.txt
```

For more switches used with the *dir* command, try the *dir /?* command and see what you get. Note that the commands differ a bit from OS to OS, so first check for all the options available on your specific OS.

Hiding Data in the Registry

The Registry is the repository that contains various configurations for the OS, the hardware, the user, and other packages. The configurations in the old days of Windows 3.0 were stored in .ini files, which were hard to manage. This gave way to what is called the *Registry* for storing the configurations and other information.

The Registry on a typical system consists of the following files:

- **In MS Windows 98**—The files User.dat and System.dat make the Registry.
- **In MS Windows Millennium Edition**—The files Classes.dat, User.dat, and System.dat make the Registry.

- **In MS Windows XP and 2003**—The Registry is a bit more complicated and is composed of the following files:
  - SAM (SAM, SAM.log, and SAM.sav)
  - Security (Security, Security.log, and Security.sav)
  - Software (Software, Software.log, and Software.sav)
  - System (System, System.log, System.alt, and System.sav)
  - NT User (NTuser.dat and NTuser.dat.log)
  - Default (default, Default.log, and Default.sav)

The .alt extension is used in Windows 2000 to store a backup copy of the hive, the .log extension contains the transaction logs, and the .sav extension carries the backup copy of the hive created at the end of the text-mode (console) phrase during Windows XP setup.

The reason for this complication in Windows XP is the improved performance coupled with new security features. The Registry uses all these files to make the blocks of the Registry called *hives*. These hives are responsible for carrying configurations pertaining to various kinds of data, as follows:

- *HKEY_CLASSES_ROOT*: This key ensures that the file opens in the program associated with it when you're using Windows Explorer to browse and open the file. (This is why a file with an *.xls extension opens in MS Excel when you double-click it.)

  This is in fact a subkey of the key HKEY_LOCAL_MACHINE\Software. As Windows 2000, XP, and up carry separate settings for different users. This information is stored in both HKEY_LOCAL_MACHINE and HKEY_CURRENT_USER. This key takes values from both the hives to make this hive in Windows 2000 and up.

- *HKEY_CURRENT_USER*: This key contains information pertaining to the current logged-in user and settings pertaining to that user profile.

- *HKEY_LOCAL_MACHINE*: This key contains information about the particular computer irrespective of the user logged in.

- *HKEY_USERS:* This key contains information pertaining to the profiles of all the actively logged-in users.

- *HKEY_CURRENT_CONFIG*: This key contains information about the computer hardware that is loaded during the system startup.

The keys HKEY_USER and HKEY_LOCAL_MACHINE are physically stored on the computer system. The other keys are symbolic links to some of the subkeys.

The values in all the keys and subkeys can be of different kinds. A list of them is shown in the following table (taken from http://support.microsoft.com/kb/256986).

Name	Data Type	Description
Binary Value	REG_BINARY	Raw binary data. Most hardware component information is stored as binary data and is displayed in the Registry Editor in hexadecimal format.
DWORD Value	REG_DWORD	Data represented by a number that is 4 bytes long (a 32-bit integer). Many parameters for device drivers and services are this type and are displayed in the Registry Editor in binary, hexadecimal, or decimal format. Related values are DWORD_LITTLE_ENDIAN (least significant byte is at the lowest address) and REG_DWORD_BIG_ENDIAN (least significant byte is at the highest address).
Expandable String Value	REG_EXPAND_SZ	A variable-length data string. This data type includes variables that are resolved when a program or service uses the data.
Multi-String Value	REG_MULTI_SZ	A multiple string. Values that contain lists or multiple values in a form that people can read are generally this type. Entries are separated by spaces, commas, or other marks.
String Value	REG_SZ	A fixed-length text string.

Name	Data Type	Description
Binary Value	REG_RESOURCE_LIST	A series of nested arrays that is designed to store a resource list that is used by a hardware device driver or one of the physical devices it controls. This data is detected and written in the \ResourceMap tree by the system and is displayed in the Registry Editor in hexadecimal format as a binary value.
Binary Value	REG_RESOURCE_ REQUIREMENTS_LIST	A series of nested arrays that is designed to store a device driver's list of possible hardware resources the driver or one of the physical devices it controls can use. The system writes a subset of this list in the \Resource Map tree. This data is detected by the system and is displayed in the Registry Editor in hexadecimal format as a binary value.
Binary Value	REG_FULL_RESOURCE_ DESCRIPTOR	A series of nested arrays that is designed to store a resource list that is used by a physical hardware device. This data is detected and written in the \HardwareDescription tree by the system and is displayed in the Registry Editor in hexadecimal format as a binary value.

Name	Data Type	Description
None	REG_NONE	Data with no particular type. This data is written to the Registry by the system or by applications and is displayed in the Registry Editor in hexadecimal format as a binary value.
Link	REG_LINK	A Unicode string naming a symbolic link.
QWORD Value	REG_QWORD	Data represented by a number that is a 64-bit integer. This data is displayed in the Registry Editor as a binary value and was first introduced in Windows 2000.

The Registry contains a lot of information, and it is really hard to trace if any secret data is stored in it, particularly in some kind of coded format.

Microsoft has listed many functions in MSDN to get and write data in the Registry. For example, the Registry function *RegGetValue* retrieves the values from the Registry and the function *RegSaveKey* can save the data in the Registry. A detailed list of the Registry's functions is available at http://msdn2.microsoft.com/en-us/library/ms724875.aspx. This makes it easy to store and retrieve data to/from the Registry with the help of a simple package.

It is important to note that the values that are not called upon by the OS or any of the loaded packages will not harm the system in any manner. Thus, you can enter loads of information in the Registry without affecting the system.

The information in the Registry can be stored in any format like binary or string or even as defined by the application. This means that in case a data-hiding application is made to hide the data in the Registry, then only that application knows how, where, and in which format the data is stored.

As you know, the Registry supports the storage of binary data in key values, so it is possible that the package that is used to hide the data in Registry itself is hidden in chunks in the Registry in binary form. Thus a simple code can take all these chunks and assemble them to run and hide the data. What is important here is that the package itself gets hidden.

Going a step farther, you might even hide a chunk in the Registry that is responsible to assemble all the chunks. This way the process of finding the hidden data becomes very tough and almost impossible.

Using Time Zone Information in the Registry

Harlan Carvey in his book on Windows forensics has brought a very fine piece of data hiding in the Windows Registry. The key HKEY_LOCAL_MACHINE\System\CurrentControlSet\Control\TimeZoneInformation contains information about the time zone on a machine. This also contains the time difference between local time and UTC. Windows reads this information into a TIME_ZONE_INFORMATION structure during startup. There are two values that can be left blank without affecting the system— DayLightName and Standardname.

These are the string values, and you can store passwords here or any other information that you want to hide. This value can be called with the function *GetTimeZoneInformation()* or can be written with the function *SetTimeZoneInformation()*. These values can also be edited manually by the user.

Carving Data Hidden in the Registry

You can view the data that is stored in the time zone values by simply browsing to the Registry key. Further, you can search for keywords in the Registry to find the stored data. For example, consider a suspect is involved in the illegal trading of drugs. You can search for keywords like *drugs*, *cocaine*, *opium*, and so on. These keywords then can be searched in the entire drive and the Registry. The search should be for "ANSI ASCII" and "UNICODE" strings.

The investigator can even reverse the piece of code as well as decompile the suspected package to find exactly how and where the data has been hidden in the Registry. The package "Regmon" from Sysinternals can be used to monitor the effects and transactions in the Registry in a live manner.

API calls to the kernel can also be monitored in a simulated environment to find the details of calls. *API Monitor* from www.rohitab.com is one such tool that can be used to find the API calls made to the Registry. The major problem arises when the package used to hide the data in the Registry is not stored on the suspected system and is not available for analysis.

One more problem with this is the encoded text or strings. The text or strings can be encoded and thus makes it tougher for the forensic investigator to search for them.

The Registry Last Write Time

Every key that is written in the Registry has a last write time, which is the time at which the key was created or modified. This time value can be calculated to find the last modified time of a Registry key, which can help a forensic investigator determine the suspicious data times and analyze them.

Harlan Carvey has developed a tool called Keytime.exe to find the last write time of a Registry key (see http://www.windows-ir.com/tools.html).

Flaw in Registry Editor

An investigator uses the tool Regedit or Regedt32 to search for a string. He or she knows it is there in the Registry, yet he or she cannot find it. How is that possible?

A flaw in the Regedit and Regedt32 tools in Windows XP and Windows 2000 are the reason for that. Any Registry value with the name from 256 to 259 characters long hides itself from the Registry Editor, yet it can be successfully executed. Take for example if one creates a Registry value with 258 characters (if it falls between 256 and 259 characters) in the key HKLM\Software\Microsoft \Windows\CurrentVersion\Run, and places some command in it to run on system startup, it will never be shown by the *Regedit* or *Regedt32* command, yet it will still be executed every time the system boots up.

Further, any subkeys in it will remain hidden despite the length of it thus hiding a whole gamut of data. Several Trojans take advantage of this flaw to remain undetected by the system administrator.

So, what is the forensic response? This flaw is not a big deal. Fortunately, the console version allows you to see these kinds of long entries. For this one, you need to use the command-line tool *reg.exe* with the suitable option. The reg.exe tool can list these long entries.

To demonstrate this point, I have created a long entry with 257 characters in the key HKLM\Software\Microsoft \Windows\CurrentVersion\Run. The output screen from the command

```
reg quary HKLM\Software\Microsoft \Windows\CurrentVersion\Run
```

shows a long entry with *"qpqp.....1423657"* as a string value in the key.

Besides manually browsing the entire Registry, you can use tools from Microsoft like Regmon and Processmon to find the Registry keys that are being accessed by a package or a process. The package works by using a VxD driver. Just running a suspected package in a virtual environment can reveal where in the Registry it is looking for input.

Data Hiding through Registry Tweaks

Most basic data-hiding software packages use one or more tweaks to the Registry to hide data for the simple reason that they are fast and good enough for any normal computer user. Here are the basic Registry tweaks used to hide data:

- **Marking the file or folder hidden and disabling the Folder View option**—
  This is one of the techniques used by several older packages. This method hides data in a particular folder, as follows:
  - The data marked to be hidden is set with the hidden attribute.
  - The File View option is set to not show hidden files and folders.

- The ability to change this option is removed from the Tools menu with a Registry tweak.

- One or more following things might also be done:

  The Regedit tool is disabled.

  The command prompt is disabled.

  The *attrib* command is disabled.

- To unhide the data, you must reverse the entire process or reset the hidden attribute.

- To get rid of such packages, you simply use the other drive to boot and work as usual. Because Windows from the suspect system is not used, it can bypass the mechanism.

- **Renaming the file extension to disguise it along with its location and name**— What happens here is that the file extension is changed to disguise the file. For example, a document file with a typical extension .doc is changed to .exe. The location is changed too. The record of such changes is kept by the package for reverting to the original position. Such files can be revealed with the help of scanners, which list the files based on the signatures.

- **Using the CLSID to hide data**—Very often, you might come across a Recycle Bin or a Control Panel on a machine that is located in a folder or a subfolder. When you double-click it, the default location (Recycle Bin/Control Panel) pops up. Why is that so? The answer lies in understanding the CLSID in Windows, which is a 128-bit number that is used by Windows to identify software applications. This unique number is stored in the Registry in a fixed format of xxxxxxxx-xxxx-xxxx-xxxx-xxxxxxxxxxxx. This ID in fact identifies a COM class object and is used for object embedding and linking.

  - In Windows, the file extension and the associated programs are tightly integrated. That's the reason when you double-click a file with the .doc extension, it opens up in the MS Word.

  - This ID is generated with the package itself and provides smooth functioning even if two objects use the same name.

  - It is interesting to note that the extension of a file can be replaced with its CLSID, and it will keep all the properties and even won't display the CLSID associated in Windows GUI.

- In Windows, items like the Recycle Bin, the Control Panel, My Documents, My Network Places, and so on all have a CLSID. If you associate the CLSID of any of these with the normal file or folder, that file or folder will appear just like the item associated with it. For example, the CLSID of the Recycle Bin is {645FF040-5081-101B-9F08-00AA002F954E}. If you rename a folder called test to test {645FF040-5081-101B-9F08-00AA002F954E}, the folder will look like the Recycle Bin. When you double-click it, your Recycle Bin will open. This is one way to hide data in the Windows GUI.

- I have seen several packages using this tweak to hide data. Use the DOS prompt to view the content of a directory; doing so reveals everything and you can see the CLSID appended therein. To get the things back to normal, you need to rename the folder and remove the CLSID extension from it.

- The CLSID can of course be used to identify the computer system on which the package was compiled.

Some Other Ways of Data Hiding

There are some other ways the data can be hidden from an investigator. Some of them are discussed in the following sections.

Hiding Data in Virtual Machines

There are several packages that create a virtual drive and save data to it. The location of such data can be the local computer or some remote location. The more well-known packages that create virtual machines are called Virtual PC from Microsoft and VMware. With these packages, you can simply create a virtual drive and work in it. The virtual machine's drive is in fact a file that is created on the hard drive of the actual machine. This file is mounted and works as a hard drive in that particular virtual machine. A forensic investigator should always look at the files pertaining to such virtual machines (for example, the *.vmdk files in the case of VMware). Be sure to also search for the installation of such virtual machines.

Sometimes the point of creating such a virtual machine is to hide data on it, so the files pertaining to the virtual drive are kept on removable drives. A forensic investigator should search for the Registry keys and other evidence related to the use of a removable drive. You should also search for memory dumps created by the Windows operating systems.

Notes

A note on memory dumps. Perhaps you have seen the blue Stop screen that says there has been an error and memory is being dumped onto the hard drive (it might say something like "Beginning dump of physical memory").

In this instance, the memory is dumped into a pre-specified location. Virtual machines can cause such problems. All of the memory is dumped here, and so you can expect to find the virtual machine data in such dumps despite the fact that the files pertaining to the virtual machine are stored on some removable medium, which is not available for the analysis.

By default, Windows XP stores this dump in the location *%SystemRoot%\Minidump*, which can be changed in the system's startup and recovery options.

Hiding Data on a Local System's Virtual Drives

The data-hiding package "Steganos" keeps data in a file that is encrypted (*.sle). These files are mounted in the package and used as a drive. This kind of data can be encrypted or unencrypted. For unencrypted data, there is not much of a problem, but when it comes to encrypted files, you need to perform some other counter-attack such as a plain-text file attack or a brute-force attack to crack the encryption.

Hiding Data on Virtual Drives on a Remote System

Some packages allow data to be stored on remote systems, either for a certain charge or even free of cost. The biggest issue with this kind of storage is that the investigator doesn't have much time to work on it. The reason is simple. The data is stored on some remote system, and the suspect can always delete it using any other machine having access to the Internet or to the server on which data is stored.

One such example is a GMail drive, which is a kind of shell extension to access the GMail account as a drive. The GMail drive contains files and folders stored on your GMail account. The GMail drive shows up in My Computer on Windows systems as any other drive.

Methodology of Analyzing the Functioning of a Data-Hiding Package

It is important to analyze how data is hidden by a particular package. Whatever strategy a package uses, hidden data is bound to make some changes to the drive on which it's hidden. Consider the following utilities and packages:

- **Uninstallers**—These packages keep track of the installations made on the drive. They take snapshots of the entire system, including files and folders, as well as the Registry. The first snapshot is taken before the package is installed and then other snapshot is taken after the package is installed. These snapshots are compared to track any differences, which are kept in log form. Whenever a package is installed through these uninstallers, the log is used to remove the files and Registry keys. An investigator can use these logs to trace the files, folders, and Registry keys added during the installations. If you find any data-hiding packages installed on the suspect system, you should try to install these packages on a test machine with some kind of uninstaller program to see what a package does during the installation phase. One of these packages is called Ashampoo Uninstaller (see www.ashampoo.com).

- **Registry-comparing utilities**—These utilities take snapshots of the Registry and compare them to show the addition and deletion of the Registry keys as well as modified values. Advanced Registry Tracer (see www.elcomsoft.com) and Active Registry Monitor (www.protect-me.com) are two such utilities.

- **File and folder comparison utilities**—These utilities compare files and folders to find any changes. The comparison is done on the binary level; every bit is compared to find the changes made, even in the file. These utilities help a lot even in finding the algorithm of a steganography package. Two such tools are Beyond Compare (see http://www.scootersoftware.com/) and ExamDiff (see http://www.prestosoft.com/edp_examdiff.asp).

  You can use these tools to determine the behavior of a package and the way it stores or hides data.

Besides these, there are other tools from Sysinternals (now with Microsoft), such as Regmon, Processmon, Filemon, Diskmon, Portmon, and so on (refer to http://www.microsoft.com/technet/sysinternals).

The following is a list of the areas on your hard drive that you should search for any hidden data:

- Host-protected area
- Drive configuration overlay
- File slack
- Volume slack

- Partition edge
- Unused space in MBR
- Unused space in extended partition boot record
- Unused space on the boot record of all the volumes
- Fake bad blocks
- Clusters marked as bad by the OS or some other utility (they might not be bad or even just logically bad sectors)
- Disk slacks

This list is by no means an exhaustive one and is, in fact, applicable mainly to FAT or NTFS systems.

Alternate Data Stream: The NTFS Way to Hide the Data

The NTFS system can store several data streams associated with a file, and these streams can be hidden from a forensic investigator. Can you imagine that a file of 1KB can contain 100MB of data? Hmm...I can see a smile on your face....

Yes, it is very possible. You can have a main unnamed stream of 1KB and an alternate data stream of 100MB. The file size is 1KB, because the main unnamed data stream is 1KB. What a place to hide data!

Lets see how this works:

1. On an NTFS system, open the command prompt.
2. Type the command **Notepad mainfile.txt** and press Enter.

    You will be asked if you want to create a new file called mainfile.txt.

3. Click OK and you will see the file opened in Notepad.
4. Write the text that you want to display here, and then save it and close it.
5. Now type the command **Notepad mainfile.txt:alternate.txt**.

    You will again be asked if you want to open a new file. Click Yes. A blank document in Notepad will open.

6. Type the text that you want to keep hidden here.
7. Save and close the document.

What you have just done is created an alternate data stream and a hidden file. A normal user will be able to see the original file with the text that you want to display. The hidden file will not be shown without the help of specific tools.

Now it is important to note that this *clubbing* can be done with other file formats as well. You can club .exe files this way and hide text from normal Windows processes. Thus, the alternate data streams can be used to launch hidden files.

Alternate data streams are hard to detect due to following reasons:

- You can attach data to any file, thus it is almost impossible to manually work on each of the files.
- The file size of the original file remains the same.
- The NTFS does not take into account the alternate streams in calculating the available space.
- The alternate stream is not visible in Windows Explorer, the command prompt, or even in the Task Manager (Windows 2000).
- The alternate stream is executed directly. It is not copied anywhere else before being executed.

Here, you can create an alternate stream with the executable file forked into a text file and observe the results:

1. Create a normal text file named carrier.txt:

```
D:\ads>echo "This is the normal text"> carrier.txt
```

2. Add the file calc.exe stored in the same directory (ads) to the alternate stream of carrier.txt:

```
D:\ads>type calc.exe>carrier.txt:calc.exe
```

3. Now try to verify the size of the file. Note in the bold line here the time of alteration:

```
D:\ads>dir /t
    Volume in drive D is PRINCE
    Volume Serial Number is 48A1-4F2B
    Directory of D:\ads


02/15/2007 02:04AM    <DIR>            .
02/15/2007 02:04AM    <DIR>            ..
08/23/2001 05:30PM            114,688 calc.exe
02/15/2007 02:04AM                 27 carrier.txt
            2 File(s)    114,715 bytes
            2 Dir(s)  411,082,752 bytes free


D:\ads>
```

4. Finally, you can launch the calc.exe by using this command:

```
D:\ads>start.\carrier.txt:calc.exe
```

The first and the very basic inconsistency to note here are the times associated with the file. Whenever a stream is attached, the file modification time changes. This allows an investigator to see the inconsistency. For example, if an executable is attached with a Windows executable like notpad.exe or calc.exe, the modification time will reflect the time that the alternate data stream was added.

There are specific tools that you can use to detect an alternate data stream:

- Streams from Mark Russinovich is a utility from Sysinternals (now a part of the Microsoft Web) that detects the alternate data streams on the NTFS volume.
- Lads is yet another utility that detects the alternate data streams; created by Frank Heyne (www.heysoft.de).
- In Windows Vista, try the command *dir /r.*
- Although Windows 2000 shows only the main process running in the Task Manager, the XP and Server 2003 Task Manager details the alternate stream running.

Changing the File Signature: A Challenge to Forensics

The simplest way to hide something like a Word document is to change the extension of the file. This reminds me of an anticorruption case that I investigated. The user thought that he was smart enough to disguise some Word files by changing their extensions to .jpeg. He placed the files in between other photographs. When I investigated the copy of the drive, I simply right-clicked the image files. I was able to see MS Word listed in the Open With command. (Remember that if you keep opening a file with a particular extension in a program that is not associated with it, that program is listed by Windows XP in the Open With dialog box.)

It was then evident that some of the MS Word files were hidden in the images. A simple tool that scanned the files based on file signatures identified the files as MS Word documents.

Understanding File Signatures

Every file format has some initial bytes that identify it as that particular type of file. These are called its *signatures*. To understand a file's signature, open a particular type of file in Notepad, and you will see some common initial bytes that can be called the signatures of that file type. These signatures have a very significant role in handling that type of file at the system level.

For example, when you open an .exe or .dll file in Notepad, you will find the following initial bytes:

MZ

Similarly, a document file with the extension .doc will have the following initial bytes:

ÐÏ à

Even if you rename the file and change the extension, the signature is not altered. You can scan such files with a scanner that uses file signatures to identify the files and therefore easily find the true nature of any file. One such scanner and data-recovery package I have come across is called Recover My Files (see http://www.recovermyfiles.com/).

The real challenge comes when a file's signature has been changed along with its file extension. In such cases, it is almost impossible to detect the file. Further, the file will not open properly in its default program. Say, for example, I rename the abc.doc file (an MS Word document) to abc.jpg and I do not change its signatures. Windows will attempt to open the file in the default picture viewer. If I try to open the file in MS Word, it certainly will open as a normal Word document.

If, however, I also change the signature of the file to match a .jpg file, that file will not open up in MS Word or the default image viewer. No signature-scanner program can detect the file; detection of such files is almost impossible.

To detect a file with an altered signature and extension is tough. You have to look for the possibly corrupted files and analyze the structure of the entire file to determine the type of file it is. As of now, I really haven't come across a scanner that scans the file based on the structure of the file for identification.

Hiding Data in Known File Types

This section discusses the default way data is hidden in some of the known file types, one by one.

Hiding Data in an MS Word File

Data can be hidden in an MS Word file. In fact, an MS Word file provides the facility to hide the data. You simply select the text you want to hide and then choose Format>Font.

Select the Hidden option in the Effects section to have the text disappear. This data can be shown depending on the option that you choose for viewing. To view the hidden text, Choose Tools>Options and in the View tab, check the Hidden Text check box in the Formatting Marks section. This will show the hidden text as well. If you're performing a forensic investigation, be sure to customize MS Word so you can see all the hidden text if there is any.

Using Font Color to Hide Data

You can also use a white font with a white background to hide the data in MS Word. Simply choose Ctrl+A (Select All) and then change the font color to the default to reveal any white text.

Hiding Data in the File Metadata

MS Word contains information in the form of metadata. You can view this metadata by right-clicking a MS Word file and clicking Properties. The metadata contains a lot of information pertaining to the owner of the document, who checked it and when, and so on. The field of special interest is the Comment field, which can contain a lot of data. When you open the file, these comments are not visible. As a forensic investigator, you want to be able to see all the data in a file. You can do this by clicking File>Open and in the File Type field, selecting the Recover Text From Any File option.

Hiding Data in a Macro

Data can be hidden in a macro by marking the data as a comment. This data can be seen only if the document is analyzed for the macro, as shown in Figure F.1.

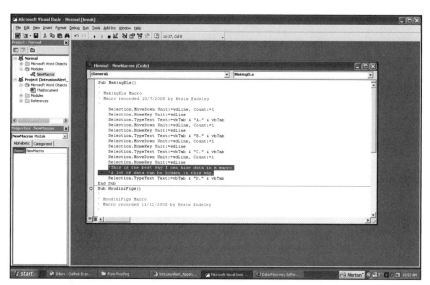

Figure F.1   Hiding Text in a Macro

You can see in the figure that the text has been inserted in the macro as a comment. As a forensic investigator, you should look through any macros that have been attached to files. Looking at the macros within VB Editor can help you find a lot of information.

SNOW (steganographic nature of whitespace) is a tool developed by Matthew Kwan that uses the whitespace in a Word or text document to hide data. This whitespace is nothing but the tabs and spaces that you normally use when preparing a text document. This tool merges two documents wherein one is shown and the other is hidden within the whitespace. The compression tool is used to fool the forensic investigator. See www.darkside.com.au/snow/ for more about SNOW.

Hiding Data in Microsoft Excel

Microsoft Excel too has some data-hiding capabilities. The first and most common way to hide data in Excel is to hide rows and columns. To do so, select the rows and columns you want to hide, right-click, and then select Hide. You can hide an entire worksheet using the Format>Sheet>Hide command. To be more secure, you can then protect the sheet or workbook with a password.

You can insert a comment in any cell and choose not to show it using the Tools>Options>View menu command. Similarly, objects can be hidden in the worksheet as well.

Besides all this, the metadata hiding techniques that we have seen in MS Word are applicable in Excel too.

There is a way to hide the sheet in such a fashion that it doesn't appear in the Hide menu and doesn't indicate that there is a hidden sheet at all.

To do this, follow these steps:

1. Go to Tools>Macro>VB Editor.

2. In the project, select the sheet you want to hide.

3. Click the Visible property of the sheet and select 2-xlSheetVeryhide.

    This will not even show up as a hidden sheet. The only way to view the sheet is to use VB Editor to make it visible.

The size of the Excel document is a good guide as to whether data might be hidden in it. If the file is too big compared to the contents, go in for a deeper search.

An important thing to note here is that the numbers contained in MS Excel are converted to binaries and thus do not appear in a keyword search by any of the major forensic packages.

You can run the drive image in a virtual environment and start Excel. Choose Tools>Options>General to reveal the number of sheets that Excel opens by default.

Check if a workbook contains fewer sheets. Even though it doesn't guarantee that you'll find a hidden sheet, this exercise is helpful in finding the suspicious files.

Password.xla is an add-in that you can use to remove sheet and workbook passwords. You can search for it in Google. It is freely available.

A Note on Glue and OLE

Object linking and embedding (OLE) is a Microsoft framework of creating and displaying multiple objects embedded in some single object. All of these objects are separate entities. This makes a document a "compound document." This allows you to insert an object in a document, which can then be edited in some other program and re-imported. Thus, you can have a Word document with an Excel sheet in it or an Excel sheet with a Word document in it.

Glue is the package that takes advantage of this feature to hide an entire file. All you need to do is launch Glue, select the Document file to work as the carrier, and the Excel file to be hidden in it. Now click Merge and the Excel document will be merged into the Word document in such a manner that when you open the file in MS Word, the Word document will open. If you open the file in Excel, the Excel sheet will open. The package can be used by changing the extension to mislead the investigator. Thus, if you want to hide the Word document part of the merged document, you can rename it with an .xls extension, whereas if you want to hide the Excel part of the file, you rename it with a .doc extension.

One way to display all the information in a file is to open the document in MS Word with the Recover Text From Any File Type option, as discussed earlier.

The other tool you can use is called Strings from Sysinternals. It can be used with the *–a* switch to display the content.

Hiding Data in Tally

Tally is one of the most commonly used accounting packages in India. There is a feature in Tally that most users are not aware of. This feature is known as Tally Audit. By default, this feature is disabled. You can enable it by changing the Company information and adding a security feature.

After the Tally Audit feature is enabled, you can simply go to Display>Statement of Accounts>Tally Audit>Vouchers to see all the vouchers that have been created or altered or even deleted. Similarly, the ledger accounts that have been created, altered, or deleted can be seen here.

This ends the section on data hiding in specific applications. Data hiding in applications is a concept that can take up an entire book, so if this is a real area of interest to you, search Google for more and updated information. This section is just the beginning!

Metasploit Anti-Forensic Project

Posing a challenge is the Metasploit anti-forensic project. The details and developments can be viewed on the Web at www.metasploit.com. This anti-forensic project has several tools as of now:

- **Timestomp**—A timestamp-changing utility that can change the MAC (Modified, Accessed, Created) timestamp for any file or folder.

- **Slacker**—An ultimate tool that can hide the data in slack space in the NTFS file system. It can use its own smart algorithm for such storages. Moreover, it can encrypt and decrypt the file so that an investigator will never now where the file is stored.

- **SAM liucer**—This tool dumps the SAM database containing the password decryption for Windows user accounts. The best part is that it never leaves any traces of this activity having happened.

- **Transmogrify**—Yet another tool that has been developed to counter the signature-analysis techniques of Encase (a forensic investigation tool suite). This tool modifies signatures in such a way that Encase is not able to detect them.

Hats off to the Metasploit team. All that you can do is to detect the traces of these tools to find out whether something has been done. One can use a variety of tools for signature alteration detection to counter Transmogrify. As of now, Slacker uses the XORing for encryption that can be easily detected. The only problem is that it doesn't have an XOR-ing mechanism with set bits. Rather, it takes bits from some existing file to XOR with.

Encryption: The Ultimate in Data Hiding

People Ran In Northern Center of Education. Kings Of Mauritius, Algeria and London who Brought On One New League In Africa were there.

Read this phrase carefully. As a forensic investigator, what might you see... Nothing? Try again and see if you can find a name in it. Check the initial capped letters.

P.R.I.N.C.E   K.O.M.A.L.   B.O.O.N.L.I.A

This is a very old method of hiding the text within text. In the old days, it was quite sufficient, but with the sophisticated technology of today, this method of hiding the data has become obsolete. As the sophistication increased, the methodology of jumbling the data became more and more complex. This gave rise to what we know these days as *encryption*.

Encryption refers to the process wherein the data is converted to some jumbled form based on some algorithm so that it is not readily accessible. One needs to reverse the entire process to get the original data back. How this reversing is done depends upon the type of encryption used. Broadly, there are two kinds of encryption processes:

- **Symmetric/private key encryption**—The encryption scheme wherein a single key is used to encrypt as well as decrypt the data. Data and the private key fits in some kind of algorithm to produce the encrypted data.

   To decrypt the data the same private key is used and the entire process is reversed.

   Microsoft Office documents use this kind of encryption. You can brute force this encryption to find the key with all the combinations of letters or perform a crypt-analysis to find the algorithm used.

- **Public key encryption**—This is a process wherein two separate keys are used for encrypting and decrypting the data. These keys are computed by the software itself.

The way the data is jumbled is known as the *encryption algorithm.* There are various algorithms being used these days . Lets have a better look at some of them here.

The RSA Algorithm

Named after its inventors (Ron Rivest, Adi Shamir, and Leonard Adleman), this algorithm is a public key algorithm. There are various values that are calculated or chosen to work with the scheme.

Step 1: You chose any two prime numbers, P and Q (Say P= 43 and Q= 37).

Step 2: Chose E such that it's greater than 1, less than PQ (E<43 X 37) or (E<1591), and relatively prime to {(P-1)(Q-1)}. Here, (P-1) X (Q-1) = (42 X 36) = 1512 and relatively prime number is say 5. So we have E=5.

Next, you compute D such that (DE-1) is evenly divisible by {(P-1)(Q-1)}. This is referred to as DE=1(mod (P-1)(Q-1)) in mathematical language. There can be several values here. One such value is 605.

D=605 and E=5 so you have (DE-1) = 3024. The value of (P-1)(Q-1) = 1512. Divide 3024 by 1512 = 2 (which is an integer).

Now you have all the values set as follows:

P= 43

Q = 37

E = 5

D = 605

Now comes the encryption and decryption process. The public key is composed of two parts. The first value is what's referred to as N, which is simply (PQ) (P multiplied by Q). In the case here, 43 X 37 = 1591. The other part is the value E, which the case here is 5.

The message is then encrypted using the following function.

C = M^E(Mod N)

where C is the encrypted value and M is the message (the unencrypted value).

Say a person wants to send the value 45 to you. The values are:

M=451

N=159

E=5

So the encrypted value will be:

C= 45^5 (Mod 1591) = 763

Thus the encrypted value is 763. To decrypt this, you use the following function:

M = C^D (Mod N)

M = 763^{605} (Mod 1591)

Looks very cumbersome for the human mind, but not for a computer.

DES (Data Encryption Standard)

This is a private key encryption and has come out of the modified version of the earlier encryption algorithm called *Lucifer*. This is a block cipher, which means that the data to be encrypted is divided into fixed length blocks and then processed for encryption. DES divides the entire data into blocks of 64 bits and processes it with a 64-bit key. Even though the key is 64-bit, only 56 bits are used for the encryption. In fact in every bit of the key (there are 8 bits in the key, of course), only 7 bits are used and the 8th bit is used as a parity bit. The parity bit is set such that the numbers of "1" in every byte are odd.

Take for example a byte that carries an initial 7 bits as 1011001. Now you have four number 1s and thus the last bit will be set to 1 to make the total number of 1s to be five, which is an odd number. When the number of 1s in the first 7 bits are odd, the last bit is set to 0 so that the total number of 1s remains odd.

Now use a table called a permutation choice 1 to find the 56-bit value K, as follows.

PC-1: Permuted Choice 1

Bit	0	1	2	3	4	5	6
1	57	49	41	33	25	17	9
8	1	58	50	42	34	26	18
15	10	2	59	51	43	35	27
22	19	11	3	60	52	44	36
29	63	55	47	39	31	23	15
36	7	62	54	46	38	30	22
43	14	6	61	53	45	37	29
50	21	13	5	28	20	12	4

Now make the substitution of bits as follows.

Take the bit and find the corresponding row and column value. Add these values and replace the resultant number's bit with that bit. For example, you take bit 13 (which might be say equal to 1) and locate the value 13 in the table. This is at column 1 and row 50. Adding these two values (1+50), you get 51. Now substitute the 51st bit in the 64-bit value with the value in bit 13 (that's 1). Similarly, you take the first byte. The value of 1 can be found in the table at column 0 and row 8. You add both the values to get the value (0+8) = 8. By this methodology, you should get the 8th bit replaced with what is written in the first bit. Now, as you know, the 8th bit is not used, so you can ignore this altogether.

Which bit will replace the first bit then? The answer is simple. You find the total of row and column = 1 only at row 1 and column 0. The value there is 57, so you know that the value of the first bit will be replaced with the value of the 57th bit.

The very next thing you do is calculate 16 48-bit keys ($SK_1 - SK_{16}$), by way of *shifting*, with the help of the following table.

Subkey Rotation Table

Round Number	1	2	3	4	5	6	7	8	9	10	11	12	13	14	15	16
Number of bits to rotate	1	1	2	2	2	2	2	2	1	2	2	2	2	2	2	1

This is done as follows:

1. Set the Rnd to 1 (indicating that you are calculating the first subkey).

2. Divide the 56-bit key (K) in two halves of 28 bits each. They are the left 28 bits (L) and the right 28 bits (R).

3. Rotate or shift the entire left half key with the number of bits shown in the table to the left. (When it's a round number, you have to rotate the 1 bit.) So the first bit will become the 28th bit, the second bit will become the first bit, the third bit will become the second bit, and so on. Repeat the same procedure with the right half key.

4. Join the resultant values to get the new K value. This value will be used to calculate the second subkey using the same procedure wherein this value will replace the original 56-bit key. (This means that the key calculated in the first round is used as the K for the second round and second subkey. The key calculated in the second round will be used to calculate the SK in the third round, and so on).

5. Use the following permutation table to get the 48-bit subkey, as you did earlier when calculating the 56-bit key from the 64-bit key.

PC-2: Permuted Choice 2

Bit	0	1	2	3	4	5
1	14	17	11	24	1	5
7	3	28	15	6	21	10
13	23	19	12	4	26	8
19	16	7	27	20	13	2
25	41	52	31	37	47	55
31	30	40	51	45	33	48
37	44	49	39	56	34	53
43	46	42	50	36	29	32

6. What you have calculated just now is the first 48-bit subkey. Now set the Rnd to 2 and start calculating the next subkey.

7. After 16 rounds, you will have 16 subkeys to work with.

At this stage, you have the processed keys. The next step is to prepare the plain text for further processing. (It's just like having cut the vegetables before cooking. The actual cooking is yet to come.)

To do this, you divide the total text/data into blocks of 64 bits. When it doesn't evenly divide, you add padding. You then process the blocks one by one, passing them through the permutation as per the permutation table shown here.

IP: Initial Permutation

Bit	0	1	2	3	4	5	6	7
1	58	50	42	34	26	18	10	2
9	60	52	44	36	28	20	12	4
17	62	54	46	38	30	22	14	6
25	64	56	48	40	32	24	16	8
33	57	49	41	33	25	17	9	1
41	59	51	43	35	27	19	11	3
49	61	53	45	37	29	21	13	5
57	63	55	47	39	31	23	15	7

Every bit of the block is replaced with the other bit depending upon the table. You do need a reverse table to do this:

IP^(-1): Inverse Initial Permutation

Bit	0	1	2	3	4	5	6	7
1	40	8	48	16	56	24	64	32
9	39	7	47	15	55	23	63	31
17	38	6	46	14	54	22	62	30
25	37	5	45	13	53	21	61	29
33	36	4	44	12	52	20	60	28
41	35	3	43	11	51	19	59	27
49	34	2	42	10	50	18	58	26
57	33	1	41	9	49	17	57	25

The inverse table is used to reverse the process completed with the initial permutation table. Using the initial permutation table, you can now prepare the text for encryption. (At this point you have the vegetables cut and have your cooking utensils ready. The next step is to begin cooking.)

Implementing the Encryption

Once the key scheduling and plain-text preparation have been completed, the actual encryption or decryption is performed by the main DES algorithm. The 64-bit block of input data is first split into two halves: L and R. L is the left-most 32 bits and R is the right-most 32 bits. The following process is repeated 16 times, making up the 16 rounds of standard DES. We call the 16 sets of halves L[0]-L[15] and R[0]-R[15].

1. R[I-1], where I is the round number, starting at 1, is taken and fed into the e-bit selection table, which is like a permutation, except that some of the bits are used more than once. This expands the number R[I-1] from 32 to 48 bits to prepare for the next step.

2. The 48-bit R[I-1] is XORed with K[I] and stored in a temporary buffer so that R[I-1] is not modified.

3. The result from the previous step is now split into eight segments of 6 bits each. The left-most 6 bits are B[1], and the right-most 6 bits are B[8]. These blocks form the index into the substitution boxes (called *S-boxes*), which are used in the next step. The S-boxes are a set of eight two-dimensional arrays, each with 4 rows and 16 columns. The numbers in the boxes are always 4 bits in length, so their values range from 0-15. The S-boxes are numbered S[1]-S[8].

4. Starting with B[1], the first and last bits of the 6-bit block are taken and used as an index into the row number of S[1], which can range from 0 to 3, and the middle 4 bits are used as an index into the column number, which can range from 0 to 15. The number from this position in the S-box is retrieved and stored. This is repeated with B[2] and S[2], B[3] and S[3], and the others up to B[8] and S[8]. At this point, you now have eight 4-bit numbers, which when strung together one after the other in the order of retrieval, give a 32-bit result.

5. The result from the previous stage is now passed into the P permutation.

6. This number is now XORed with L[I-1], and moved into R[I]. R[I-1] is moved into L[I].

7. At this point, you have a new L[I] and R[I]. Here, you increment I and repeat the core function until I = 17, which means that 16 rounds have been executed and keys K[1]-K[16] have all been used.

When L[16] and R[16] have been obtained, they are joined back together in the same fashion they were split apart (L[16] is the left-hand half, R[16] is the right-hand half). The two halves are then swapped; R[16] becomes the left-most 32 bits and L[16] becomes the right-most 32 bits of the pre-output block. The resultant 64-bit number is called the *pre-output*.

The tables used for this process can be seen on the Web at http://www.aci.net/Kalliste/ des.htm. M.J. Orlin Grabbe has provided a very good working example under the heading "The DES Algorithm Illustrated." (Adapted with modifications from http://www. tropsoft.com/strongenc/des.htm.)

Triple DES

This is an improved version of DES where two keys are used in the encryption process. The initial data is processed with key 1, as is done with DES. The entire process is the same as is done in DES. Then, this encrypted data is decrypted, or reversed, using the second key. Because you are using a separate key, the resultant data is not the data you originally worked with. The last step is to encrypt it again using the first key. This has some very interesting implications. Brute force and the known plain-text attack can be used to crack this encryption.

Blowfish Algorithm

This algorithm was produced by B. Shneier and is free for use. This is a symmetric block cipher and uses as variable length key that can vary between 32 bits and 448 bits. The algorithm consists of two parts, as in the case of DES. The first part is a key expansion, wherein the original key is used to produce several subkey arrays totaling to 4168 bytes. These arrays are used to encrypt the data in a 16-round network. Each round consists of a key-dependent permutation as well as key- and data-dependent permutations and substitutions. These operations involve XORing on 32-bit word size. One less-complicated version known as *Mini Blowfish* is available as well.

Encrypting File System (EFS)

This is the default NTFS encryption. It is tightly integrated into Windows Explorer and a click away for added security.

EFS encryption works as follows. The computer system generates a key called the *file encryption key* (FEK), which is a pseudo-random number. This number is used to encrypt the data with the algorithm *Data extended standard X* (DESX). The FEK is then encrypted using the public key of the user and stored with the file. To access this, the computer uses the private key of the user and decrypts the FEK. This decrypted key is then used to decrypt the file on the fly. The private and public keys are automatically generated once you start using the encryption. The entire process is so tightly integrated into the OS that the users never know what is going on behind the scenes. All the users have to do is right-click the file to open the Properties tab and use the Advanced button to access the extra security with encryption.

Now as an administrator of the local system, you can always take ownership and disable the encryption from any file. When the system is a member of the domain controller, the keys are stored on the domain controller.

Microsoft has clearly established the recovery agent policies that are implemented by default in case something goes wrong. It is important to note that this information is stored as a *certificate* on the local machine. If that machine is reformatted, the recovery of that certificate becomes almost impossible.

On the file system level, the NTFS file system stores the list of encrypted FEKs with the encrypted files in special EFS attributes called *data decryption fields* and *data recovery fields*.

The need to have two levels of encryption comes from the fact that symmetric encryptions are faster than asymmetric encryptions. Thus, a symmetric encryption scheme is required. However, to keep the files secure from users who have physical access to the system, there was a need to link all this information to something that is not specific to the system but is user specific. This resulted in the need for a asymmetric scheme. Both of these schemes were implemented with the well-known encryptions DOSX and RSA.

The entire process can be explained with the following figure.

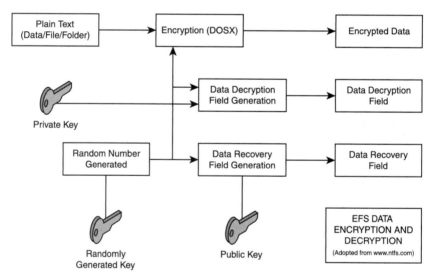

Figure F.2   EFS Data Encryption and Decryption

Can you use encryption as a technique for data hiding? If you get only encrypted data, what can you do? The encryption cannot be reversed. Unless and until you do get the decrypted data, it is of no use to you as a forensic investigator. The only option in such cases is to find the encryption key or the password.

Understanding Password Implementation

Passwords are a good way to protect data from unauthorized uses. Passwords actually protect the data, rather than hiding it. A forensic investigator is bound to face this fact sooner or later. The password on any file can be implemented in one of the following ways:

- *Passwords being stored in the file in plain text:* A very old technique, yet there are possibilities of finding cases where it is still being implemented. This is the most insecure way of password protection and such passwords can be cracked instantly. The legacy DOS packages used these kind of passwords.

- *Passwords that are stored in the document in some kind of jumbled format:* This was an improvement over the plain-text passwords. The password was kept in the file itself, but it is in some kind of encrypted/ciphered/jumbled format. Passwords of this nature are comparatively hard to crack, and the level of difficulty depends upon how the password has been secured and what algorithm has been used. The jumbling of the password can be in reversible form or non-reversible form.

- *A combination of more than one technique or several rounds in some kind of permutation or combination of one of these listed methods can be used.*

- *Finally, the pure encrypted format wherein the password is not stored in the file.* All that happens is the user input is taken and the data is encrypted/decrypted. The password is not stored anywhere in this case. Whenever the user keys in any password, it is used to decrypt the encrypted data and the output is compared to the structure of that file. If it matches (which is possible only if the correct password is keyed in), the file opens. Otherwise, an error is displayed.

- *Password protection wherein the password is more of an entry point rather than the key for encryption.* In these cases, the package specifies whether any password is prescribed in the document. If it is, it asks for the password and matches the password with the one that is stored in the file in some form. When no such password is prescribed, the package simply displays the data. This is much like a security guard posted at an open gate. When a guard is posted, he or she will ask you for identity and when the guard is gone, you can enter straight away. The guard does not close the doors. In such cases, all you need to do is remove the guard and enter the gate.

When cracking a password, you'll see three commonly used words:

- **Password**—This is the actual keystroke that you use to enter the password. This is what is called a plain-text password.

- **Key**—The password as such might not be used (especially in encryption). Instead, a key is produced based on the password input. This key is used for the encryption.

- **Hashing**—This is the process of taking the variable length of the password and converting it with some algorithm to a fixed-length key.

The next sections cover the basics of password cracking. There are several ways in which a password can be cracked. All that is required is the basic understanding of how the password is stored to develop a strategy to crack it.

Password Guessing

You love someone and she loves you. She marries someone else. You marry someone else. Her name becomes the password of your mail account.

It's a joke. But not really for a serious forensic investigator. Very often, people use something known and something that they can easily remember for their passwords. Have a close look at their life, and you may get the clues related to the passwords. At times this works. However, in my personal experience, these types of personal passwords are used mainly by the following people:

- People with very little knowledge about computers.
- People who tend to forget a lot.
- People who have little to hide.

The people who are computer-savvy seldom choose these kinds of passwords for anything they really want to secure.

Reversing the Algorithm

When the password is in some kind of jumbled format and is stored in the file itself, it is possible to crack that password instantly by reversing the algorithm. I am not talking about one-way encryptions schemes here. Take for example the password type used with MS Office 95 documents. These passwords were stored by XORing the password with the data in the file. Such passwords can be instantly revealed and recovered. The packages that crack these passwords simply reverse the algorithm to reveal the password. One such encryption is ROT 13; it shifts the characters by 13 letters.

One-Byte Patching

As the name goes, there is just a patch that can do the trick. There are packages that store the password or work with the password this way. As mentioned earlier, a few packages act like guards standing at an opened door. When the file is opened in the package, the package asks for the password for authentication and then lets you access the data. There is nothing in the data that is encrypted. In such cases, you simply have to patch the program itself so that it doesn't require a password anymore.

The most common techniques at the assembly level use a condition with the jump. In low level assembly, two values are compared. If they are equal, the program is instructed to jump to a particular location (open the data) and, when they are not equal, it jumps to the other location (display an error). As a bypass mechanism, you can always change or reverse these instructions and thus open the data, even when you cannot provide a correct password.

Bypassing a Password

Few applications allow you to bypass a password. Take for example in Windows 9x, when you forget your password, you can enter the system by simply pressing the Esc key. Similarly, a bypassing mechanism has been demonstrated on the Tally 4.5 Accounting package.

Searching the Drive

Why do you need to crack the password if you can find a file that you are looking for on the hard drive in unencrypted format? Most programs create temporary files when they open documents. As you make changes to a document, you should always be able to discard them. This is possible due to temporary files. Most packages use a well-known mechanism. They simply create a copy of the file as a temporary file and store the data in it. As soon as you click the Save button, the new data is written to the main file or, rather, I must say that the temporary file overwrites the main file. Most MS Office programs use this methodology. When you close the program, temporary files are typically deleted by the program. The following figure shows some temporary files created in MS Word, with their tilde character (~).

Figure F.3   Temporary Files Can Be Your Gateway to Passwords and Secured Data

When these temporary files are deleted, they are not wiped off the hard drive, thus you can find such files during recovery processes. Besides this, there are lot of locations where you can find temporary files. For example, compression packages like Winzip first extract the files to some location before working on them.

Dictionary Attacks

The dictionary attack uses several passwords to find the password in question. A dictionary of words are tried one by one to find the password. The idea behind this is simple. Most people want to remember the password. The best way to do so is to use some common word that can be remembered. You cannot expect users to remember *jtsrduk* easily, yet it's easier to remember *analysis*. The dictionary attack preys on this fact. The dictionary that you use can be downloaded from the Internet or even customized to include names and telephone numbers. The attack is used mainly for decrypting the files encrypted with a nonreversible scheme and long encryption keys.

Brute-Force Attacks

This attack is used when most other attacks fail. This is based on the assumption that the password is typically keyed in from a keyboard. Why not try all the possible combinations to find the password? This process in fact tries each and every possible combination of keys on the keyboard to access a password. The chances of getting the password is 100%, but the time it takes can be practically infeasible. Take for example a document that can take all the keys on the keyboard.

There are 26 (A-Z) letters, 26 variations of it (a-z) case sensitive, 10 numbers (0-9), and approximately 32 special characters. This makes a total of 94 characters. For a single-letter password, it takes about 94 attempts for guaranteed recovery. For two-letter password, it takes 94 * 94 or 8836 attempts.

If the password is eight letters long (very common these days), it takes 94^8, or 6095689385410816 attempts to crack the password. With the best package running on multiple systems, it will take years to get the result. Thus this technique is not at all recommended if the password is more than eight letters.

The best way to get protection against brute-force attacks is to increase the length of your passwords. But at times this is not practical. Can you imagine a normal user having to remember a 15-character password made up of random letters and numbers? Certainly not. The other option is to increase the number of keys. This has an exponential impact. Some of the packages now use ASCII passwords. The idea is to use the entire ASCII table as input, thus allowing the use of special characters like NULL and so on in the password. This increases the number of keys from 94 to 128. The impact is significant when the length of the password increases.

Hybrid Attacks

This kind of attack merges the common methods to increase the efficiency. At times people use substitution. A user might replace A with 4, since they look alike. Now, if a password is Paper, the user stores it as P4per. A traditional dictionary attack cannot crack this password, but a hybrid attack can eventually do so.

Rule-Based Attacks

These attacks are launched when the attacker has some information about the password. The information can be of any kind, such as password length, the password carries one or two numbers, the password carries some special characters, or the password starts with certain letters or has certain letters in it. These conditions then can be fed into the password-cracking package, which significantly reduces the number of attempts needed to crack the password.

Xieve Attack

This attack is a variant of the brute-force attack. The only difference here is that while attempting the brute-force attack, an intelligent decision is made to skip nonsense passwords. This makes such an attack faster and more efficient, as compared to the traditional brute-force attack.

Search the Drive Attack

More of a dictionary attack, this is based on the theory that the password is stored somewhere on the drive, either deliberately by the user or unknowingly by a program. Say a user keys in a password and then the system crashes. In such cases, the memory dump might contain the password. The Access Data toolkit uses this information in an interesting manner. It searches the entire drive to make its dictionary and then launches the attack with that customized dictionary. Practically, it is very effective.

Known Plain-Text Attack

The only program still using plain-text passwords are zip programs. There is every possibility that a file that resides in the password-protected file in a zip archive might be available out of it as well as somewhere on the machine or network or even on the Internet. At times such files can even be constructed with certain knowledge and trials. These files then can be compared with the encrypted file. This makes it a lot easier to find the key, particularly when the algorithm is known. Take for example, the DES encryption process. Now to hit this blindly causes a lot of problems. When the plain text as well as the encrypted text is available, you can fit the text into the analysis to calculate the encryption key faster. This is one of the best attacks I have come across that produces positive results.

Using Rainbow Tables

This is one of the most effective ways to crack a password. This process works on a simple concept. We know that when we encrypt a piece of data with a certain key we get the same encrypted text (hash) every time. We have the encrypted data with us to decrypt. Why not store all the possible keys in a database along with the hashes? This means that you can use the hash and look for the matching value for the password against it. The data in the hash table can occupy terabytes of space and is tough to search. The way out now is to keep the initial record of the hash so that groups of it are made. Once a matching value is found, the brute-force attack is applied within the group to obtain the password.

The hashes are generated and commonalities in a set of hashes are stored. This commonality is matched and then the brute-force method is applied within the set to get the password.

The way to get rid of a rainbow table is to add a string after the password. This is known as *salt*. When this salt is added, hackers have to compute every combination for the salt as well. This, coupled with the final calculations in the password, makes it too time-consuming for a rainbow table to be of any practical use. This can be depicted as

```
Hash = MD5 (Password. salt)
```

for the MD5 algorithm.

Using Key Loggers

Key loggers as password recovery? Yes it is possible. Key loggers are the software or hardware that keeps a record of keys used by the users. These loggers can work as a last resort in several cases. The idea goes like this.

Take the system for analysis and install the key logger. Return the same. As human psychology goes, the culprit checks his secret data first. All what he does is logged. This can then be used to check for passwords. Theoretically, it might sound crazy, but practically it does work.

Do You Recover the Password or the Key?

As the concept of encryption goes, the passwords you use are converted to keys called the encryption keys. In symmetric encryption, the same key is used to encrypt as well as decrypt the password. You can decrypt the password in two ways. The first one is using the password and the other is applying the key directly. This gives rise to two possibilities. You can either brute-force attack the password or use the key. The decision is simple. Find the method that requires fewer attempts.

If the expected password length is more than eight letters (64 bits) and the encryption scheme uses 40-bit encryption, for example, it is always better to use encryption keys than brute forcing. But when the encryption uses 128-bit or 256 bits, use the brute-force method to crack the password.

The next sections discuss how password protection is implemented in some of the well-known packages and covers how to crack these methods.

Cracking Microsoft Office File Passwords

Microsoft Office versions before 97 used a weak standard and thus are very easily crackable. All they do is XOR the content with the password. The encryption scheme on Office 97, 2000, and XP uses the RC4 encryption standard. The RC4 standard uses 40-bit keys to encrypt the document. It doesn't matter what password length you use (it allows 1-15 letter passwords); it simply converts the password to a 40-bit hash. This is then used as the password for encryption. It's interesting to note that 40 bits is somewhat equal to a password of five letters in length. This can be cracked with a brute-force attack. The calculation goes like so.

With 40-bit encryption, there are 2^{40} combinations. This is equal to 1,099,511,627,776 combinations. With the speed of 100,000 passwords per second, it takes about 1,099,512 seconds to crack any password. This is about eight days.

Due to this, MS Office encryption is considered pretty weak. Further, if you use the rainbow table, it will be a matter of minutes before you crack the password.

The latest versions of Office XP come with the 128-bit encryption, which is comparatively secure. There are several packages available that are capable of cracking the security of MS Office documents. When not much information is available, the rainbow table–based attack is the best option.

Excel provides the capability to hide a worksheet, hide the rows and columns, and then protect the sheet or the workbook. This protection requires a password to open it. This is in fact a very weak protection and can easily be cracked. This process converts the password into 2 bytes (a 16-bit hash). This means that 2^{16} combinations of the keys are required at most. This comes to 65,536 combinations. A password cracker using the 100,000 keys per second will take less than a second to crack the password.

There are Excel add-ins available that perform the task free of cost. One such add-in is called Password.xla. To use these packages, you need to lower the security and allow macros to run. It is interesting to note that since it is a 16-bit hash it is very easy to get a different password that results in the same hash. Thus it is possible to use one password to protect the sheet and use the other one to unprotect it.

Cracking Winzip Passwords

Winzip up to version 8 uses a very weak encryption. It allows executing a known plaintext attack and recovering the password in minutes. When the archive stores more than five or six files, it is easy to crack. Winzip 9 and up use a strong AES encryption, thus you can only rely on brute-force attacks for these. This is quite time consuming if the password length is more than eight characters. The vulnerability is in the IBDL32.dll used by Winzip, because it uses the 12 bytes before the data to be encrypted for encryption. Most other packages use 12 random bytes, whereas Winzip uses 12 known bytes, which increases the chances of hackers finding the key.

Cracking RAR Passwords

RAR 2.x and up use a very strong encryption scheme, and it is almost impossible to crack it if the key length is long. It should be noted that RAR uses a slow encryption process, which means that only a few hundred passwords per second can be tested. This makes the brute-force process even slower. Known plain-text attacks are also not applicable here.

Cracking ARJ Passwords

The ARJ program uses a very weak encryption. It simply XORs the key with the content, and thus these passwords can be recovered instantly.

Notes

Note on temporary files: Users often open archives and access files in them by simply double-clicking them. Once they view the file, they then close the archive. What happens in the background is that the file the user opened is uncompressed into a "temp" folder and then opened. This means that it is possible that an unzipped version of the file exists in the temporary folder for hackers to find.

Cracking PDF File Passwords

PDF files use two levels of protection. The first one is a user-level protection, which allows viewing the file, and other is the administrative-level protection, which allows altering the document. PDFs use 40-bit encryption for version 1.4 and below, whereas later versions use 128-bit AES encryption. Even though the encryption standard is AES, the implementation is poor, which makes it vulnerable to opening the document instantly. Guess which password is easier to crack—the user or administrative one?

It's the administrative password that can be more easily bypassed. You have to crack the read/view password first. This is a 40-bit RC4 encryption, and the later version allows 128-bit encryption. This can be cracked with the dictionary attack or the brute-force attack. Once the document is decrypted and is open, it is simply a matter of bypassing the admin's password, as it does not use encryption. This implementation flaw allows the admin password to be accessed with what is called *single-byte patching*.

The exact vulnerability is out of the scope of this book, yet you can look for the password-cracking packages in the "Tools of the Trade" section later in this appendix.

Bypassing NT Authentication

It is a well-known fact that Windows NT–based systems, including Windows 2000 and XP, use the SAM database to keep the password hashes. These password hashes are the encrypted form of passwords in a fixed length. The SAM database is stored in C:\%Windir%\system32\config (where *%windir%* is the Windows directory). There are various ways to crack this database, as discussed here.

- **Rename the SAM**—The first way is to boot the system from some other boot disk, rename the SAM file, and then reboot the system. This will remove the passwords and hashes. A new blank file will be generated with no password hashes, and you can log in to it without a password.

- **Know the password**—The other way is to simply use tools like SAMDUMP2 to get the dump of hashes. Now use those hashes in the password tools like John the Ripper or LC4 (Earlier L0phtcrack) to get the password. LC4 can take the hashes automatically as well.

- **Use Linux boot CD to replace the password hash with the new password hashes**—There are boot CDs available that can simply replace the hashes with new hashes of the password you provide. It is as good as the Reset Password option. The Winternals ERD Commander is also a great tool for password resetting.

- **Using Windows XP boot CD for password cracking**—You can easily change or wipe out your administrator password during a Windows XP repair.

Cracking Oracle Database Passwords

The Oracle database uses salting and encryption, but this is done in such a fashion that it is possible to crack its passwords. The process goes like this:

1. The user inputs the password.

2. The password is salted with the username.

3. The resultant text is converted to uppercase.

4. The plain text is then converted to multi-byte storage format; ASCII characters have the high byte set to 0x00.

5. You encrypt the plain-text string using DES (in cipher block chaining) with the fixed key value of 0x0123456789ABCDEF.

6. You use the last block of the resultant encryption text as K.

7. You then encrypt the plain-text string using the key K to produce the hash.

So where is the vulnerability? The vulnerability lies in the way this scheme is made or used. First of all, the salt is the username itself, thus the utility of salting is reduced substantially. Then the plain text is converted to uppercase, which substantially reduces the number of keys that have to be tried during brute forcing. You can now use only uppercase or lowercase keys. The encryption is quite fast; it allows about 800,000-900,000 passwords per second on a good machine. This means that the passwords can be cracked within a time span of about 20-25 days using brute force.

Cracking SQL Passwords

It really took a long time to find out the way SQL hashes its passwords. It was only when David Litchfield of NGSSoftware published his observations that things became clear. He observed that the same user with the same password produces different hashes. This indicated that a time factor was playing a role. Because the same password was producing different hashes, that password is being salted with a time factor. When a single letter is used multiple times in uppercase, you see that the hash is repeated at some location.

This means that there are in fact two passwords stored—one in uppercase and one in lowercase. This means that the character sets can be reduced substantially for a dictionary attack or brute-force attack. This duplication of hashes also allows you to isolate the salt hashes, thus reducing the task substantially. Now the attack can be executed to get the password in uppercase. Once the uppercase password is found, it is just the matter of seconds to get the actual password.

The process of resetting the password in MySQL is quite simple. All you need to do is follow these steps:

1. If the server/daemon is running, stop it.

2. Start the daemon again with the *–skip-grant-tables* option.

3. Start the client with the *-u root* option.

4. Execute the command *UPDATE mysql.user SRT password=PASSWORD('new password')*, where *User='root'*.

5. Execute the *FLUSH PRIVILAGES* command.

You have reset the password for the root.

These examples provided here are just the tip of the iceberg. There are several applications, all with multiple versions. Most of them have one or two vulnerabilities to be explored; plan for the right strategy for password recovery.

Tools of the Trade

There are several cracking packages available, as follows:

- The Passware toolkit from www.lostpassword.com.

  This is a complete toolkit that recovers lost passwords for MS Office, EFS, Adobe Acrobat files, archives including .zip, .rar, and .arj, all protected storages, Lotus Notes, MYOB, Peachtree, and many more. This is all in all a superb utility. It should be noted that Passware provides the guaranteed recovery services.

- Elcomsoft is an all-in-one password-recovery package.

  This is a comprehensive password-recovery toolkit that recovers passwords for most of the commonly known file formats and packages. Similar to the Passware toolkit.

- Access-Data Password recovery toolkit.

  PRTK is one of the strongest password-recovery programs in the forensic world. Access-Data provides for rainbow tables as well as distributed network attacks.

- Packages by Rixler Software.

  Rixler provides password recovery for Internet activities, Mail clients, MS Office files (they have an instant recovery solution with online processing as Decryptum), FTP passwords, DUN passwords, and so on.

- Orabf.exe from www.toolcrypt.org is a free Oracle password-recovery utility.
- L0phtcrack and Cain & Abel are for administrative password cracking on Windows 2000, XP, and Server 2003.
- Advanced zip password recovery.
- SQL Key from Passware and NGS Squirrel from Next Generation Security software for SQL password recovery.

I could keep adding to this list, but to provide a complete list of tools is not the object of this book. My goal is to make things clear as to how things are done and why they are done that way.

With this, you have come to the end of the password section. You will now switch to yet another and perhaps the most powerful data-hiding technique—steganography.

Steganography: The Art of Hiding Data

Derived from the Greek word *steganos*, which means covered, *steganography* is an art of hiding messages in such a way that no one except the intended recipient knows about the message. In a broader sense, you can view steganography as a process wherein some data is inserted into other data so that the inserted data remains invisible and the data in which it is inserted seems to be unaltered.

The *carrier file*, or the cover, is the file that is used to hide the data. In fact, this is more often an image/audio/video file. The *stego medium*, or file, is the cover file with the hidden data and the key (if used). In fact, the carrier file is the file before hiding the data and stego file is the same file after hiding the data.

People typically choose an image/audio/video file to be the carrier file because these files are such that they doesn't display much distortion when the binaries of the file to be hidden are inserted in between its binaries. Take the example of an MS Word document. If you inserted any binary into a Word file, it's easily detected due to distortion in the original file. Further, the image/audio/video files are large enough to carry a sufficient amount of data. This makes them prime choices for the carrier file.

Adding or hiding data doesn't increase the size of the file by much. The bytes of the file to be hidden usually replace the bytes of the carrier files.

Steganography involves hiding the information under cover of some other information. This can be hiding text in an image or in some other text, hiding images in some other carrier files, or other symbolic methods of information transmission.

But as this appendix is concerned with the "system forensics," it focuses on the very specific part that pertains to hiding files in some other files. Throughout this appendix, I use steganography in this narrow sense only.

Hiding Data in Images: An Introduction

The tool called S-Tools is a very old steganography tool. Let's consider an example using S-Tools here. If you open the S-Tools program and drop on it an image, such as ole.bmp. This ole.bmp image file is the carrier for hiding the data.

Now you add the file to be hidden in the image called release_Notes.rtf by dragging it into the S-Tools window. The program immediately asks for a passphrase and the encryption algorithm to be used. You enter these details and click OK to hide the file release_Notes. rtf in the file ole.bmp. A new window pops up with the copy of the original image, now including the hidden file. Save this as a copy of ole.bmp.

Now, when you check the file size of the file ole.bmp and the copy of ole.bmp, you can see they are exactly the same.

The size of the hidden file is 106190 bytes, or 103 KB. This means that you have success-fully hidden the file of size 103KB in the image file ole.bmp. When you see both of these images, you do not find any difference whatsoever in the image. Where have these bytes gone? To analyze this, you use a file-comparison utility. This utility reveals the differences in the binary pattern of both the files. The file is being hidden in the file by modifying the binaries of the file. So you might ask how you modify the binaries and cannot detect any differences. The answer to this lies in the following sections.

Creating a Simple Algorithm for Steganography

A simple algorithm:

- Take a text file that contains only the letter *S*.
- Now hide this text file in an image.
- It is a 1-byte file and the binary for it is 1010011.
- Now take an image and open it in a hex editor.
- Find the offset from where the bitmap data starts.
- Select the first byte from there and note the hex value of the same.
- Convert that hex value to binary and check the last bit.
- If it is 1, keep it as is. If it is 0, change it to 1.
- Check the second byte and replace its last bit of the same with 0.
- Take the third byte and replace the last bit of the same with 1.
- Keep doing that until you have inserted the entire value 1010011.
- Complete the process. You have added the text file in the image manually.

Hiding Data in Sound Files

Sound files are one of the best types of files to hide data, for the following reasons:

- The deterioration in the quality of sound is very minimal.

- Sound files are comparatively large and thus support a large amount of data hiding.

- You can find several .wav files in a computer system that are used by the system for some default purposes. These can be used to hide the data without raising doubts unless and until they are scanned for changes in the hashes to be compared with the database of known hashes.

As with the case of image data hiding in the sound file, there are several algorithms you can use. As of now, the best possible algorithm seems to be LSB (least significant bit), wherein the LSB is substituted with the data. This produces the subtle difference that can not be detected by the human ear.

There are several methods for hiding information in audio files. Some of them are discussed here:

- **LSB hiding**—There are LSBs for image files and LSBs for sound files, so just as you can hide data in image files, you can hide data in sound files as well.

  Let's again start with an example. Say that an audio file uses the 16-bit CD quality audio. This means that every pulse is stored in 16 bits. In that case, the LSB is the last bit of the 2 bytes: the 16th bit. The LSBs have been replaced with the stored data.

- **Parity coding**—The audio is divided into regions of samples, and the parity bit is then used to store the data. To match the parity, one of the bits is reversed if required. The process goes like this:

  1. Take the region to store the bit.

  2. Check the parity bit with the condition Parity bit (P1) = Message Bit (M1) where the message bit is the bit that must be hidden.

  3. If the condition evaluates to be true, use the parity bit to store the message bit.

  4. If the condition is false, reverse one of the bits in the region. Now if the region contains, say, 32 bits, any of them can be flipped to match the condition, as this will reverse the parity and make the parity bit equal to the message bit. Take for example a region that contains an even number of 1s; the parity bit will be 0. In case the bit to be hidden is 0, you need not make any adjustment. But if you need to store the binary digit 1, you need to flip one of the bits (0 to 1 or 1 to 0). This will make the total number of 1s odd. Now the parity bit will be 1, and the condition will match.

The biggest advantage of using this method is that you get a large amount of bits that you can change, and thus more options. You can simply change one bit such that the sample matches closely to the nearest sample, which means it becomes very hard to trace the distortion.

- **Echo hiding**—In this method, an echo is introduced in a discrete signal to embed the secret information. The bit specifies the delay in the echo. Say, for example, you need to hide the data 10110110. You add echo to the sound. The echo is then manipulated according to the bits of data to be hidden. The first bit with value 1 results in an echo delay of 1 ms, and the value of 0 results in an echo delay of 0.5 ms. The delay is such that the human ear cannot discriminate between the delays. Similarly, other aspects like amplitude or decay can be manipulated to hide secret information. The process goes like this:

    1. Divide the sound file into segments equal to the bits you want to hide.

    2. Decide which parameter of echo will be altered for data hiding. This can be delay, amplitude, or decay. Choose the delay for this example.

    3. Insert the data bit in the delay field; that is, place the bit responsible for the delay in the stereo left and right channels.

The bit 0 will result in 0.5 ms of latency and 1 will result in 1 ms of latency. As this is spread across the file, the switching from 1 to 0 or 0 to 1 is not frequent. The delay difference is just 0.5 ms and thus not discernable by the human ear. The problem arises when the data is large enough to produce rapid changes and thus produces shaky sound. In such cases, a more complex algorithm can be used where in more than one channel is used in such a fashion that one takes care of the other; thus, if there is a 1 in the first channel, it will have a 0 in the corresponding channel and vice versa. Therefore, when they are finally mixed, they produce a comparatively better output.

Hiding Data in an Executable File

I can guess that most people reading this or using steganography packages are saying, "Is this man crazy? Changing a single bit in an executable can render it useless." That would have been my response too if I had not seen the tool called *Hydan*. Hydan is a tool that has been developed by El-Khalil in his research during his computer science master's degree work at Columbia University.

Adding 50 to a number is as good as subtracting 50 from that number. Logically and functionally, there is no difference at all. You can replace one by another. But by choosing one in place of other, you get 1 bit of space for covert storage.

Khalil exploits these redundancies in order to effectively hide the data to the tune of about 1 in 110 bytes (1 byte can be hidden in 110 bytes). Even though this ratio is far less than what is expected from a good steganography package, it is still worthwhile, as there are very few who will doubt an executable program. More details can be obtained from the Web at www.crazyboy.com/hydan/.

The beauty of this package is that it can hide data in Windows as well as Linux executables, but it doesn't work well with self-modifying executables.

Data Hiding in Spam Mails

Well, I was literally beating my head when I saw this. Here is an example for your consideration:

Dear Friend , This letter was specially selected to

be sent to you . This is a one time mailing there is

no need to request removal if you won't want any more

! This mail is being sent in compliance with Senate

bill 1622 ; Title 6 ; Section 306 . This is NOT unsolicited

bulk mail ! Why work for somebody else when you can

become rich within 12 DAYS . Have you ever noticed

most everyone has a cell phone & nearly every commercial

on television has a .com on in it ! Well, now is your

chance to capitalize on this . WE will help YOU process

your orders within seconds & deliver goods right to

the customer's doorstep ! You can begin at absolutely

no cost to you ! But don't believe us . Prof Anderson

who resides in New Hampshire tried us and says "Now

I'm rich many more things are possible" . We are licensed

to operate in all states . Because the Internet operates

on "Internet time" you must hurry ! Sign up a friend

and your friend will be rich too . Best regards ! Dear

Sir or Madam ; Especially for you - this amazing announcement

. If you no longer wish to receive our publications

simply reply with a Subject: of "REMOVE" and you will

immediately be removed from our club ! This mail is

being sent in compliance with Senate bill 1625 , Title

6 , Section 309 ! This is different than anything else

you've seen . Why work for somebody else when you can

become rich as few as 30 days ! Have you ever noticed

nearly every commercial on television has a .com on

in it and nearly every commercial on television has
a .com on in it . Well, now is your chance to capitalize
on this . WE will help YOU decrease perceived waiting
time by 120% plus SELL MORE ! You can begin at absolutely
no cost to you ! But don't believe us . Ms Simpson
who resides in Wyoming tried us and says "Now I'm rich
many more things are possible" . We assure you that
we operate within all applicable laws ! We urge you
to contact us today for your own future financial well-being
. Sign up a friend and you get half off ! Thanks !
Dear Salaryman , We know you are interested in receiving
amazing news ! This is a one time mailing there is
no need to request removal if you won't want any more
. This mail is being sent in compliance with Senate
bill 1622 , Title 2 ; Section 305 ! THIS IS NOT A GET
RICH SCHEME ! Why work for somebody else when you can
become rich as few as 18 WEEKS . Have you ever noticed
nobody is getting any younger and people love convenience
. Well, now is your chance to capitalize on this !
WE will help YOU decrease perceived waiting time by
100% & use credit cards on your website ! You can begin
at absolutely no cost to you . But don't believe us
! Mrs. Ames of Oklahoma tried us and says "Now I'm rich
many more things are possible" . We are licensed to
operate in all states ! We implore you - act now !
Sign up a friend and you'll get a discount of 20% .
Thanks .

I am not promoting spam here. Mail me at boonlia@gmail.com to get a copy of this email. Now simply copy the text and paste it in the Decode section at www.spammimic.com. Now press the Decode to see the message hidden in it. The hidden message in this email was "Now its ur turn to beat the head. Prince"

I don't know yet exactly how this works and am looking to find the clues. Whatever the algorithm, it is just a new way to hide data. Yes, the spam might contain some information.

A full discussion of steganography might require more than 1,000 pages to get a fair enough picture of what is happening. In fact, there are ways to hide data in HTML files, dot net assemblies, and more. One can hide data in the whitespace of an MS Word document. I even came across an article on hiding data in audio tapes with a fair amount of reliability. There seems to be no end at all.

Unfortunately, I do have to end this section at some point. So let's now jump to the other and more important topic: steganalysis.

Steganalysis: The Art of Finding Data

Steganalysis is the art of discovering and rendering useless covert messages. This is what you as a forensic investigator are expected to do—detect the steganography and unmask the hidden message.

On any typical system, you'll find a number of images, sound, and even video files stored on it. I have yet to come across a system that doesn't have any of them as a standalone system. Searching and performing steganalysis on every system is neither practical nor possible. What you should look for is some footprints.

What kinds of footprints might these be?

The first and foremost thing that you should look for while starting with forensics is for information about the suspect. Is he or she computer-savvy?. If not, it's very rare to find some steganography in the computer system in question. If you do not find any other signs of steganography being used, you can be fairly sure that there has been no steganography used.

The second clue to look for are packages installed, including any steganography package or tool. I have mentioned the Registry keys to look for on a Windows computer. You can simply check the Run MRU and shortcuts on your computer system. In Windows XP, you can use the image in a virtual environment with the help of Live View. You right-click on images and check for the programs in the Open With box. If steganography is frequently used, you will find some signs in all these places.

Check for the large images, particularly stored in the BMP format. The best way to hide data is within larger and brighter images. As far as sound files are concerned, the best way to hide data is within files with louder and varied sounds.

Check known files for changes. Most of the forensic tools carry hash sets for known files. You can create your own hash sets as well, which are simple databases of hashes for common files. These often include the files pertaining to the operating system, commonly used packages like MS Office, and so on. If you see some discrepancies in these common files, you can suspect something is wrong.

Check for temporary file locations and memory dumps. All steganography packages copy or rather extract the file somewhere before using it. If the file has been frequently extracted, it is probable that you will find some signs of the file in the temporary files, in memory dumps, or in pagefile remains and fragments.

Still nothing suspicious?

As a last step, I suggest you run a steganalysis tool against all the files.

Still nothing suspicious? You can safely presume that steganography has not been used on the system in question.

Attacking the Steganography

Once you have performed any foot printing and found something suspicious, the next step is to launch a counter-attack on the suspicious data. Types of counter-attacks, whereby you attack the steganography, are covered in the following sections.

Stego Only Attack

This attack is launched when only the stego file is available and no other information is available. This is the initial situation in nearly all examples of forensic examination. The investigator is blind. He or she can then perform the attacks that you have read about: the visual attack to find any hidden text, statistical tests to guess if the data is hidden, and if hidden then if it is some kind of encryption. In case of audio files, you can listen to them. Some visual analyzers for sound can prove to make a difference here.

Packages from www.acoustic.com can help a lot. "Diagnostic system for sound fields" is a very powerful tool to analyze steganography in sound files. This tool can be downloaded from www.ymec.com.

The beauty of this package is the way it segregates the information in the sound file. You can see the echo delay pattern and the decay pattern in a file. You can visualize the channels separately, and so on. The package even has a noise measurement system with it.

Known Signature Attack

When you suspect that a certain package might have been used to hide data, you can use a known signature attack, whereby the signatures left in the image are analyzed and compared against the signatures of the known steganography packages to identify the package used.

Known Carrier Attack

This type of counter-attack is launched when both the carrier and stego files are available for analysis. In other words, you have the file before data was hidden in it and after the data was hidden in it. These two files can be compared to find the pattern of storage and some general clues. This gives you an idea of the hiding scheme.

Known Message Attack

Here, the hidden message or a part of it is known. This helps in identifying the hiding mechanism and thus helps unmask the hidden file.

Chosen Stego Attack

Here, the stego medium and algorithm are both known. The task is simply to extract the data.

Chosen Message Attack

More for analysis purposes. The message as well as the algorithm are known and a stego is created for analytical purposes.

Known Stego Attack

The carrier, stego, and algorithm are available.

What if you know the algorithm or the package used to hide the data? The very next step is to extract the data. This again is the tough part. The data that has been hidden might be encrypted and not readily available for analysis. You need to find the decryption keys. You can deploy any of the counter-attacks as discussed in this appendix.

There are known tools that can help you with this process. Some of them are discussed in the next section.

Tools of the Trade

Try these steganography tools:

- S-Tools (ftp://ftp.funet.fi/pub/crypt/mirrors/idea.sec.dsi.unimi.it/code/s-tools4.zip): Hides data in image and sound files.
- Snow by Matthew Kwan: It explores the whitespace used to hide data, just like a polar bear hides in the snow (see http://www.cs.mu.oz.au/~mkwan/snow/).
- Hide4PGP: Hides data in BMP, WAV, and VOC files (http://www.rugeley.demon.co.uk/security/hide4pgp.zip).
- Hide and Seek: (http://www.rugeley.demon.co.uk/security/hdsk50.zip).
- Jpeg-Jsteg: Hides data in JPEG image files. Uses DCT coefficient to hide the data. (See ftp://ftp.funet.fi/pub/crypt/steganography.)
- Steganos: A complete suite for security and data hiding. Creates encrypted storage as well as hides data in image files.

Try these steganalysis tools:

- *Gargoyle from Wet Stone Technologies:* This is a commercial tool that has the database of most of the known steganography packages. It searches the drive for the packages installed and uses the known signature database along with hashes. The tool is the first line of attack. If you know the tools used, further attacks become easy, as you can then try to find the algorithm and related information.

- *Steg-Detect:* This tool from www.outguess.org can detect the steganographic content in images. It works on the files hidden using the following packages:

  Jsteg

  JPHide

  Invisible Secrets

  Outguess

  F5 (Header analysis)

  AppendX and camouflage

- *Stegobreak:* The package launches the dictionary attack against JSteg-Shell, JPHide, and OutGuess 0.13b.

- *Stegspy:* A tool from www.spy-hunter.com that detects the messages hidden through the following packages:

  Hiderman

  JPHideandSeek

  Masker

  JPegX

  Invisible Secrets

- *Chi-Square:* A tool from http://www.guillermito2.net/. This tool can perform a chi-square test on the image to find the randomness in the LSBs.

- *Bmp2enhancedlsb:* A tool from http://www.guillermito2.net/ that can enhance the LSBs for detecting the plain text hidden in the BMP files (24-bit).

- *Winhex:* A hex editor that can be used to see the raw data in hex format. This can be used for manual analysis of the suspected file.

In fact there are fewer tools for detecting any steganography then there are to perform it. The challenge here is that you'll often need to analyze clues on a case-by-case basis.

Summary

This appendix started with the very basics in data hiding. Then, you looked at a few advanced techniques and Registry tweaks. You looked at the ADS and then tried to develop a methodology to identify how a package hides the data. You then looked at data hiding in a few of the known packages.

With the growing developments in IT as well as growing concerns with security, we are bound to face even tougher situations in the future. These processes are still evolving and seem to be a never-ending quest between forensics and anti-forensics.

INDEX

T